Employee Rights in Corporate Insolvency

This book analyses corporate rescue laws, processes and policies prescribed in corporate insolvency or bankruptcy laws, and employment laws of the UK and the US, with a particular focus on how extant employee rights are treated when a debtor employer initiates corporate insolvency proceedings.

The commencement of formal insolvency proceedings by an employer affects employees' rights and interests. Employment laws seek to protect employees' rights and interests, while insolvency laws seek to promote corporate rescue, which may entail workforce changes. Consequently, this creates a tension between whose interest insolvency law should give primacy of protection. The book analyses how corporate rescue processes such as administration, pre-pack business sales, company voluntary arrangements, receivership and liquidation impact employee rights and protection during corporate rescue proceedings in both jurisdictions. It goes on to address how the federal system of government in the US and the diffusion of power between federal and state law jurisdictions impact a uniform code of employee protection during Chapter 11 bankruptcy reorganisation proceedings. The book considers how an interpretative approach to law (Dworkin's Interpretative Theory of Law) may be used to balance both employee protection and corporate rescue laws during corporate insolvency in the UK and the US.

Of interest to academics, students and employment law practitioners, this book examines the tension between corporate rescue laws and employment protection laws during corporate insolvency in the US and the UK and how this tension may be remedied or balanced.

Dr Hamiisi Junior Nsubuga is a Lecturer in Law at Middlesex University London. He obtained his LLB from the University of London, LLM (Corporate Law) and a PhD (Law) from Nottingham Trent University, UK. Dr Hamiisi is a Member of INSOL Europe (YANIL), the British Institute of International and Comparative Law and a member of the Cross-Border Insolvency and Commercial Law Research Group (CI&CL). Dr Hamiisi's main research interests are in Corporate Law, Comparative Insolvency Law, Comparative Labour Law and Legal Theory, especially, the theoretical and conceptual underpinnings of corporate insolvency law/regimes of the UK, the USA and Uganda and how these corporate insolvency regimes impact the economic and social policies in these jurisdictions.

Routledge Research in Corporate Law

Available titles in this series include:

Regulation and Inequality at Work
Isolation and Inequality Beyond the Regulation of Labour
Vanisha Sukdeo

Regulation and the Credit Rating Agencies
Restraining Ancillary Services
Daniel Cash

Law and Responsible Supply Chain Management
Contract and Tort Interplay and Overlap
Edited by Vibe Ulfbeck, Alexandra Andhov and Kateřina Mitkidis

Shareholder Primacy and Global Business
Re-clothing the EU Corporate Law
Lela Mélon

Corporate Law, Codes of Conduct and Workers' Rights
Vanisha Sukdeo

Insolvency Law and Multinational Groups
Theories, Solutions and Recommendations for Business Failure
Daoning Zhang

Employee Rights in Corporate Insolvency
A UK and US Perspective
Hamiisi Junior Nsubuga

For more information about this series, please visit: https://www.routledge.com

Employee Rights in Corporate Insolvency

A UK and US Perspective

Hamiisi Junior Nsubuga

Routledge
Taylor & Francis Group
LONDON AND NEW YORK

First published 2020
by Routledge
2 Park Square, Milton Park, Abingdon, Oxon OX14 4RN

and by Routledge
52 Vanderbilt Avenue, New York, NY 10017

Routledge is an imprint of the Taylor & Francis Group, an informa business

British Library Cataloguing-in-Publication Data
A catalogue record for this book is available from the British Library

Library of Congress Cataloging-in-Publication Data
Names: Nsubuga, Hamiisi Junior, author.
Title: Employee rights in corporate insolvency : a UK and US perspective / Hamiisi Junior Nsubuga.
Description: New York : Routledge, 2020. |
Series: Routledge research in corporate law | Includes bibliographical references and index.
Identifiers: LCCN 2019029785 (print) | LCCN 2019029786 (ebook) | ISBN 9780367321543 (hardback) | ISBN 9780429329685 (ebook)
Subjects: LCSH: Bankruptcy—United States. | Bankruptcy—Great Britain. | Employee rights—United States. | Employee rights—Great Britain. | Business failures—Law and legislation—United States. | Business failures—Law and legislation—Great Britain. | Corporate reorganizations—United States. | Corporate reorganizations—Great Britain.
Classification: LCC K1375.N78 2020 (print) | LCC K1375 (ebook) | DDC 344.4101—dc23
LC record available at https://lccn.loc.gov/2019029785
LC ebook record available at https://lccn.loc.gov/2019029786

ISBN: 978-0-367-32154-3 (hbk)
ISBN: 978-0-429-32968-5 (ebk)

Typeset in Galliard
by codeMantra

Contents

Preface vii
Acknowledgements ix
List of abbreviations xi
Table of cases xiii
Table of legislation xvii
Table of government reports, guidance reports and other documents xix

1 Corporate rescue and employment protection – concepts, policies and processes 1

2 Bankruptcy legal theory: the traditionalist and proceduralist theoretical models 24

3 Employee rights under US Chapter 11 bankruptcy reorganisations 43

4 Institutional challenges – the federal vs state law conundrum 69

5 Interpretation as a balancing tool in the US – applying Dworkin 81

6 Employee rights and protection in the UK – TUPE transfers and business sales 94

7 Balancing corporate rescue and employment protection in the UK – applying Dworkin 122

8 Conclusion – latest legislative developments and substantive matters 149

Index 157

Preface

The commencement of formal insolvency proceedings by an employer affects employees' rights and interests. Employment laws seek to protect employees' rights and interests while insolvency laws seek to promote corporate rescue which may entail workforce changes. Consequently, this creates a tension between whose interest insolvency law should give primacy of protection.

The inequality in the level of protection to employees' rights and interests during corporate rescue is, arguably, precipitated by the tension that is created by the divergent policy objectives of employment law and insolvency law during corporate insolvency. While insolvency law's main objective is the rehabilitation and rescue of insolvent but viable businesses, employment law's main objective is the protection and continuity of employment relationship between the debtor employer and employees. Therefore, the divergence in the policy objectives sought by both employment law and insolvency law creates a tension between the two policy objectives.

This book focuses on the treatment of employees' rights in the insolvency of their corporate employer in the UK and the US. This book argues that there exists a form of legislative protection to employees' rights and interests during corporate insolvency involving their debtor employers in both the UK and the US. However, the level of protection afforded to employees is considerably minimal in contrast to other stakeholders, such as secured creditors. It is urged in this book that the level of protection to employees' interests on their debtor employer's insolvency ought to be commensurable with the employees' input into the going concern value of their debtor employer's business.

Employees provide the human capital in the form of labour that is employed alongside financial capital in the production of goods or provision of services that the employer sets out to achieve. However, in corporate insolvency, employees' rights and interests are mainly considered as general unsecured debts or claims of the debtor company by the insolvency laws in both the UK and the US which creates a degree of inequality of protection between extant stakeholders.

Moreover, the theoretical perspectives from what has been termed the traditionalist and proceduralist theoretical schools that dominate the field of insolvency, arguably, do not provide satisfactory avenues through which a balance may be achieved between employment protection and corporate rescue.

While traditionalists' perspectives consider the interests of extant stakeholders as a whole and support fairness in distributive imperatives in insolvency, they do not provide clear answers on how these perspectives may be balanced and applied to corporate insolvencies. Proceduralists, however, provide clear answers to the factors to be taken into account during corporate insolvency but their perspectives give primacy to maximising creditors' returns rather than an inclusive distributive approach, which may be an unsatisfactorily narrow approach to stakeholders as a group. Therefore, this book applies Dworkin's interpretative approach to law as a remedy that would provide an approach through which a balance may be achieved between employment protection and corporate rescue objectives during corporate insolvency.

Acknowledgements

I would like to thank Nicola Sharpe and Caroline Church of Taylor and Francis – Routledge Publishing, for their involvement in the production of this book. Particular thanks go to my work colleague Prof. Erica Howard of Middlesex University, London, for her support and guidance since the submission of this book's proposal to Routledge to its final production.

Special thanks go to Prof. Rebecca Parry and Ms Kay Wheat of Nottingham Trent University, who supervised my PhD research project upon which this book is based. I benefited from your research expertise, support and guidance that shaped me into a better researcher. Lastly, I would like to thank my family for their continued support and encouragement.

Abbreviations

General

ARD	Acquired Rights Directive
Cir. Court	Circuit Court
CA	Court of Appeal
CJEU	Court of Justice of the European Union
ETO	Economic, Technical, or Organisational
EAT	Employment Appeal Tribunal
ET	Employment Tribunal
EA 2002	Enterprise Act 2002
ECR	European Case Report
EC	European Community
EU	European Union
OECD	Organisation for Economic Co-operation and Development
TUPE	Transfer of Undertakings (Protection of Employment) Regulations
UK	United Kingdom
US	United States

Table of cases

United Kingdom

Abellio London Ltd (formerly Travel London Ltd) v Musse & others [2012] IRLR 360.
Addison v Community Integrated Care [UKEAT/250779/11].
Allders Department Stores Ltd (in administration) Re [2005] EWHC 172.
Bateman v Asda Stores Ltd [UKEAT/0221/09].
Bernadone v Pall Mall Services Group Ltd [2001] ICR 197.
Berriman v Delabole Slate [1985] ICR 546. (CA).
Bolwell v Redcliffe Homes Ltd [1999] IRLR 485.
Bulmer v Bollinger [1974] EWCA Civ. 14.
Carmichael & Another v National Power Plc., [1999] ICR 1226 (HL).
Catamaran Cruisers v Williams and others [1994] IRLR 384.
Celtec Ltd v Astley [2005] IRLR 647.
Condon, Ex parte James Re (1874) LR 9 Ch. App 609.
Corkery v Carpenter [1951] 1 KB 102.
Crawford v Swinton Insurance Brokers Ltd [1990] IRLR 42, (EAT).
Credit Suisse First Boston (Europe) Ltd v Lister [1998] IRLR 700.
Credit Suisse First Boston (Europe) Ltd v Padiachy [1998] IRLR 504.
Crystal Place F.C Ltd and Another v Kavanagh and Others [2014] IRLR 139, (CA)
Delaney v Staples [1992] 1 AC 687.
Elliot v Grey [1960] 1 QB 367.
Enterprise Managed Services Ltd v Dance and Others [UKEAT/0200/11].
Green v Elan Care Ltd [UKEAT/0018/01].
Hartlebury Printers Ltd Re [1993] BCLC 902.
Hay v George Hansen [1996] IRLR 427.
Hazel v Manchester College [2014] EWCA Civ. 72.
Heydon's Case [1584] EWHC Exch J36.
Hollister v The National Farmers Union [1979] IRLR 238 (CA)
Home Office v Evans [2007] EWCA Civ. 1089 (CA).
Horst v High Tables Ltd [1997] EWCA Civ. 2000.
Huddersfield Fine Worsteds Ltd and Ferrotech Ltd and Granville Technology Ltd Re [2005] EWCA Civ. 1072.

Ibex Trading v Walton & Other [1994] ICR 907, (EAT.)
IRC v Wimbledon Football Club Ltd. [2004] BCC 638.
Jackson v Computershare Investor ServicesPlc [2007] EWCA Civ. 1065 (CA).
Jefferies v Powerhouse Retail Ltd [UKEAT 1328].
Kavanagh and others v Crystal Palace F.C (2000) Ltd and Others [2013] IRLR 291, (EAT).
Krasner v McMath [2006] I.C.R 205.
Ladies Health and Fitness Clubs v Eastmond [UKEAT94/03] (Unreported).
Leeds United Association Football Club Ltd Re [2007] EWHC 1761 (Ch.).
Litster v Forth Dry Dock and Engineering Company Ltd [1989] 1 All ER 113.
London Metropolitan University v Sackur & Others [UKEAT/0286/06].
Macer v Abafast Ltd [1990] IRLR 477 (HL).
Martin & Others v South Bank University [2004] ICR 1234.
Meade & Baxendale v British Fuels Ltd [1998] ICR 387, (CA).
Meter-U Ltd v Ackroyd [2012] IRLR 367.
Milligan & Another v Securicor Cleaning Ltd [1995] IRLR 288, (EAT).
Nationwide Building Society v Benn & Others [UKEAT/0273/09/JOJ].
New ISG Ltd v Vernon and Others [2008] IRLR 115.
Nokes v Doncaster Amalgamated Collieries Ltd [1940] AC 1014.
North Wales Training & Enterprise Council Ltd v Astley and Others [2006] UKHL 29 (HL).
Oakland v Wellswood (Yorkshire) Ltd [2008] UKEAT 0395/08.
OTG v Barke and Others [2011] IRLR 272.
Panama, New Zealand and Australian Royal Mail Company Re (1870) LR 5 Ch. App. 318.
Perth and Kinross Council v Donaldson & Ors (2004) IRLR 121 (EAT).
Powdrill v Watson [1995] 2 A.C. 394.
Ralton v Havering College of Further and Higher Education [2001] IRLR 743, (EAT).
RR Donnelley Global Document Solutionss Group Ltd v (1) Besagni and (2) NSL Ltd [UKEAT/0397/13].
Secretary of State for Employment v Spence [1986] ICR 672.
Secretary of State for Trade & Industry v Cook [1997] IRLR 150.
SISU Capital Fund Ltd v Tucker [2006] BCC 463.
Smith v Hughes [1960] 1 WLR 380.
Smith v Trustees of Brooklands College [EAT/0128/11].
Spaceright Europe Ltd v Baillavoine and another [2011] EWCA Civ. 1565.
Stirling District Council v Allan [1995] ICR 1082.
T & D Industries Plc Re [2000] B.C.C 956 (Ch).
Tapere v South London and Maudsley NHS Trust [2009] IRLR 972.
Thompson v SCS Consulting Ltd [2001] IRLR 801, (EAT).
Transbus International Ltd Re [2004] 2 BCLC 55.
Wheeler v Patel [1987] IRLR 211.
Whent v T. Cartledge Ltd [1997] IRLR 153.
Whitehouse v Blatchford and Sons ltd [1999] IRLR 492.

The United States

Adventure Res., Inc. v Holland, 137 F. 3d 786, 798 (4th Cir. 1998).
Bay Plastics Inc. v BT Commercial Corporation 187 B. R. 315 (CD Cal. 1995).
Brotherhood of Railways, Airline and Steamship Clerks v REA Express, Inc., 523 F. 2d 164 (2nd Cir. 1975).
Butner v United States, 440 U.S. 48 (1978).
Caesers Entertainment Operating Company Inc., In re 134 S. Ct 1188, 1194 (Bankr. D. Delaware 2015).
Century Brass Prods. Inc., In re 795, F. 2d 265, 272 (2nd Cir. 1986).
Chateagay Corp., In re 80 B.R 279, 286–87 (Bankr. S.D.N.Y. 1987).
Del Grosso, In re 115 B.R 136, 138 (Bankr. N.D 111 1990).
Delta Air Lines, In re 359 B.R 468, 473 (Bankr. S.D.N.Y. 2006).
Fall River Dyeing & Fishing Corp. v NLRB, 482 U.S. 27 (1987).
FCX Inc., In re 60 B.R 405, 411–12 (Bankr. E.D.N.C. 1986).
General Motors Corp., In re 407 B.R 463, 505 (Bankr. S.D.N.Y. 2009).
Gulf Air Inc., In re 112 B.R 152, 154 (Bankr. W.D. La 1989).
Hutton v Watters, 132 Tenn.527, 179 S.W 134 (1915).
John Wiley & Sons, Inc. v Livingston 376, U.S. 543 (1963).
Mammoth Mart Inc., In re 536 F. 2d 955, (1st Cir. 1976).
Mansfield Ferrous Castings Inc., In re 96 B.R 779,781. (Bankr. N.D. Ohio).
NLRB v Burns Int'l Sec. Serv., 406 U.S. 272 (1972).
NLRB v Bildisco & Bildisco, 465 U.S. 523 (1984).
Nw. Airlines Corp., In re 346 B.R 307, 322 (Bankr. S.D.N.Y. 2006).
Patriot Coal Corp., In re 482 B.R 718, 739 (Bankr. S.D.N.Y 2012).
Payne v Western & A.R.R. 81 Tenn. 507, 519 – 20 (1884).
Petermann v International Brotherhood of Teamsters, 344 P. 2d 25 (Cal. App. 1959).
Pomona Valley Medical Group, Inc., In re 476 F.3d 665, 670 (9th Cir. 2007).
Prime Motor Inns, In re 124, B.R. 378, 381 (Bankr. S.D. Fla. 1991).
Salant Corp., In re 53 B.R.158, 161. (Bankr. S.D.N.Y. 1985).
Structurlite Plastics Corp., In re 86 B.R 922, 932. (Bankr. S.D. Ohio 1988).
Sun City Investments, Inc., In re 89 B.R. 245, 249 (Bankr. M.D. Fla. 1988).
Tres – Ark Inc., In re 09–12589 (Bankr. W.D Texas 2012).
Truck Drivers Local 807 v Carey Transportation, 816 F. 2d 82 (2nd Cir.1987).
UAL Corporation, In re 428 F. 3d 677, 684 (7th Cir. 2005).
US v Whiting Pools Inc. (1983) 462 U.S. 198, 203.
W.T Grant Co., In re 620 F. 2d 319,321 (2nd Cir. 1980).
Wheeling-Pittsburgh Steel Corp. v United Steel Workers of Am., 791 F. 2d 1074, 1091 (3rd Cir. 1986).
WorldCom Inc., In re 346 F. 2d 628 (Bankr. S.D.N.Y 2004).

The European Union

Case C-101/87 *P. Bork International A/S v Foreningen af Arbejdslederen i Danmark* [1989].

Case C-126/16 *Federatie Nederlandse Vakrereninging v Smallsteps BV C* [2017].
Case C-132/91 *Katsikas v Konstantinidis* [1993] IRLR 179.
Case C-135/83 *Abels v Bedrijfsvereniging voor de Metallindustrie en de Electrotechnische Industrie* [1985] ECR 469.
Case C-186/83 *Arie Botzen and others v Rotterdamsche Droogdok Maatschappij BV* [1985].
Case C-319/94 *Jules Dethier Equipement SA v Dassy & Another* (1998) ICR 541 (ECJ).
Case C-324/86 *Foreningen AF Arbedjsldere I Denmark v Daddy's Dance Hall* [1988].
Case C-362/89 *D'Urso v Ercole Marelli Ellectromeccanica Generale SPA* [1991] ECR 1–4105.
Case C-426/11 *Alermo-Herron and Others v Parkwood Leisure Ltd* [2013].

Table of legislation

United Kingdom

Companies Act 2006 c. 46.
Employment Protection Consolidation Act 1978 c. 44.
Enterprise Act 2002 c. 40.
European Communities Act 1972 c. 68.
European Union (Withdrawal) Act 2018, c.16.
Fraudulent Conveyance Act (13 Eliz. Ch.7 (1570).
Insolvency Act 1986 (Prescribed Part) Order 2003 (2003 No. 2097).
Insolvency Act 1986 c. 45.
Insolvency Rules 1986 (1986 No. 1925).
Limitation Act 1980 c. 58.
Trade Union and Labour Relations (Consolidation) Act 1992. c. 52.
Transfer of Undertakings (Protection of Employment) (Amendment) Regulations 2014 (SI 2014/ 16).
Transfer of Undertakings (Protection of Employment) Regulations 1981 (SI 1981/1794).
Transfers of Undertaking (Protection of Employment) Regulations 2006 (SI 2006/246).

United States

Bankruptcy Act of 1800 (2 Stat. 19).
Bankruptcy Code 1978 (Title 11 of the US Code).
Bankruptcy Reform Act 1978 (Pub L. No.95–598, 92 Stat. 2549).
Civil Rights Act 1964 (Pub. L. 88–352, 78 Stat. 241).
Employment Retirement Income Security Act 1974 (Pub L. 93–406, 88 Stat. 829).
Government Organization and Employees Act 1979 (Pub. L. 89–554, 93 Stat. 381).
National Labour Relations Act 1935 (29 U.S.C. ss.151–169).
The Bankruptcy Venue Statute (1984) (28 U.S.C. s.1408).
The Delaware Code – Title 19 (DEL. CODE ANN. tit. 19).

The European Union

Council Directive 77/187/EC of 14 February 1977 on the approximation of the laws of the Member States relating to the safeguarding of employees' rights in the event of transfers of undertakings, businesses or parts of businesses [1977] OJ L 61/26.

Council Directive 98/50/EC of 29 June 1998 1977 amending Directive 77/187/EC on the approximation of the laws of the Member States relating to the safeguarding of employees' rights in the event of transfers of undertakings, businesses or parts of businesses [1998] OJ L 201.

Council Directive 2001/23/EC of 12 March 2001 on the approximation of the laws of the Member States relating to the safeguarding of employees' rights in the event of transfers of undertakings, businesses or parts of undertakings or businesses [2001] OJ L 82/16.

European Commission, *Proposal for a Directive on Preventive Restructuring Frameworks, Second Chance and Measures to increase the Efficiency of Restructuring, Insolvency and Discharge Procedures and amending Directive 2012/30/EU.* (Com (2016) 723/0359) final.

European Commission, *Commission Recommendation of 12 March 2014 on a New Approach to Business Failure and Insolvency*, (2014/125/EU).

Table of government reports, guidance reports and other documents

United Kingdom

Association of Business Recovery Professionals, *Statement of Insolvency Practice16: Pre-packaged Sales in Administrations* (London: R3, 2009).

Department of Employment, *Contracting Out in the Context of the Provisions of Community Law and National Laws relating to the Transfer of Undertakings* (House of Commons Deposited Papers, Ref. HINF 94/1363).

K. Cork, Sir (Chairman), *Insolvency Law and Practice: Report of the Review Committee* (1982) [Cmnd 8558].

The Insolvency Service, *Enterprise Act 2002 – Corporate Insolvency Provisions: Evaluation Report*, (London: 2008).

The Insolvency Service, *Report on the Operation of SIP 16: 1 January to 31 December 2010* (London: IS 2011).

United States

United States Congress, *United States Statutes at Large*, 95th Congress, 1st Session, (H.R Report No. 595, 1977)

United States Department of Labor, *Economic News Release: Union Members Summary*, (Bureau of Labor Statistic, 2016).

1 Corporate rescue and employment protection – concepts, policies and processes

Introduction

In modern market economies, a company is a place of social relationships from which members, such as employees, derive their livelihood.[1] Capital and labour are the two most important factors of production in a company. Employees provide human capital in the form of labour that facilitates the day-to-day running of the company that enables the company to enhance its going concern value.[2] Therefore, human labour is a strategic asset[3] without which a company may struggle to achieve its economic goals.[4]

Shareholders invest money in companies in anticipation that such companies will prosper and generate profits that will enhance their economic well-being. Likewise, employees seek employment in these companies in order to gain a source of income. This income would facilitate and enhance their economic well-being, provide for their relations and meet their living costs.[5] Job satisfaction and job security are regarded as important aspects of quality of life.

However, on the insolvency of their employer, employees not only face the prospect of having their economic well-being in terms of job security and income interrupted, but also face the possibility of having their jobs permanently ended where their employer is liquidated.[6] In addition to losing their job security and income, employees may also suffer social disruptions to their well-being.[7] Social

1 J. E. Stiglitz, "Employment, Social Justice and Societal Well-being" (2002) 141 *Int'l Labour Rev.* 9–29.

2 The term 'going concern value' refers to the value of the company as a going entity for the foreseeable future as opposed to being liquidated. See also, Edith Penrose, *The Theory of the Growth of the Firm* (Oxford, Basil Blackwell, 1959).

3 Michael Armstrong, *A Handbook of Personnel Practice* (4th edn, London, Kogan Page, 1991).

4 Lester C. Thurow, *The Future of Capitalism* (New York, W. Morrow & Co, 1996).

5 The term economic well-being in the context of employees relates to remunerative employment through which they are paid wages or salaries for services rendered. See, Margaret M. Blair and Lynn A. Stout, "A Team Production Theory of Corporate Law" (1999) 85 *VA. L. Rev.* 247.

6 M. Stephens, "The Long-Run Consumption Effects of Earning Shocks" (2001) 83 *Rev. Econ. Stat.* 28–38.

7 Richard H. Price, "Psychological Impact of Job Loss on Individuals and Families" (1992) 1(1) *Curr. Dir. Psychol. Sci.* 9–11.

effects, such as marriage and family breakdown, increase in crime and other anti-social practices, such as alcoholism and neighbourhood nuisance, have been to some extent attributed to job losses.[8] Therefore, job security is an important aspect of an employee's economic security.

However, following the global economic recession in 2007/2008 that economically affected companies both in the US and the UK, most companies have become more risk-averse[9] to financial investments and business activities that may potentially affect their companies' business productivity, or risk the companies' economic and financial stability. Therefore, some companies in these jurisdictions have continued to engage in corporate restructuring[10] as a measure of either improving their business productivity or protecting the financial stability of their companies' businesses.

However, the forms of corporate restructuring that these companies adopt often involve cutting or lowering production costs, which often point towards labour costs reduction. Reduction in labour costs may involve cutting jobs or introducing new working practices, such as 'zero-hours' contracts[11] or implementing changes to the terms and conditions of employment. Some companies may consider moving production and service centres to locations where labour and service costs are relatively cheaper both locally and internationally. All these practices by the employers threaten employment security; therefore, a need to balance the interests of employees and employers during corporate insolvency.

The genesis of corporate rescue and employment protection in the UK and US

The United Kingdom

In the UK, many of the policies underlying social employment protection during corporate insolvency derive from the European Union (EU) Social Policy influenced by the sociopolitical and economic culture. The social employment protection policies that are influenced by the EU are codified in three main EU social policy directives that set out to preserve and protect workers' rights in the event of the employers' insolvency.

The first is Council Directive 2001/23/EC[12] which provides for specific provisions for the protection of employees by providing for prohibition on unfair

8 J. Gruber, "The Wealth of the Unemployed" (2001) 55 *Ind. Labour Relat. Rev.* 79, 94.

9 A 'risk-averse' company is one that chooses to invest in business transactions with known risks that may provide low returns than unknown risks with higher predictable returns.

10 These are approaches a company may take to review its organisational, operational or capital structures. See, Oliver Hyams, *Employment Aspects of Business Reorganisation* (Oxford, OUP, 2006).

11 Ian Brinkley, "Flexibility or Insecurity? Exploring the Rise in Zero-hours Contracts" *The Work Foundation* (1 August 2013) <www.theworkfoundation.com/Reports/339/Flexibility-or-insecurity-Exploring-the-rise-in-zero-hours-contracts> (accessed 10 June 2019).

12 Council Directive 2001/23/EC of 12 March 2001 on the approximation of the laws of the Member States relating to the safeguarding of employees' rights in the event of transfers of undertakings, businesses or parts of undertakings or businesses [2001] OJ L 82/16.

dismissal of employees and variations to employees' terms and conditions of employment because of the business sale or transfer of the undertaking. The Directive also provides for the continuity of employment by requiring automatic transfer of employees' employment contracts on a business sale or relevant transfer subject to specific insolvency exceptions. This Directive was transposed into UK law via the Transfer of Undertakings (Protection of Employment) Regulations 2006.[13]

The second is the Collective Redundancy Directive – Council Directive 98/59/EC.[14] This Directive sets out provision for standards to be followed by employers for consultations with employees' representatives when employers are contemplating collective redundancies and dismissals. Where an employer intends to lay off 20 employees over a period of 90 days or the lesser of 10 percent or 30 employees over 30 days, that employer must provide relevant information to employees' representatives and also, consult with employees' representatives to reach agreements over ways and means of avoiding projected collective redundancies or reducing the number of employees to be affected among other mitigating circumstances.[15]

This is to afford employees in Member States a certain level of protection against collective dismissals while taking into account the need for balanced economic and social development within the European Union. The provisions in this Directive were implemented in the Trade Union and Labour Relations (Consolidation) Act 1992,[16] especially, ss. 181–189 that deal with information and consultation requirements for employers during collective redundancies.

The third is the Employers in Insolvency Directive, Council Directive 80/987/EEC[17] which offers additional protection to employees in the event of their employer's insolvency in the form of a guarantee for payment of outstanding claims arising from contracts of employment and other employment-related interests. This Directive provides for Member States to apply or introduce measures favourable to employees in the pursuance of these protective measures. The provisions in this Directive are implemented in the Insolvency Act 1986, particularly Schedule 6 under the title of preferential debts.

In the UK, employees' unpaid wages and accrued holiday pay are given preferential priority in distribution ahead of unsecured claims out of the assets of the company on the insolvency of their employer. However, this is subject to a statutory limit as set out in IA 1986, Schedule 6. In addition, as a matter of adhering to Directive 80/987/EEC, the UK government established a state National Insurance Fund from which employees affected by their employer's

13 Transfer of Undertakings (Protection of Employment) Regulations 2006 (SI 2006/246). (TUPE 2006).

14 Council Directive 98/59/EC of 20 July 1998 on the approximation of the laws of the Member States relating to collective redundancies [1998] OJ L 255.

15 Ibid, Section II, Art. 2(1) and (2).

16 Trade Union and Labour Relations (Consolidation) Act 1992, c.52.

17 Council Directive 80/987/EEC of 20 October 1980 on the approximation of the laws of the Member States relating to the protection of employees in the event of the insolvency of their employer [1980] OJ L283.

insolvency may claim certain unpaid debts arising out of their employment. In addition to EU-derived social employment protection legislation, other UK statutes such as Employment Rights Act (ERA) 1996[18] have provisions that govern the employee-employer concerns during corporate insolvency in the UK.[19]

On the other hand, insolvency law policies in the UK were first influenced by the Cork Committee Report[20] and later by the consultation documents[21] that led to the Enterprise Act.[22] This was following the UK government's appointment of the Cork Committee to review both corporate and personal insolvency laws of the UK and to make recommendations for reform.

The Cork Committee's report advised the provision of 'means for the preservation of viable commercial enterprises capable of making a useful contribution to the economic life of the country'.[23] The Cork Committee recommended two new procedures: the company voluntary arrangement (CVA) and the administration procedure to supplement the existing administrative receivership,[24] reconstruction,[25] scheme of arrangement procedures[26] and the informal 'London Approach'.[27]

The Cork Committee's recommendations for the provisions of the administration process and CVA were first introduced under the Insolvency Act 1985,[28] which was consolidated as the Insolvency Act 1986 (IA 1986).[29] The policies underlying corporate rescue in the UK derive from the IA 1986, Schedule B1, Paragraph 3(1) that governs the administration process in the UK during corporate insolvency. Schedule B1, Paragraph 3(1) sets out the three hierarchical objectives to be pursued by the insolvency practitioner (administrator) during administration proceedings with the main objective being the rescue of the company as a going concern.[30] The second objective is achieving a better result for the company's creditors as a whole than would be likely if the company were

18 Employment Rights Act (1996), c.18. (ERA 1996).
19 ERA (1996), Part XII on Insolvency of employers and rights of employees on insolvency of employers.
20 Report of the Review Committee, Chairman Sir Kenneth Cork, *Insolvency Law and Practice* Cmnd 8558 (London: HMSO, 1982) (Cork Report).
21 For example, see, Insolvency Service, *A Review of Company Rescue and Business Reconstruction Mechanisms*, Report by the Review Group (DTI, 2000) (IS 2000); Insolvency Service, *A Review of Company Rescue and Business Reconstruction Mechanisms*, Interim Report (DTI, September 1999). See also, I. Fletcher, "UK Corporate Rescue: Recent Developments – Changes to Administrative Receivership, Administration and Company Voluntary Arrangements – the Insolvency Act 2000, the White Paper 2001 and the Enterprise Act 2002" (2004) 5 *Eur. Bus. Organ. Rev.* 119.
22 Enterprise Act 2002, c40.
23 Cork Report, p. 55, para. 198(j).
24 IA 1986, s.29.
25 IA 1986, s.110.
26 Companies Act 2006, Part 26.
27 The 'London Approach' is a set of informal restructuring processes aimed at supporting financially struggling companies to restructure their debts regulated by the Bank of England.
28 IA 1985, c65.
29 IA 1986, c45.
30 IA 1986, Sch. B1, Para.3 (1) (a).

wound up,[31] while the third objective is realising property in order to make a distribution to one or more secured or preferential creditors.[32]

The United States

In the US, the policies underlying social employment protection under the US social policy derive from both federal and state legislation mandating employment protection policies during bankruptcy reorganisation proceedings due to a federal system of government.[33] Therefore, the policies underlying employment protection are mainly set out in the National Labor Relations Act 1935 (NLRA 1935).[34] For example, under Section 7, the NLRA (1935) mandates collective bargaining rights on employees through forming, joining or assisting a labour organisation to bargain collectively on matters relating to their employment through labour union representation.[35] The NLRA 1935 makes it an unfair labour practice where an employer interferes with, coerces or restrains employees from exercising these rights.[36]

However, corporate rescue or bankruptcy reorganisation policies in the US derive from Title 11 of the US Code which is known as the US Bankruptcy Code that governs bankruptcy reorganisation proceedings. Bankruptcy Code provisions such as s. 362[37] – mandating moratoria on creditor actions against the debtor after filing for bankruptcy, s.365[38] – allowing a debtor to assume or reject executory contracts upon bankruptcy filing and s.1113[39] – allowing a debtor to assume or reject collectively bargained agreements are some of the provisions that set out the policy objectives of the US Bankruptcy Code which is to augment the reorganisation and rescue prospects of the financially struggling company.

Corporate rescue and employment protection in the US

In the US, bankruptcy reorganisation proceedings are governed by Chapter 11 of the US Bankruptcy Code which was enacted in 1978 as Title 11 of the US Code.[40] The US Bankruptcy Code prescribes a traditional Chapter 11 filing process

31 IA 1986, Sch. B1, Para.3 (1) (b).
32 IA 1986, Sch. B1, Para.3 (1) (c).
33 M H. Redish, "Doing it with Mirrors: *New York v. US* and Constitutional Limitations on Federal Power to Require State Law Legislation" (1993) 21 *Hastings Const. L. Q.* 593, 604.
34 29 U.S.C. ss.151 - 169 (2017). Enacted by the 74th United States Congress on July 6 1935, Pub. L. 74–198, 49 Stat. 449 to create a National Labor Relations Board and to regulate labour disputes between employers and employees that may burden or obstruct interstate and foreign commerce. This statute is also known as the Wagner Act.
35 29 U.S.C. s.8 (a) (5).
36 29 U.S.C. s.158.
37 11 U.S.C. s. 362.
38 11 U.S.C s.365.
39 11 U.S.C. s.1113.
40 11 U.S.C. ss. 101 - 1330 (2012) Enacted by the Bankruptcy Reform Act 1978 (Pub. L. No.95 - 598, 92 Stat. 2549).

through which outcomes, such as s.363 business sale or a pre-pack plan, may be achieved by a US debtor company during bankruptcy reorganisation proceedings.

In a traditional Chapter 11 route, the debtor negotiates with the affected stakeholders to agree a reorganisation plan. The debtor will solicit for votes to approve the plan, and then the reorganisation plan, together with a disclosure statement, is presented to the court for confirmation.[41] This route is, however, initiated without a defined exit plan, unlike in a pre-packaged or pre-arranged Chapter 11 plan.

In a pre-packaged route, a lot is done in advance of the filing for bankruptcy. The debtor company negotiates a reorganisation plan with the affected stakeholders, distributes disclosure statements to the stakeholders and solicits for votes for the approval of the plan. The adequacy and viability of the proposed plan and the disclosure statement are scrutinised at a joint hearing. If well presented, and therefore holding good prospects, together with a defined exit plan, a Chapter 11 reorganisation plan is commenced, which is usually shorter in duration than the traditional route.[42]

Alternatively, a debtor company may choose to utilise a s.363 business sale[43] to end the uncertainty of bankruptcy. The provisions in s.363 afford the trustee or the Debtor-in-Possession (DIP)[44] power to use, sell or lease, other than in the ordinary course of business, the assets of the debtor company's estate, following a notice and hearing processes. Although this has been the subject of varied debates,[45] it is a route that can enable a quick sale of the struggling business, sidestepping liabilities that were incurred by the debtor company pre-petition.

However, unlike a s.363 business sale, the ultimate aim of a Chapter 11 reorganisation plan is to afford a financially struggling company, a second chance to regain solvency. This is inherent in the contention that a business is more profitable and beneficial to its stakeholders, as a going concern than when liquidated piecemeal.[46] Moreover, the US Supreme Court, in *US v Whiting Pools Inc.*,[47] described the objective of a Chapter 11 reorganisation plan, by referring to the intentions of the US Congress in drafting Chapter 11 of the Bankruptcy Code. This was the anticipation that, where a company adopts a Chapter 11 reorganisation plan, its business would continue to enhance its going concern value, save jobs, satisfy creditors' claims and produce a return to its owners.[48]

41 11 U.S.C. s.1129.

42 Jennifer Payne, "Debt Restructuring in English Law: Lessons from the United States and the Need for Reform" (2014) 130 *L. Quart. Rev.* 282.

43 11 U.S.C. s.363.

44 The term Debtor-in-possession is used in the US to refer to pre-petition management of the company that is undergoing bankruptcy reorganisation. See David A. Skeel Jr, "Creditors' Ball: The New Corporate Governance in Chapter 11" (2003) 152(2) *U Pa L Rev.* 917 regarding the influence of creditors on the debtor-in-possession.

45 G. Moss, "Comparative Bankruptcy Cultures: Rescue or Liquidation? Comparison of Trends in National Law – England" (1997) 23 *Brooklyn J. Int. L.* 115.

46 M. Herbert, *Understanding Bankruptcy* (New York, LexisNexis Legal Text Series, 2005) 303.

47 *US v Whiting Pools Inc.* (1983) 462 U.S. 198, 203.

48 See, H.R Report No. 595, 95th Congress, 1st session, 220 (1977).

Therefore, to an employee, a successful Chapter 11 reorganisation plan would potentially be a lifeline as jobs could be saved. For the management DIP, a successfully executed Chapter 11 reorganisation plan would not only potentially save their jobs, but would also restore their reputation as the stigma of failure in the first instance may be remedied.[49]

Corporate rescue and employment protection in the UK

In the UK, outside of insolvency settings, that is, before a debtor employer files for formal insolvency proceedings, employees are generally protected against unfair employer prerogatives, such as employer decisions to dismiss employees without 'just cause' or changes to employees' terms and conditions of employment. The ERA 1996 protects employees from unfair dismissals from their employers,[50] This Act gives employees a right to compensation where an employee is made redundant by the employer,[51] a right to a written statement of employment setting out the terms and conditions of employment,[52] a right to continuity of employment where the employer's business is the subject of a transfer to a new buyer as a going concern,[53] among other protection.

In addition to the above, employees are further protected by the Transfer of Undertakings (Protection of Employment) Regulations (2006) (TUPE 2006) and The Collective Redundancies and Transfer of Undertakings (Protection of Employment) (Amendment) Regulations 2014 (TUPE 2014) where their employer is the subject of a relevant business sale or transfer as a going concern. However, inside formal and quasi-formal insolvency proceedings, the level of employee protection is dictated by the procedural and legal framework within which each particular corporate rescue process operates.

Formal and quasi-formal corporate rescue processes in the UK

Formal corporate rescue processes in the UK are the administration procedure[54] and the CVA.[55] Administrative receivership can also be used to rescue companies in limited circumstances[56] and the scheme of arrangement has also been used for this purpose and has gained in popularity in this regard in recent years, in particular with larger companies with complex financial arrangements.[57] Prepack business sales are also a common approach to financial distress, recognised

49 B. A. Henoch, "Post Petition Financing: Is There Life After Debt?" (1991) 8 *Bankr. Dev. J.* 575, 577.

50 ERA 1996, s.94.

51 ERA 1996, s.218.

52 ERA 1996, s.86 (2).

53 ERA 1996, s.218.

54 IA 1986, Schedule B1.

55 IA 1986, Part 1, and the Insolvency Rules 1986, Part 1.

56 See generally, IA 1986, s.29.

57 CA 2006, Part 26, ss.895 – 901 and Part 27 (special rules for public companies).

through case law[58] and guidance statements[59] from professional bodies but they are not legislatively established by the UK insolvency laws. The UK Insolvency Service, as a regulatory body, plays a major role by maintaining a monitory and regulatory role in the pre-pack process by ensuring compliance and adherence to established codes of conduct by insolvency practitioners.

Administration

The administration procedure is a corporate rescue process used by companies in the UK seeking to reorganise or restructure their company businesses during corporate insolvency. This procedure was introduced in 1985 by the Insolvency Act 1985, consolidated as the Insolvency Act 1986 (IA 1986) and recently streamlined by the Enterprise Act 2002 (EA 2002).[60] This was through the introduction of the out of court route for administration orders to be obtained by the company or its directors or a qualifying floating charge holder, upon the giving of notice and the filing of documentation with the court.[61] Administration is one of the most commonly used insolvency procedures in the UK.[62] It is designed to help in the rescue of financially struggling but viable companies in the UK.

Administration allows for the reorganisation of a company or the realisation of a company's assets whilst it is under the protection of a statutory moratorium.[63] The moratorium is a useful mechanism as not only does it freeze the enforcement of security by creditors seeking to recover their debts, but it also stays creditors from presenting petitions for the winding-up of the struggling company.[64] Thus, the moratorium that comes with the administration procedure, at least as it was originally intended to operate affords the company time to negotiate with its creditors to find a way in which the business can be saved without it being wound-up.

Administration lasts for up to 12 months from the date at which the administrator's appointment took effect,[65] unless extended by the court or by the consent of creditors but the extension of the administrator's term of office (with the consent of creditors) cannot exceed six months.[66] The provisions governing the administration process in the IA 1986[67] place a hierarchy of three objectives to

58 See *Re T & D Industries Plc* [2000] B.C.C 956 Ch.; *Re Transbus International Ltd* [2004] 2 BCLC 550.

59 See for example, Association of Business Recovery Professionals (R3), *Statement of Insolvency Practice 16: Pre-packaged Sales in Administrations* (London: R3, 2009); See, Insolvency Service (IS), *Report on the Operation of SIP 16: 1 January to 31 December 2010* (London: IS 2011).

60 Enterprise Act 2002, c40.

61 S. Frisby, "In Search of a Rescue Regime: The Enterprise Act 2002" (2004) 67 *Mod L. Rev.* 247.

62 V. Finch, "Corporate Rescue: A Game of Three Halves" (2012) 32(2) *Legal Stud.* 302–324.

63 IA 1986, Sch. Bl, Para. 42(1).

64 IA 1986, Sch. Bl, Para. 42(2).

65 IA 1986, Sch. Bl, Para. 76(1).

66 IA 1986, Sch. Bl, Para. 76(2)(a) and (b).

67 IA 1986, Sch. Bl, Para. 3(1).

be pursued by the administrator with the main objective being the rescue of the company as a going concern.[68]

This objective of the administration process is aimed at the rescue of the company as a going concern as opposed to liquidation but this is rarely achievable. It is only where the administrator thinks that this main objective is not reasonably practicable to achieve[69] that the administrator may consider the second objective of 'achieving a better result for the company's creditors as a whole than would be likely if the company were wound up'.[70]

The administrator is only required to pursue this objective if it would achieve a better result for the company's creditors as a whole,[71] which may include, for example, saving jobs for employees and maintaining the continuity of the chain of employment, as well as optimising the amounts available for creditors. However, where the administrator thinks that neither the first, nor the second objectives, are reasonably practicable to achieve,[72] the administrator may consider pursuing the third objective[73] of 'realising property in order to make a distribution to one or more secured or preferential creditors'.[74]

The appointment of an administrator does not necessarily terminate the employment contracts of the employees or trigger the operation of TUPE Regulations obligations on the transferor or transferee. TUPE Regulations obligations on the transferor and transferee are triggered where there is a business transfer or changes in employer. TUPE Regulations' automatic transfer provision in regulation 4(1), the protection from variations to contract terms and condition in regulation 4(4) and employee protection from dismissals because of the business sale or transfer will be invoked upon a relevant transfer of a business or an undertaking in the UK. With this protection in operation, the employees remain employed by the insolvent but viable company as it attempts to trade out of its financial difficulties. The administrator has 14 days in which to decide whether or not to adopt employees' contracts of employment.[75]

Where the contracts of employment are adopted by the administrator after the 14 day period, accrued sums due to unpaid wages, salaries, holiday payments et cetera, in the adopted contracts are given a super priority status[76] and therefore, treated as expenses in administration.[77] However, where the administrator decides not to adopt the contracts of employment after the 14 days' period,

68 IA 1986 Sch. B1, para 3(1)(a).
69 IA 1986 Sch.B1, para 3(3) (a).
70 IA 1986 Sch.B1, para 3(1) (b).
71 IA 1986 Sch.B1, para 3 (3) (b).
72 IA 1986, Sch. B1, para. 3(4) (a).
73 IA 1986 Sch.B1, para 3(1) (c).
74 IA 1986 Sch. B1 para 3 (4) (b).
75 As per the reasoning in *Powdrill v Watson* [1995] 2 AC. 394.
76 IA 1986, Sch. B1 para 99 (6); *Krasner v McMath* [2006] I.C.R 205.
77 IA 1986, Sch. B1, Paragraph 99(6). For judicial authority on the nature of employee claims that may have super priority payment, see, *Re Allders Department Stores Ltd (in administration)* [2005] EWHC 172; *Re Leeds United Association Football Club Ltd* [2007] EWHC 1761 (Ch.).

consultations on redundancy with affected employees may be initiated where certain thresholds under s.188 of the Trade Union and Labour Relations (Consolidation) Act (TULCRA) 1992 are met.[78]

The threshold under s.188 of the TULCRA 1992 places a duty on the employer to consult with employees' appropriate representatives where the employer proposes to dismiss as redundant 20 or more employees at one establishment within a period of 90 days or less. The employer must also consult with employees' appropriate representative for at least 45 days where proposals are to dismiss as redundant one hundred or more employees before the first of the dismissal takes effect.[79]

However, where the administrator chooses to pursue the second and third objectives of administration[80] because the main objective of 'rescuing the company as a going concern' is not reasonably practicable to achieve, employee protection, especially, the automatic transfer of employment following the sale or transfer of their employer's business to a new owner, may be compromised. The second objective of 'achieving a better result for the company's creditors as a whole than would be likely if the company were immediately wound up'[81] may take different forms other than keeping the company operating on a going concern basis. For instance, the administrator may decide that dismissing some of the employees or making changes to employees' terms and conditions of employment may help to achieve a better result for the company creditors as a whole[82] which may benefit creditors at the expense of employee protection.

Moreover, the third objective[83] of 'realising property in order to make a distribution to one or more secured or preferential creditors does not give primacy to employment protection. This, therefore, creates tensions between corporate rescue objectives and employment protection objectives since rescuing the company as a going concern may entail changes in the workforce, among other factors. This tension is in need of remedy if both the objectives of corporate rescue and of employment protection are to be pursued simultaneously.

Pre-pack administration

A pre-pack process is an arrangement which involves negotiations between the struggling company's management or directors and secured creditors to agree to a sale of all or some of the company's assets informally in advance of the appointment of an insolvency practitioner. It is a quasi-legal rescue process as it starts out informally, turning into the formal administration process following the appointment of an administrator to oversee the implementation of the agreed sale.[84]

78 Trade Union and Labour Relations (Consolidation) Act 1992, C 52, (TULCRA 1992).
79 TULCRA, 1992, s. 188 (1) – s.188 (1) (A).
80 IA 1986, Sch. B1, para. 3(1) (b) and (c).
81 IA 1986, Sch. B1, para 3(1) (b).
82 This was one of factors in *Crystal Palace F.C Ltd and Another v Kavanagh and Others* [2014] IRLR 139, CA.
83 IA 1986 Sch.B1, para 3 (4) (a).
84 A. Kastrinou, "An Analysis of the Pre-pack Technique and Recent Developments in the Area" (2008) 29(9) *Company Lawyer* 259, 263.

The insolvency practitioner plays a central role in the pre-pack business sale process as he or she is often involved as an advisor to the management or directors of the company before the commencement of full administration and, later, more formally as the administrator when the company is properly in administration. Upon appointment, the insolvency practitioner, who is now the administrator, quickly implements the pre-agreed sale of the business via a formal administration process, often to the existing owners or the directors of the business. In other words, in a pre-pack sale of a business, all of the preparatory work in relation to the sale in question is usually carried out in advance of formal administration commencing and prior to the creditors of the company being told about the failure of the business.[85]

Although pre-packs are commonly used alongside administration proceedings, drawing them closer to within the boundaries of formal processes, such as CVAs and administration proceedings, a pre-pack business sale is nonetheless, seen as a hybrid procedure due to the fact that the process is neither statutorily defined by the IA 1986, nor the Enterprise Act 2002 but rotates between the borders of formal and informal insolvency procedures.[86] However, despite pre-pack business sales not being legally established by the UK statutes, their status as a corporate rescue process has been established by caselaw.[87]

The inherent advantage of a pre-pack business sale from the perspective of employees is that a successful pre-pack business sale would trigger the operation of the automatic transfer of employees via regulation 4 of TUPE 2006 Regulations. A pre-pack is not a case of irretrievable insolvency and cessation of business. Rather, in a pre-pack process, goodwill is maintained and the business is transferred as a going concern to a buyer.[88] Therefore, a pre-pack business sale may lead to the preservation and the continuity of employment, which is beneficial for employees.[89]

However, the underlying policy objectives of pre-pack business sales have attracted criticisms and continue to be the subject of varied debates.[90] The key issues in the debates from the perspective of employees are the limited involvement of employees in the activities leading to the sale of their employer's business, and the lack of transparency and open marketing of the business. The quick and speedy sale of the business raises questions whether other alternatives to the pre-pack sale are considered by the insolvency practitioner.

85 P. Walton, "Pre-packin' in the UK" (2009) 18 *Int. Insolv. Rev.* 85, 104.

86 V. Finch, "Corporate Rescue: A Game of Three Halves" (2012) 32(2) *Legal Stud.* 302–324.

87 See *Re T & D Industries Plc* [2000] B.C.C 956 Ch; *Re Transbus International Ltd* [2004] EWHC 932 (Ch.).

88 See *Jules Dethier Equipement SA v Dassy & Another* (1998) ICR 541 ECJ; *Perth and Kinross Council v Donaldson & Ors* (2004) IRLR 121 EAT.

89 For instance, see *Federatie Nederlandse Vakrereninging v Smallsteps BV* C- 126/16 [2017] (also known as *Estro / Smallsteps* case) concerning a Dutch pre-pack business transfer where the CJEU held that employees' rights in the event of transfer of undertakings may be maintained where a pre-pack is put in effect following insolvency.

90 See for example, Jessica Klein, "Pre-Pack Administrations: A Comparison between Germany and the United Kingdom: Part 1" (2012) 33(9) *Company Lawyer* 261, 268; Kastrinou (n 112), Walton (n 113), Finch, (n 114).

Employees are often considered as the most important asset of a company when the human capital contributions they make in a company are taken into account.[91] It has been opined that when employees make firm-specific human capital investment in a company or business, their contributions rank in importance as, or even more important than, the shareholders' investment of finance capital.[92] However, in a pre-pack business sale process, employees are not involved in the matters relevant to the business sale process, yet they have interests, such as their job security and unpaid wages that may be compromised, if not ended.

All the above factors combined, make the pre-pack business sale process a less inclusive rescue process, as the process is driven by the company's management or directors and secured creditors with little or no say for other parties with interest in the company, such as employees. The lack of a transparent and open marketing approach of the insolvent but viable business may fare negatively to the protection of employment and continuity.

There was hope that the transparency requirement on insolvency practitioners in the Statement of Insolvency Practice 16 (SIP 16)[93] would provide details to unsecured creditors on how the valuations of the business and the details of the entire pre-pack process would serve to improve transparency in the pre-pack process. However, full compliance from insolvency practitioners in relation to this requirement has yet to be achieved.[94]

The information that is usually provided to unsecured creditors, such as employees, is provided after a pre-pack business sale is agreed. At this point, the provision of information to unsecured creditors may be seen as effectively a filing obligation to provide assurance as to the appropriateness of the pre-pack process, not a procedural requirement prior to a decision being taken to agree to a pre-pack business sale.[95] From the perspective of employees, pre-pack business sales often leave them under represented and less involved in comparison to other stakeholders, such as secured creditors.

Company voluntary arrangements

A CVA is a formal corporate rescue process which is used by companies in the UK attempting to respond to their corporate financial difficulties. The aim is to either attempt to save the company from liquidation or to save the company's business as a going concern through a compromise agreement with creditors.

91 Michael Armstrong, *A Handbook of Personnel Practice* (4th edn, London, Kogan Page, 1991).

92 Wanjiru Njoya, "Employee Ownership and Efficiency: An Evolutionary Perspective" (2004) 33(3) *Ind. L. J.* 211–241.

93 SIPs are a series of guidance papers that set out principles and procedures that insolvency practitioners should follow. See, Association of Business Recovery Professionals (R3), *Statement of Insolvency Practice16: Pre-packaged Sales in Administrations* (London, R3, 2009).

94 See, Insolvency Service, "*Report on the Operation of the Statement of Insolvency Practice 16: 1 January to 31 December 2010* (London: Insolvency Service, undated) pg. 3.

95 R. Smiles, "SIP 16: Does it do what it says on the tin or is it a can of worms?" (Winter 2009) *Recovery* 28.

The procedure was introduced by the Insolvency Act 1985 which was consolidated as Insolvency Act 1986.[96] The process had been recommended by the Cork Committee, under the chairmanship of Sir Kenneth Cork, who sought to make companies in England and Wales able to enter into contractually binding agreements with their creditors in satisfaction of their debts. This was after establishing that the insolvency procedures that existed at the time were too cumbersome.[97] Therefore, if a company decides to use a CVA for its business restructuring or reorganisation processes, the company directors, the liquidator or the administrator (where the company is undergoing administration or liquidation proceedings) submits a proposal to the nominee.[98]

A nominee is the person designated by the IA 1986 to supervise the implementation of the CVA process and must be a qualified insolvency practitioner.[99] Upon accepting the proposal, the nominee files a copy of the proposals with the court, followed by summoning a shareholders' and creditors' meeting to approve the proposals. If approved by the creditors' meeting with a majority of over 75 percent in value of creditors voting in person or by proxy, the CVA would bind all persons who had notice of the meeting and were entitled to vote[100] except secured creditors.[101] Once implemented, the nominee becomes the supervisor[102] of the CVA and would be answerable as an officer of the court in relation to the monitoring and implementation of the CVA.[103]

Procedural and substantive requirements above put aside, the overall aim of a company adopting a CVA is to facilitate the reorganisation and continuation of the company's business as a going concern, as opposed to liquidation. For the employees, continued trading on a going concern basis would create employment continuity.

However, a CVA does not bind secured creditors.[104] This would have the effect that where the CVA proposal leads to a diminution in the secured creditor's entitlement, it may be vetoed by the secured creditor.[105] Where a secured creditor vetoes the agreement, a CVA may fail in its implementation. Where this is the case, employment protection and continuity predicated on the successful implementation of the CVA may be compromised.

Under a CVA, employees do not form a specific class of creditors with specific voting and approval rights in respect of proposals put forward by insolvency practitioners. Rather, they form a subset of unsecured creditors. This would

96 See, IA 1986, Part 1, and the Insolvency Rules 1986, Part 1.

97 Insolvency Law Review Committee, *Insolvency Law and Practice* (Cmnd 8558, 1982) Chapter 9 paras. 400, 418.

98 Insolvency Rules 1986, Rule 1.12.

99 IA 1986, Part 1, s.1(2).

100 IA 1986, s.5(2).

101 IA 1986, s.4(3).

102 IA 1986, Part 1, paras 1(2) & 7(2) (b).

103 At this point the nominee becomes an officer of the court and bound to act honourably in the implementation of the CVA. See also, the rule in *Re Condon, Ex parte James* (1874) LR 9 Ch. App 609.

104 IA 1986, s.4(3).

105 *IRC v Wimbledon Football Club Ltd.* [2004] BCC 638.

imply that when a CVA proposal is put forward to the nominee, it is not a requirement on the director or the administrator to make provisions for the equal treatment of employees as non-preferential unsecured creditors in comparison to secured and preferential creditors.[106]

Although aggrieved parties may bring unfair prejudicial claims against the company where they feel the terms of the CVA were prejudicial to their interests,[107] to the employees, it would require time and costs to initiate the claims and employees may lack the procedural knowledge of how to initiate such claims which may dissuade them from pursuing such actions. All these factors create tensions precipitated by the imbalances in corporate rescue laws and processes which further, impact on employment protection policy objectives and corporate rescue policy objectives that ought to be addressed to achieve a fair representation of employees' and employers' interests during corporate insolvency.

Administrative receivership

Administrative receivership is a procedure that arises under the terms of the charge between a floating charge holder and the company, giving the holder of the charge power to appoint an administrative receiver to take over the control of the business of the company in pursuit of the floating charge holder's interest.

An administrative receiver may be defined as either

a a receiver or manager of the whole (or substantially) the whole of the company's property appointed by or on behalf of the holders of any debentures of the company secured by a charge which, as created is a floating charge and one or more other securities; or

b a person who would be such a receiver or manager but for the appointment of some other as the receiver of part of the company's property.[108]

Administrative receivership is a procedure that was in common usage formerly, having been recognised by the courts since the late nineteenth century in the UK.[109] However, it has been virtually abolished due to the impact of the EA 2002. One of the most notable changes that the EA 2002 made to administrative receivership was the restriction on the floating charge holder's ability to appoint administrative receivers on floating charges created after the coming into effect, of the EA 2002 on 15 September 2003. However, the restriction is subject to the narrow exceptions under s.72A – G of the IA 1986. This restriction is not retrospective in effect as holders of floating charges created before

106 See the reasoning in *IRC v Wimbledon Football Club Ltd* [2004] BCC 638, para.18.

107 See the reasoning of the House of Lords in *SISU Capital Fund Ltd v Tucker* [2006] BCC 463, 68.

108 IA 1986, s.29.

109 See for example, *Re Panama, New Zealand and Australian Royal Mail Company* (1870) LR 5 Ch. App. 318.

15 September 2003 are able to exercise their rights to appoint an administrative receiver.[110]

Therefore, once appointed, the administrative receiver may facilitate a going concern sale of the business to achieve a better result for his appointor than would be possible on a piecemeal sale of the business assets of the company.[111] The main objective of administrative receivership is neither to liquidate nor to save the company but rather to enforce the floating charge holder's interest. This may be achieved through the sale of the whole or part of the company's business to a new buyer as a going concern. Where this is the case, employee jobs would be saved due to the continuity of employment chain.

Moreover, where the whole or part of the business is sold on a going concern basis, the automatic transfer of employment provisions of TUPE Regulations (2006) would be triggered, which would further protect employees from job terminations and changes to their terms and conditions of employment, courtesy of regulation 4 of TUPE (2006). However, administrative receivership does not provide employees with the same level of protection and involvement that it does to the floating charge holder.

In addition to the above, employee participation in administrative receivership is considerably minimal. There is a lack of collectivity in the procedure as a whole. The main point of concern for the administrative receiver is the interest of his appointer, the floating charge holder. Although the administrative receiver once appointed is deemed an agent of the company, and therefore, required to act in good faith,[112] the administrative receiver is able to dispose of business assets without regard to the interests of employees. Employees may have valuable skills and knowledge that may greatly contribute to rescue of their employer's business but their views may not be considered the main concern for the administrative receiver.

Moreover, administrative receivership restricts the use of other procedures like administration. While other corporate rescue processes, such as a CVA may use administration process alongside it to improve the prospect of achieving the intended rescue objectives, the appointment of an administrative receiver blocks the appointment of an administrator.[113] Therefore, if the business is not sold piecemeal by the administrative receiver, administrative receivership would have the effect that although the debts of a floating charge holder would be reduced or discharged, debts to other creditors would remain outstanding. Such debts may affect the prospects of an insolvent but viable business to trade out of its financial difficulties[114] which would lead to liquidation of the business assets which may also lead to job losses.

110 IA 1986, s.72A (4)(a).

111 See, R. Mokal, "Administrative Receivership and Administration – An Analysis" (2004) 57 *Curr. Legal Probl.* – Available at ssrn.com <https://ssrn.com/abstract=466701> (accessed 1 June 2019).

112 I A 1986, s.42.

113 I A 1986, s.9(3).

114 J. Armour and S. Frisby, "Rethinking Receivership" (2001) 21 *Oxford J. L. Stud.* 73–90.

Administrative receivership is presently not of great significance in comparison to other rescue processes, such as administration. However, where used by holders of floating charges created prior to the coming into effect of the EA 2002, the lack of an inclusive and a collective approach in the process may affect corporate rescue prospects of insolvent but viable businesses. In addition, the drive for increased enterprise growth and productivity may also be affected. Administrative receivership gives primacy of protection to the floating charge holder. Likewise, employment protection and continuity may be compromised as employment protection is not the main concern for the appointed administrative receiver.

Liquidation

Liquidation is a procedure that brings the existence of the company to an end. Liquidation proceedings may be sanctioned by company members. This is known as Members' Voluntary Liquidation (MVL). MVL is a solvent winding-up of the company. Creditors can also sanction the winding-up process of the company. This is known as Creditors' Voluntary Liquidation (CVL). In both MVL and CVL, the winding-up process is not mainly necessitated by financial difficulties. Rather, other factors, such as internal management concerns of the company may necessitate liquidation.[115]

Liquidation proceedings may also be initiated via a court order. This is known as compulsory liquidation. A court in England and Wales may issue a winding-up order of the company on the grounds that such a company is unable to pay its debts upon demand for payment from creditors.[116] Once appointed, the liquidator's main duty is to assume powers from the directors to oversee the winding-up process, which includes realisation of company assets to settle outstanding company debts in the order of priority prescribed by law. Liquidation proceedings can be initiated as a stand-alone procedure, or alongside other rescue processes, such as receivership, administration or CVA as an exit route.[117]

Unlike other corporate rescue processes such as administration and CVAs whose main aim is the rescue of the company as a going concern, liquidation proceedings are aimed at termination of the company. Therefore, the fate of employment protection differs procedurally and substantively. For example, under compulsory liquidation, employee protection provisions under TUPE Regulations such as regulation 4 – on the automatic transfer of employment contract and regulation 7 – on the prohibition from employee dismissal because of the business sale or transfer are inapplicable.[118] This is because the rationale for

115 For example, see, IA 1986, s.996 and IA 1986, s.122(1)(g).

116 IA 1986, s.122 and s.123.

117 I. Fletcher, "UK Corporate Rescue: Recent Developments – Changes to Administrative Receivership, Administration and Company Voluntary Arrangements – The Insolvency Act 2000, the White Paper 2001 and the Enterprise Act 2002" (2004) 5 *Eur. Bus. Organ. Rev.* 119.

118 These TUPE provisions are broadly discussed in Chapter 6 of this book.

winding-up of the company is not to save the company as a going concern, in which case, employee jobs may be saved.[119] Rather, liquidation brings the life of the company to an end. Therefore, all existing employment contracts are deemed terminated.

Where an insolvent practitioner (liquidator) transfers the affected company's business either via an MVL or CVL, regulations 4 and 7 will not apply as both the MVL and CVL are not relevant insolvency proceedings[120] initiated to rescue the company as a going concern. Unless there is an express agreement between the liquidator and the transferee (new buyer) to take on existing employees, all existing employee contracts will be terminated. In this situation, affected employees may claim for accrued wages, outstanding holiday payments, redundancy payments, et cetera from the government via the National Insurance Fund.

Conclusion

In the both the UK and the US, managerial decisions to restructure their businesses may involve sacrificing some of the employees' jobs, making changes to terms and conditions of employment or a reduction in the employees' working hours as measures to lower labour costs.[121] Besides labour being key to converting capital into goods and services that enhance the going concern value of the business, labour is also one of the biggest costs of production and service delivery. Therefore, an employer seeking to restructure operational and production costs may unavoidably, look at reducing labour costs. However, this freedom and flexibility is constricted by employment protection laws which prohibit employers from making business decisions that would potentially enable successful reorganisation and rescue for fear of burdensome liabilities or consequences for breaching these employment protection laws.

Much as employment protection is the main policy objective of both the UK general employment legislation and the EU social employment legislation in the form of the TUPE Regulations and other measures on the one hand, corporate rescue is the main policy objective of the UK insolvency law on the other hand. Corporate rescue as the main objective of the UK insolvency law's administration process is enshrined in (IA 1986) Schedule B1, Paragraph 3(1) (a). The objective is to afford insolvent but viable businesses in the UK a chance at corporate rescue through the sale or transfer of their businesses or part of the businesses to the available buyers as going concerns.[122]

119 See the reasoning in *D'Urso & ors v Ercole Marelli Ellectromeccanica Generale SpA & ors* Case C-362/89 [1991] ECR 1- 4105.

120 See TUPE 2006, Regulation 8(6).

121 P. A. Gibbs, "Determinants of Corporate Restructuring: The Relative Importance of Corporate Governance, Takeover Threat and Free Cash Flow" (1993) 14 *Strateg. Manage. J.* 51–68.

122 Sandra Frisby, "In Search of a Rescue Regime: The Enterprise Act 2002" (2002) 67(2) *Mod. L. Rev.* 247, 272.

However, sometimes business rescue is more achievable in reality as opposed to corporate rescue despite the apparent objectives of the IA 1986.[123] This is because corporate rescue is about saving the company, that is, the legal entity that was incorporated to carry forward the business of the company.[124] Business rescue, however, would involve either selling or transferring the business assets that are more cohesive as a productive unit to a new owner and the business may continue to operate under the new ownership as a going concern rather than saving the company as a whole.

This may be supported by the fact that it is the business of the company that progressively enhances its going concern value, thereby generating revenue, and perhaps, creating new jobs due to growth and expansion. Therefore, on corporate insolvency, a sale of a viable business would easily appeal to potential buyers in contrast to a sale of the company as a whole. However, irrespective of which of the two is achieved first, the overall advantage that may be born out of corporate rescue is the avoidance of corporate liquidations and the opportunity for the continuity of the business. This arguably, protects employee jobs and maintains the chain of continuity of employment.

However, the 'road' to a successful rescue of an insolvent but viable business is quite treacherous. This is because during proceedings for the sale or the transfer of an insolvent but viable business, the policy objectives of employment protection, especially, under TUPE Regulations, and the policy objectives of corporate rescue enshrined in the IA 1986 potentially conflict with each other.

TUPE provisions, such as regulation 4(1) on the automatic transfer of employees on the same terms and conditions of employment, the prohibition on the employer from varying employee terms and conditions of employment during business sales and transfer of undertakings in regulation 4(4) together with the protection to employees from being dismissed by their employers where the sole or principal reason for the dismissal is the business sale or transfer may restrict the employer's flexibility to execute business and entrepreneurial decisions for fear of breaching these TUPE provisions.[125]

On the other hand, a potential or prospective buyer may be disincentivised from buying an insolvent but viable business due to fear of inheriting contingent and non-contingent liabilities born out of TUPE Regulations obligation on the transferor and the transferee. This may negatively impact on the employer's flexibility to sell the business as a going concern. This may not only affect the policy

123 R. Mokal, "Administrative Receivership and Administration – An Analysis" (2004) 57 *Curr. Legal Probl.*, <https://ssrn.com/abstract=466701> (accessed June 2019).

124 J. Armour and R. Mokal, "Reforming the Governance of Corporate Rescue: The Enterprise Act 2002" (2004) *ESRC Business Research Working Paper No. 288*, <https://ssrn.com/abstract=567306> (accessed 5 June 2019).

125 S. Hardy and N. Adnett, "Entrepreneurial Freedom Versus Employee Rights: The Acquired Rights Directive and EU Social Policy post-Amsterdam" (1999) 9 *J. Eur. Soc. Policy* 127; A. Garde, "Recent Developments in the Law of Transfers of Undertakings" (2002) 39 *Common Mkt L. Rev.* 523.

objectives underlying the drive for corporate rescue but might also, grossly affect the entrepreneurship and enterprise norms that would otherwise boost going concern business sales, a catalyst for economic growth and stability.[126]

In the US, employer power plays a significant role in the way the employment relationships are handled. The main form of protection to employees in the private sector workforce is through collective bargaining and labour union movement between the employer and the employees through their respective labour unions. The National Labour Relations Act (NLRA) 1935[127] grants employees the right to bargain collectively over wages, hours of work and other terms and conditions of employment.[128] Collective bargaining is a means of ensuring that employee participation centres on the duty to consult in good faith and in the performance of mutual obligations.[129]

However, few employees in the private sector workforce are members of labour unions. Rather, a majority of employees in the private sector workforce are non-unionised. For example, a 2017 Economic News Release by the Bureau of Labor Statistics, United States Department of Labor, on 26 January 2017 reported that the percentage of wage and salary workers that were members of unions in 2016 was at 10.7 percent down 0.4 percent from the overall membership in 2016.[130] This represents a proportionately low level of union representation which leaves a significant majority of employees lacking protection as they fall outside of the scope of labour union protection.[131]

The rationale for protecting employees with some priority during insolvency or bankruptcy proceedings may be drawn from a number of justifications. For example, the commencement of Chapter 11 reorganisation plan gives employees hope that the business may continue and that a number of future constituent interests, such as future employment may be attained.[132] Employees are arguably unable to diversify risks of losing their jobs in comparison to other stakeholders with interests in the debtor company such as secured creditors who may diversify their risks by investing in other business transactions. Employees can only normally hold one full-time job at once.

126 J. McMullen, "TUPE: Ringing the (Wrong) Changes – The Collective Redundancies and Transfer of Undertakings (Protection of Employment) (Amendment) Regulations 2014" (2014) 43 *ILJ* 149.

127 29 U.S.C. ss.151 – 169 (2016).

128 29 U.S.C. s.158 (d).

129 Clyde W. Summers, "The Rights of Individual Workers: The Contract of Employment and the Rights of Individual Employees: Fair Representation and Employment at Will" (1984) 52 *Fordham L. Rev.* 1082, 1085.

130 See an Economic News Release by the Bureau of Labor Statics, United States Department of Labour, <www.bls.gov/news.release/union2.nr0.htm> (accessed 9 June 2019).

131 David A. Skeel Jr, "What is So Bad about Delaware?" (2001) 54 *Vand. L. Rev.* 309; Lynn. M. LoPucki and J W. Doherty, "Delaware Bankruptcy: Failure in the Ascendancy" (2006) 73 *U. Chi. L. Rev.* 1387.

132 Donald R. Korobkin, "Employee Interests in Bankruptcy" (1996) 4 *Am. Bankr. Inst. L. Rev.* 5, 6.

However, the protection that is inherent in the US legislation that ought to safeguard such expectations is not uniformly available to all employees, as most are not members of certain labour unions or collective groups. There is a lot of lobbying between labour unions with the government in the US. However, lobbying has only led to unionised employee protection as non-unionised employees lack a significant voice to influence the government which defeats the policies underlying the need for employment protection. This creates an imbalance between the policies underlying the need for employment protection and the policies underlying the need for encouraging bankruptcy reorganisation to avoid unnecessary liquidations.

Bibliography

Books

Armstrong, M, *A Handbook of Personnel Practice* (4th edn., London, Kogan Page, 1991).
Herbert, M, *Understanding Bankruptcy* (New York, LexisNexis Legal Text Series, 2005).
Hyams, O, *Employment Aspects of Business Reorganisation* (Oxford, OUP, 2006).
Penrose, E, *The Theory of the Growth of the Firm* (Oxford, Basil Blackwell, 1959).
Thurow, C Lester, *The Future of Capitalism* (New York, W. Morrow & Co, 1996).

Cases

United Kingdom

Crystal Palace F.C Ltd and Another v Kavanagh and Others [2014] IRLR 139, CA.
IRC v Wimbledon Football Club Ltd. [2004] BCC 638.
Jules Dethier Equipement SA v Dassy & Another (1998) ICR 541 ECJ.
Krasner v McMath [2006] I.C.R 205.
Perth and Kinross Council v Donaldson & Ors (2004) IRLR 121 EAT.
Powdrill v Watson [1995] 2 AC. 394.
Re Allders Department Stores Ltd (in administration) [2005] EWHC 172
Re Condon, Ex parte James (1874) LR 9 Ch. App 609.
Re Leeds United Association Football Club Ltd [2007] EWHC 1761 (Ch.).
Re Panama, New Zealand and Australian Royal Mail Company (1870) LR 5 Ch. App. 318.
Re T & D Industries Plc [2000] B.C.C 956 Ch.
Re Transbus International Ltd [2004] 2 BCLC 550.
SISU Capital Fund Ltd v Tucker [2006] BCC 463.

United States

US v Whiting Pools Inc. (1983) 462 U.S. 198, 203.

European Union

C-126/16 *Federatie Nederlandse Vakrereninging v Smallsteps BV* [2017].
C-362/89 *D'Urso & ors v Ercole Marelli Ellectromeccanica Generale SpA & ors* [1991] ECR 1-4105.

Journal articles

Armour, J, and Frisby, S, "Rethinking Receivership" (2001) 21 Oxford J. Legal Stud. 73–90.

Armour, J, and Mokal, R, "Reforming the Governance of Corporate Rescue: The Enterprise Act 2002" (2004) ESRC Business Research Working Paper No. 288 <https://ssrn.com/abstract=567306> (accessed 5 June 2019).

Blair, M Margaret, and Stout, A Lynn, "A Team Production Theory of Corporate Law" (1999) 85 VA. L. Rev. 247.

Finch, V, "Corporate Rescue: A Game of Three Halves" (2012) 32(2) Legal Stud. 302–324.

Fletcher, I, "UK Corporate Rescue: Recent Developments – Changes to Administrative Receivership, Administration and Company Voluntary Arrangements – The Insolvency Act 2000, the White Paper 2001 and the Enterprise Act 2002" (2004) 5 Eur. Bus. Organ. L. Rev. 119.

Frisby, S, "In Search of a Rescue Regime: The Enterprise Act 2002" (2004) 67 Mod. L. Rev. 247.

Garde, A, "Recent Developments in the Law of Transfers of Undertakings" (2002) 39 Common Mkt. L. Rev. 523.

Gibbs, PA, "Determinants of Corporate Restructuring: The Relative Importance of Corporate Governance, Takeover Threat and Free Cash Flow" (1993) 14 Strateg. Manage. J. 51–68.

Gruber, J, "The Wealth of the Unemployed" (2001) 55 Ind. Labour Relat. Rev. 79, 94.

Hardy, S, and Adnett, N, "Entrepreneurial Freedom Versus Employee Rights: The Acquired Rights Directive and EU Social Policy post-Amsterdam" (1999) 9 J. Eur. Soc. Policy 127.

Henoch, BA, "Post-Petition Financing: Is There Life After Debt?" (1991) 8 Bankr. Dev. J. 575, 577.

Kastrinou, A, "An Analysis of the Pre-pack Technique and Recent Developments in the Area" (2008) 29(9) Company Lawyer 259, 263.

Klein, J, "Pre-Pack Administrations: A Comparison between Germany and the United Kingdom: Part 1" (2012) 33(9) Company Lawyer 261, 268.

Korobkin, R. Donald, "Employee Interests in Bankruptcy" (1996) 4 Am Bankr. Inst. L. Rev 5, 6.

LoPucki, M Lynn, and Doherty, JW, "Delaware Bankruptcy: Failure in the Ascendancy" (2006) 73 U. Chi. L. Rev. 1387.

McMullen, J, "TUPE: Ringing the (Wrong) Changes – The Collective Redundancies and Transfer of Undertakings (Protection of Employment) (Amendment) Regulations 2014" (2014) 43 Ind. L. J. 149.

Moss, G, "Comparative Bankruptcy Cultures: Rescue or Liquidation? Comparison of Trends in National Law – England" (1997) 23 Brooklyn J. Int. L. 115.

Njoya, Wanjiru, "Employee Ownership and Efficiency: An Evolutionary Perspective" (2004) 33(3) Ind. L. J. 211–241.

Payne, J, "Debt Restructuring in English Law: Lessons from the United States and the Need for Reform" (2014) 130 L. Quart. Rev. 282.

Price, H Richard, "Psychological Impact of Job Loss on Individuals and Families" (1992) 1(1) Curr. Dir. Psychol. Sci. 9–11.

Redish, HM, "Doing it with Mirrors: *New York v. US* and Constitutional Limitations on Federal Power to Require State Law Legislation" (1993) 21 Hastings Const. L. Q. 593, 604.

Skeel, DA Jr, "What is So Bad About Delaware?" (2001) 54 Vand. L. Rev. 309.
Skeel, DA Jr, "Creditors' Ball: The New Corporate Governance in Chapter 11" (2003) 152(2) U. Pa. L Rev. 917 regarding the influence of creditors on the debtor-in-possession.
Smiles, R, "SIP 16: Does It Do What It Says on the Tin or is it a Can of Worms?" (Winter 2009) *Recovery* 28.
Stephens, M, "The Long-Run Consumption Effects of Earning Shocks" (2001) 83 Rev. Econ. Stat. 28–38.
Stiglitz, JE, "Employment, Social Justice and Societal Well-being" (2002) 141 Int'l Labour Rev. 9–29.
Summers, W. Clyde, "The Rights of Individual Workers: The Contract of Employment and the Rights of Individual Employees: Fair Representation and Employment at Will" (1984) 52 Fordham L. Rev. 1082, 1085.
Walton, P, "Pre-packin' in the UK" (2009) 18 Int. Insolv. Rev. 85, 104.

Legislation

European Union

Council Directive 80/987/EEC of 20 October 1980 on the approximation of the laws of the Member States relating to the protection of employees in the event of the insolvency of their employer [1980] OJ L283.
Council Directive 98/59/EC of 20 July 1998 on the approximation of the laws of the Member States relating to collective redundancies [1998] OJ L 255.
Council Directive 2001/23/EC of 12 March 2001 on the approximation of the laws of the Member States relating to the safeguarding of employees' rights in the event of transfers of undertakings, businesses or parts of undertakings or businesses [2001] OJ L 82/16.

United Kingdom

Statutes

Companies Act 2006, c.46.
Employment Rights Act (1996), c.18.
Enterprise Act 2002, c40.
Insolvency Act 1986, c.45.
Trade Union and Labour Relations (Consolidation) Act 1992, c.52.

Others government reports

Insolvency Law Review Committee, *Insolvency Law and Practice* (Cmnd 8558, 1982).
Insolvency Service, "*Report on the Operation of the Statement of Insolvency Practice 16: 1 January to 31 December 2010* (London: Insolvency Service, undated).
Insolvency Service, *A Review of Company Rescue and Business Reconstruction Mechanisms*, Report by the Review Group (DTI, 2000) (IS 2000).
Insolvency Service, *A Review of Company Rescue and Business Reconstruction Mechanisms*, Interim Report (DTI, September 1999).
Report of the Review Committee, Chairman Sir Kenneth Cork, *Insolvency Law and Practice* Cmnd 8558 (London: HMSO, 1982).
Transfer of Undertakings (Protection of Employment) Regulations 2006 (SI 2006/246).

United States

11 U.S.C. ss. 101–1330 (2012) Enacted by the Bankruptcy Reform Act 1978 (Pub. L. No.95–598, 92 Stat. 2549).

29 U.S.C. ss.151–169 (2016).

29 U.S.C. ss.151–169 (2017). Enacted by the 74th United States Congress on July 6 1935, Pub. L. 74–198, 49 Stat. 449 to create a National Labor Relations Board and to regulate labour disputes between employers and employees that may burden or obstruct interstate and foreign commerce.

H.R Report No. 595, 95th Congress, 1st session, 220 (1977).

2 Bankruptcy legal theory

The traditionalist and proceduralist theoretical models

Introduction

There have long been debates from insolvency scholars, academics and practitioners on what the legitimate goal of insolvency law is or ought to be in a legal system.[1] One of the leading scholars of insolvency, Prof. Douglas Baird is of the view that engaging debates on insolvency law's legitimate goal are mainly contested between two theoretical schools, the traditionalists and the proceduralists.[2]

As termed by Prof. Baird, traditional bankruptcy lawyers and scholars are proponents of the traditionalist theoretical school whose main focus is on the rich store of bankruptcy cases that have developed over time.[3] Their approaches are built on the conviction that bankruptcy law plays a special role in a legal system and advances substantive goals that are distinct and important. Traditional bankruptcy lawyers and scholars include, for example, Karen Gross,[4] Donald Korobkin,[5] Elizabeth Warren,[6] Samuel L. Bufford[7] and Harvey R. Miller[8] among others.

On the other hand, Prof. Baird describes proceduralists as entirely academics whose distinct characteristic is the focus on procedures.[9] They believe that a coherent bankruptcy law must recognise how it fits into the rest of the legal system

1 E. Warren, "Bankruptcy Policy" (1987) 54 *Uni. Chi. L. Rev.* 775; E. Warren, "Bankruptcy Policymaking in an Imperfect World" (1993) 92 *Mich. L. Rev.* 336, 387; D Baird and TH Jackson, "Corporate Reorganizations and the Treatment of Diverse Ownership Interests: A Comment on Adequate Protection of Secured Creditors in Bankruptcy" (1984) 51 *U Chicago L. Rev.* 97; DR Korobkin, "Contractarianism and the Normative Foundations of Bankruptcy Law" (1993) 71 *Tex. L. Rev.* 554.

2 Douglas G Baird, "Bankruptcy's Uncontested Axioms" (1998) 108 *Yale L. J.* 573, 578.

3 Ibid., 576.

4 Karen Gross, *Failure and Forgiveness: Rebalancing the Bankruptcy System* (New Haven, Yale University Press, 1997).

5 Korobkin, (n 1) 554.

6 Warren, (n 1), 775.

7 Samuel L Bufford, "What is Right About Bankruptcy Law and Wrong About Its Critics" (1994) 72 *Wash. U. L. Quart.* 829.

8 Harvey R. Miller, "The Changing Face of Chapter 11: A Re-emergence of the Bankruptcy Judge as the Producer, Director, and Sometimes Star of the Reorganization Passion Play" (1995) 69 *Am. Bankr. L. J.* 431.

9 Baird, (n 1) 577.

and a vibrant market economy.[10] Proceduralist bankruptcy scholars include, for example, Douglas G. Baird,[11] Thomas H. Jackson,[12] Alan Schwartz,[13] Barry E. Adler[14] among others. Prof. Baird's categorisation of the traditionalist and proceduralist theoretical schools has also been expounded by other academic writers on the subject of corporate bankruptcy and insolvency such as Prof. Roy Goode,[15] Ziad R. Anzari,[16] Charles W. Mooney Jr[17] and Edward J. Janger.[18]

These two theoretical schools offer differing conceptual perspectives on the role that insolvency law should, or ought to play in the reorganisation and rescue of insolvent but viable businesses, the substantive law that is, or ought to be, applied in a bankruptcy process, the role of judges in interpreting insolvency laws and whether judges should be afforded a certain degree of judicial discretion during insolvency proceedings where the subject matter of adjudication is not covered by relevant judicial precedents.[19]

For example, proceduralists look at insolvency law's main objective as a means of maximisation of value for creditors and therefore, this can be seen to be creditor biased. They contend that insolvency law should focus on addressing issues that only arise within bankruptcy. They believe that non-insolvency creditor claims or entitlements should not be protected by insolvency law unless doing so maximises value for creditors.[20] They prefer using economic models as a basis for analysing corporate insolvency and market solutions, as opposed to seeking judicial intervention for resolving issues arising on corporate insolvency.[21]

10 Ibid., 579.

11 Douglas G. Baird, "The Uneasy Case for Corporate Reorganisations" (1986) 15 *J. Legal Stud.* 127; D Baird and T H Jackson, "Corporate Reorganizations and the Treatment of Diverse Ownership Interests: A Comment on Adequate Protection of Secured Creditors in Bankruptcy" (1984) 51 *U Chicago L. Rev.* 97.

12 Thomas H. Jackson, "Bankruptcy, Non-Bankruptcy Entitlements and the Creditors' Bargain" (1982) 91 *Yale Law J.* 857, 860; Thomas H. Jackson, "Avoiding Powers in Bankruptcy" (1984) 36 *Stan. L. Rev.* 725.

13 Alan Schwartz, "A Contract Theory Approach to Business Bankruptcy" (1998) 107 *Yale L. J.* 1807, 1851.

14 Barry E. Adler, "Financial and Political Theories of American Corporate Bankruptcy" (1993) 45 *Stan. L. Rev.* 311; Barry E. Adler, "Finance's Theoretical Divide and the Proper Role of Insolvency Rules" (1994) 67 *S. Cal. L. Rev.* 1107.

15 R. Goode, *Principles of Corporate Insolvency Law* (3rd edn, London, Sweet & Maxwell, 2005) 41, 42.

16 Ziad R. Anzari, "Bankruptcy Policy, Legal Heritage and Financial Development: An Agenda for Further Research" (2008) 24(2) *Emory Bankr. Dev. J.* 382.

17 Charles W. Mooney Jr, "A Normative Theory of Bankruptcy Law: Bankruptcy as (Is) Civil Procedure" (2004) 61 *Wash. & Lee L. Rev.* 931.

18 Edaward J. Janger, "Crystals and Mud in Bankruptcy Law: Judicial Competence and Statutory Design" (2001) 43 *Ariz. L. Rev.* 559, 566.

19 See for example, Thomas H. Jackson, "Bankruptcy, Non-Bankruptcy Entitlements and the Creditors' Bargain" (1982) 91 *Yale L. J.* 857; Elizabeth Warren, "Bankruptcy Policy" (1987) 54 *U. Chi. L. Rev.* 775.

20 Schwartz, (n 13) 1809.

21 See, for instance, R. Posner, *The Economics of Justice* (Cambridge, MA, HUP, 1983) pgs. 60–87 on his account on wealth maximisation as an ethical principle, a typical law and economics perspective.

Traditionalists however take a stand that is opposite to that of the proceduralists in that they advocate for a more inclusive approach to stakeholder interests consideration during corporate insolvency. They believe that all stakeholder interests should be given equal weight of consideration on corporate insolvency. They are against the notion that insolvency law exists to only serve the interests of creditors.[22]

In light of these varying views and perspectives and the theoretical divide and limitations, it may be argued that there is a theoretical deadlock between the two theoretical schools on the proper approach to be adopted in addressing the debtor-creditor concerns during corporate insolvency in a balanced manner. Moreover, employment protection concerns, such as the proper treatment of employees' interests during their employer's insolvency is an area where these theories would lead to conflicting views.[23]

The theoretical divide analysed

A theory is a factual concept or framework describing a given phenomenon, the way it is or it ought to be.[24] Although there exist various theories on different disciplines, where theories are used in insolvency disciplines, they are explored as normative phenomena as they prescribe evaluation of why insolvency is the way it is or ought to be in a given state or society.[25] Although it may be argued that theories on their own cannot solve underlying insolvency issues in a given state, they however provide the basis upon which substantive insolvency laws and policies in different jurisdictions can be prescribed and provide arguments for constructing different insolvency regimes.[26]

The role of a legal system in an insolvency setting

Modern insolvency regimes have approaches that deal with the debtor-creditor relationships during corporate insolvency. However, these insolvency regimes restrict the coordination of the debtor-creditor relationship to one particular collective approach in place of individual bargaining. Parties to a contractual agreement are restricted by that particular insolvency regime from inserting clauses in their contractual agreements that prescribe using alternative bankruptcy or insolvency regimes to address their contractual rights and obligations upon the commencement of formal proceedings.[27]

22 Warren, "Bankruptcy Policymaking" (n 1) 336, 387.
23 Giles Saint-Paul, "The Political Economy of Employment Protection" (2002) 110 *J. Pol. Econ.* 672, 673.
24 Brian H. Bix, *Jurisprudence: Theory and Context* (6th edn, London, Sweet & Maxwell, 2012) 4.
25 Ibid., 7.
26 Hamiisi J. Nsubuga, "Corporate Insolvency and Employment Protection: A Theoretical Perspective" (2016) 4(1) *NIBLeJ* 4.
27 Schwartz, (n 13) 1809.

These insolvency laws are influenced by governmental policies that dictate the way the debtor-creditor relationship is resolved. These may include, for example, policy goals of boosting corporate rescue or policies designed to curb rising levels of unemployment in a given legal system which could be jeopardised by individual creditor actions.[28] Therefore, when bankruptcy strikes, the dictates of the debtor-creditor relationships that arise outside bankruptcy settings give way to the particular legal system's insolvency laws in coordinating their resolution, yet the same insolvency laws, of course, do not play a part in regulating these debtor-creditor arrangements pre-bankruptcy.[29]

There is sense in the argument that where contractual arrangements are not regulated by a particular system of laws, creditors and debtors would enter into contractual arrangements that might not only be detrimental to each other but might also bring burdensome effects to the economy as a whole.[30] However, bankruptcy laws are designed to address these coordination problems during corporate insolvency, rather than regulating substantive contractual transactions that lead businesses to bankruptcy in the first place.

This has led to questions being asked by different actors in the bankruptcy field, such as business owners, employees, bankruptcy scholars and commentators on the role that a state or legal system should or ought to play in coordinating the debtor-creditor relationships during corporate insolvency.[31] How far should a legal system strive to keep a financially struggling company continuing trading as a going concern? How should bankruptcy policies be implemented in a legal system and what role should judges play in balancing overlapping stakeholder interests during corporate insolvency and bankruptcy? Traditionalists and proceduralists answer these questions in different ways.

Encouraging corporate reorganisations and rescue

Traditionalists believe that affording a financially struggling company a chance to reorganise is one of the essential aims of insolvency law.[32] This is a form of maintaining the going concern value of the business and the company itself is preserved. Traditionalists believe that corporate liquidations create grave effects for employees and other involuntary and tortious victims, such as the community and governmental bodies, such as tax authorities. For instance, a community may lose its interests from a company if liquated.

28 Robert K. Rasmussen, "An Essay on Optimal Bankruptcy Rules and Social Justice" (1994) *U. Ill. L. Rev.* 1, 43.

29 O. Kimhi and A. Doebert, "Bankruptcy Law as a Balancing System: Lessons from a Comparative Analysis of the Intersection between Labor and Bankruptcy Law" (2015) 23 *Am. Bankr. Inst. L. Rev.* 491, 529.

30 Paul F. Kirgis, "Arbitration, Bankruptcy, and Public Policy: A Contractarian Analysis" (2009) 17 *Am. Bankr. Inst. L. Rev.* 503, 544.

31 See for example, Rasmussen, (n 28).

32 Baird, (n 1) 577.

A community may lose a retail store such as Tesco which arguably, offered affordable prices to local residents and the store is replaced, for example, by Waitrose, which may be slightly expensive to local and community residents. A community may also face increasing levels of unemployment due to local business closures or liquidations.[33] Therefore, liquidation should be avoided as much as possible, by aiming to enact legislation to support financially struggling companies to reorganise and continue trading as going concerns.[34]

Proceduralists however, view the role of insolvency in a legal system from a different dimension. They are of the view that the substantive goal of insolvency law is to maximise the value of the debtor's bankruptcy estate for the benefit of creditors.[35] They believe that a business entity should be able to 'live or die' in the market.[36] They believe that the only aim of insolvency law is to avoid premature liquidations arising out of uncoordinated creditor actions through the adoption of a collective debt collection regime.

According to the proceduralists, it is the collective nature of the debt collection procedure that governs how insolvency law deals with extant creditor interests. Therefore, insolvency law should exclusively and procedurally aim to address debt collection problems arising out of extant creditor interests and avoid addressing issues, such as redistribution or modifications to non-insolvency creditor interests that are beyond collective imperatives.

A company should die or live in the market

Proceduralists are of the view that the role of insolvency law in a legal system is neither to support the liquidation nor reorganisation of a financially struggling company. Rather, insolvency law should be used to ensure that a struggling company's assets are put to their best use.[37] Proceduralists argue this point of view by reference to a two-stage analysis of a company's financial struggles. These stages are economic distress and financial distress.

A company is in economic distress where its assets cannot generate adequate revenue to facilitate its operating costs to the extent that its value is best achieved by breaking it up to realise any available returns rather than trying to rescue it as a going concern. An insolvency practitioner may sell off any realisable assets of the company that are of saleable value, rather than attempting to rescue and sell the business as a package.

33 Karen Gross, "Taking Community Interests into Account in Bankruptcy: An Essay" (1994) 72 *Wash. Univ. L. Q.* 1031; Ronald J. Mann, "Bankruptcy and the Entitlements of the Government: Whose Money is it Anyway" (1995) 70(5) *N.Y.U L. Rev.* 1040.

34 Donald R. Korobkin, "Rehabilitating Values: A Jurisprudence of Bankruptcy" (1991) 91 *Colum. L. Rev.* 717.

35 Thomas H. Jackson, "Bankruptcy, Non-Bankruptcy Entitlements and the Creditors" Bargain' (1982) 91 *Yale L. J.* 857.

36 Ibid., 578.

37 Schwartz, (n 13); Kirgis, (n 32) 503, 544.

An example of economic distress may be best illustrated by the 2008 administration process of Woolworths stores in the UK. In order to recover any available value in the company, having failed to achieve a going concern business sale, the administrators opted to sell any item or property that they could, which included selling shop-racks, back-office furniture and shelf-products. However, a company is in financial distress when it is unable to pay its debts and invoices as they fall due.[38] This may be a temporary financial situation that a company may be experiencing that may arguably be solved through reorganisation.

According to proceduralists, insolvency law's main aim should not be the reorganisation of financially struggling companies. To them, a market economy functions well if companies that cannot compete for their market place are allowed to fail.[39] However, traditionalists are of the view that keeping a company intact through insolvency is an independent goal of insolvency law. A company is not a pool of assets for stakeholders to collect or sell piecemeal but a collection of diverse interests that may be severely affected by a company's liquidation. Therefore, if a company in financial distress is not supported by a legal system through its reorganisation process, it may be forced into liquidation by a selfish debt collection regime that secured creditors adopt to recoup their debts or interests. This would have grave consequences for all interested stakeholders.[40]

However, it should be noted that choosing rehabilitation of the company over liquidation curtails a secured creditor's security and recovery options.[41] Although giving a debtor company a chance and time to execute a reorganisation plan may seem reasonable, there is no guarantee that such a company will utilise its reorganisation plan effectively and emerge out of insolvency successfully. There is a possibility that the costs of reorganisation may result in lower returns to creditors.

To traditionalists, saving an insolvent but viable company is the very essence of insolvency law as the company is allowed to continue trading as a going concern and employees may keep their jobs. However, to proceduralists, this is a form of prolonging the life of a bad company with no guarantees that such a company would emerge out of reorganisation successfully.[42]

Uniform application of laws inside and outside bankruptcy

The US Supreme Court's decision in *Butner v United States*[43] observed that a uniform application of the law inside and outside bankruptcy 'serves to reduce

38 G. Andrade and Steven N. Kaplan, "How Costly is Financial (Not Economic) Distress? Evidence from Highly Leverage Transactions That Became Distressed" (1998) 53 *J. Fin.* 1443, 1444.

39 Franco Modigliani and Merton H. Miller, "The Cost of Capital, Corporation Finance and the Theory of Investment" (1958) 48 *Am. Econ. Rev.* 261.

40 Karen Gross, *Failure and Forgiveness: Rebalancing the Bankruptcy System* (New Haven, Yale University Press, 1997) 253.

41 Ibid., 129.

42 Modigliani and Miller, (n 42) 261.

43 *Butner v United States*, 440 U.S. 48 (1978).

the uncertainty' and prevents a party from receiving a windfall merely by reason of the happenstance of bankruptcy.[44] Therefore, unless a federal interest requires a different result, there is no reason why bankruptcy should be analysed differently simply because an interested party is involved in a bankruptcy proceeding. This is a point of view supported and advocated for by the proceduralists as they believe that law, be it inside or outside bankruptcy, should uniformly be applied.[45]

Proceduralists believe that bankruptcy law should mirror and replicate substantive stakeholder interests and entitlements of the non-insolvency setting and avoid insolvency specific changes, such as redistribution or expropriation of non-insolvency entitlements into insolvency.[46] Insolvency should preserve the absolute priority rules of the non-insolvency setting according to the proceduralists.[47]

In a non-insolvency setting, secured creditors have absolute priority of distribution over the proceeds from the sale of the company assets or collateral. Proceduralists contend that secured creditors should have the same absolute priority in an insolvency setting. However, this right is affected where calls for fairness or equality of distribution, such as to employees and other constituent stakeholders are invoked as normatively advocated for by the traditionalists. Proceduralists are of the view that questions of fairness, equity of treatment and minimum right of compensation should have no place in insolvency unless they are given effect outside bankruptcy.[48]

This contention is further supported by the contractarian approach to insolvency law,[49] an offshoot of the proceduralist view of insolvency law. This approach looks at certain provisions of a legal system, such as legal rules and principles, as either mandatory rules or mandatory structural rules. For example, Alan Schwartz describes mandatory rules as rules in an insolvency context that seek to enhance or augment the value of the bankruptcy estate even if doing so unfairly leaves the other party at loss.

Alan Schwartz cites, for example, 11 U.S.C. 362 and 11 U.S.C. 365 of the US Bankruptcy Code[50] as mandatory rules in the current US Bankruptcy Code that seek to augment the value of the bankruptcy estate. This is through staying creditors' recovery actions against the debtor company and also affording the debtor company's trustees or DIP power to either assume or reject employment

44 Ibid., 55.

45 Douglas G. Baird and Thomas H. Jackson, "Corporate Reorganizations and the Treatment of Diverse Ownership Interests: A Comment on Adequate Protection of Secured Creditors in Bankruptcy" (1984) 51 *U. Chi. L. Rev.* 97, 102.

46 Thomas H. Jackson, "Translating Assets and Liabilities to the Bankruptcy Forum" (1985) 14 *J. Legal Stud.* 73, 114.

47 Schwartz, (n 13) 1821.

48 Kirgis, (n 32) 503, 544.

49 Schwartz, (n 13) 1819.

50 The US Bankruptcy Code is codified as 11 U.S.C. ss. 101 – 1330 (2012) Enacted by the Bankruptcy Reform Act 1978 (Pub. L. No.95 – 598, 92 Stat. 2549).

contracts or collective bargaining agreements (subject to court approval) upon filing for a bankruptcy petition.[51]

Alan Schwartz describes mandatory structural rules in a bankruptcy context as rules that seek to maintain the integrity of the bankruptcy system by maximising value for creditors, rather than creating inefficient incentives to parties in their earlier economic relationship. Non-structural mandatory rules, that is, rules that seek to enhance and achieve a fair redistributive aspect of the bankruptcy system are regarded as inefficient and therefore, should not form part of the bankruptcy system.

There is no good distributional reason to benefit one set of interest holders, such as the secured creditors at the expense of subsequent stakeholders, such as employees.[52] Therefore, mandatory rules in insolvency should only be structural; that is, they should seek to maintain the integrity of the insolvency system and uphold creditors' pre-insolvency arrangements. By following absolute priority rules in insolvency, debts are paid in the order stipulated pre-insolvency in contractual arrangements between the debtor and creditor.

This contention is however, not supported by traditionalists. Traditionalists believe that as part of the rehabilitation and reorganisation processes, modifications to stakeholder non-insolvency interests and rights that are involved in the insolvency process may be desirable, where it would serve the interests of all stakeholders and preserve the company from liquidation.[53] Traditionalists support changes to the law outside insolvency, where such changes enhance the prospects of rehabilitation of financially struggling companies enabling them to avoid liquidation.

Per Prof. Elizabeth Warren;

> When dealing with redistributive issues, it is necessary and inherent to bankruptcy policy to define moral choices. Bankruptcy is not merely procedural or derivative in nature; to the contrary, it also reflects a deliberate decision to pursue different distributional objectives from those the *de facto* scheme of general collection law embodies.[54]

For traditionalists, effecting insolvency specific modifications to employment protection provisions would moderate the rigidity of labour protection laws, to allow debtor employers to reorganise their businesses, which would benefit employees as a group. This is because insolvency law can be a vehicle for reorganisation that may help a struggling company to restructure its business.

Proceduralists however, see insolvency and reorganisation changes as a gateway to using bankruptcy filing for strategic gains. Proceduralists are of the view that moderating certain labour protection laws and policies in insolvency

51 Schwartz, (n 13) 1807, 1840.
52 Ibid., 1809.
53 Warren, "Bankruptcy Policy" (n 1).
54 Warren, "Bankruptcy Policymaking in an Imperfect World" (n 1).

proceedings may incentivise some debtor companies to file for bankruptcy to gain the advantages and protection that bankruptcy filings afford that debtor company. Proceduralists are of the view that this would amount to bankruptcy abuse and it would be a form of weakness within a legal system.[55]

Proceduralists believe that if a particular policy is worth implementing in the general law, it should also be implemented in bankruptcy. For example, if a legal system adopts a policy on curbing unjust enrichment or fraudulent transactions in contract law, that policy should also be applicable and implementable in insolvency law. It should not be only applicable in one specific area as it may arguably, create inconsistencies within a legal system[56] and provide perverse incentives for its use.

To proceduralists, insolvency is a foreseeable risk that should be fairly co-ordinated by a legal system like any other risk. In a non-insolvency setting, a legal system does not protect stakeholders and companies against misfortunes, such as property damage, fire or theft. Although certain areas of the law, such as the law of equity seek to protect stakeholders and consumers on matters of misrepresentation and fraud that may be borne out of unconscionability, beyond this imperative, stakeholders or investors take out protective remedies, such as insurance policies or remedial contract clauses to curb potential risks. Therefore, insolvency law should be treated the same as any other area of the law within a legal system and redistribution is not justified.

The role of judges in an insolvency setting

Insolvency is or ought to be a platform where competing stakeholder interests are addressed or coordinated to limit avoidable losses. However, the problem, and therefore, the point of contention between the traditionalists and proceduralists arises because the current bankruptcy system in the US revolves around one decision making vehicle. This is the bankruptcy court. While there exist specialist bankruptcy courts in the US that govern bankruptcy proceedings, in contrast, the UK insolvency proceedings are presided over by general non-insolvency specialist judges who do not tend to be required to decide upon re-distributive matters during insolvency proceedings. However, they can still be called upon to interpret the law when there are disputes, such as contentious issue during insolvent relevant transfers.[57]

Legal systems may bestow powers upon courts to regulate insolvency proceedings. These courts may make strategic decisions, such as deciding whether a company faced with financial difficulties is worthy of a chance to reorganise

55 Douglas G. Baird, "Bankruptcy's Uncontested Axioms" (1998) 108 *Yale L. J.* 573, 591.

56 Douglas G. Baird and Thomas H. Jackson, "Corporate Reorganizations and the Treatment of Diverse Ownership Interests: A Comment on Adequate Protection of Secured Creditors in Bankruptcy" (1984) 51 *U. Chi. L. Rev.* 97, 102.

57 For example, see, *Re Huddersfield Fine Worsteds Ltd and Re Ferrotech Ltd and Granville Technology Ltd* [2005] EWCA Civ. 1072 where the UK judges were called upon to interpret legislative provisions involving judicial discretion during in bankruptcy proceedings.

rather than be liquidated and whether, in a US context, a petition for rejection of executory contracts, such as employment contracts and collective bargaining agreements by the debtor employer may be granted or declined. In the US, this power is bestowed onto bankruptcy courts[58] by the US Congress through provisions in the Bankruptcy Code[59] to regulate the bankruptcy process.[60] However, in the UK the legislation tends to place such factors in the hands of insolvency practitioners, subject to court oversight if needed.[61]

A company's disputes with its employees and other creditors generally present a court with an opportunity to solve a number of different problems. These problems may range from coordination of debt collection to mitigating the effects that insolvency would have on employees, such as changes in their livelihood or a break in the chain of continuity of employment. The court may also be able to mitigate the rigidities in individual debt collection regimes to give a struggling company a second chance, which in turn saves employee jobs.

However, one point of contention between the proceduralists and the traditionalists in discussing the US system is as to whether the court is afforded too many powers and too much flexibility in the execution of its roles. The judge makes the most important decisions based on the factual arguments or matters before the court. The judge makes decisions that direct the way the debtor-creditor relationship is coordinated during bankruptcy proceedings, yet traditionalists and proceduralists offer differing perspectives on the role that a judge ought to play in a bankruptcy setting.

For example, proceduralists view the role of a judge in bankruptcy proceedings as that of a disinterested arbiter.[62] Proceduralists believe that the judge's role during insolvency proceedings should be to direct and control competing stakeholders' collection processes but that they should not be committed to any particular outcome.[63] To proceduralists, judges should allow creditors to make their own decisions and destinies.[64] The judge's task is to control parties' conflicting interests and to ensure transparency and integrity in the bankruptcy process.[65]

However, on the other hand, traditionalists view the judges' role in the interpretation and enforcement of insolvency laws as a paramount aspect. Traditionalists believe that a judge should implement insolvency's equity goals on a case by case basis and that judges should exhibit broader discretionary powers in

58 Bankruptcy courts include federal district courts and state bankruptcy courts. However, federal district courts have broader jurisdiction over state courts in deciding matters that arise under the Bankruptcy Code or matters related to a bankruptcy case. See, 29 U.S.C. s.1334 (b).

59 See provisions, such as, 11 U.S.C. s.105 (a), s.305 (a) and s.1129 (a) of the US Bankruptcy Code.

60 Christopher W. Frost, "Bankruptcy Redistributive Policies and the Limits of the Judicial Process" (1995) 74 *N. C. L. Rev.* 75.

61 IA 1986, Sch.1 and IA 1986, Sch.B1, particularly, see, IA 1986, Sch.B1, para.59 that sets out the powers of administrator as an insolvency practitioner.

62 Douglas G. Baird, "Bankruptcy's Uncontested Axioms" (1998) 108 *Yale L. J.* 573, 580.

63 Ibid., 579.

64 Ibid., 580.

65 Ibid., 579.

discharging their roles. This is to ensure that bankruptcy goals are justifiable and are fairly and reasonably used to meet the interests of competing stakeholders, such as employees.[66]

Traditionalists believe that because each case is different with different facts and stakeholders, a legal system should not have a specific or particular system or standard that fit every legal question at hand.[67] This is because, it may be difficult to ascertain or predict with certainty, competing and underlying diverse values and policy dimensions that may necessitate or inform a legal decision. However, for employees, the presence of a judge in the bankruptcy process may reassure them that their interests are fairly considered.[68]

In comparison, proceduralists do not support the idea of broad judicial discretion. According to the proceduralists, judicial use of discretion is only useful if a judge is well positioned to use such discretion to make informed decisions. Proceduralists believe that judges have no magical powers to make business decisions or predict market behaviour that may enhance the going concern value of a company.[69]

Theoretical limitations analysed

From the discussion above, it may be established that proceduralists provide clear answers as to the factors to be taken into account during corporate insolvency. For example, proceduralists' argument that companies should be allowed to live or die in the market clearly aligns with the notion that a competitive market structure or economy is controlled by market forces. Therefore, if a firm cannot fight for its market place, it should be allowed to die out of business which would enable competitors to take up that market place.

Consequently, the cycle of jobs to employees, revenue to government tax authorities and community interests and services would arguably continue to flow. This is opposed to prolonging the life of a bad company through reorganisation with no assurances that such a company would come out of reorganisation successfully. Hence, the contention that a free market approach is to the benefit of businesses and employees.

However, proceduralists' perspectives give more primacy to maximising creditors' returns during insolvency yet these returns are arguably most enjoyed by secured creditors who already enjoy priority over other creditors, such as employees and the theoretical approach neglects the position of other stakeholders. This may arguably, be perceived as being unsatisfactory and unfair to the interests of

66 Harvey R. Miller, "The Changing Face of Chapter 11: A Re-emergence of the Bankruptcy Judge as a Producer, Director and Sometimes Star of the Reorganization Passion Play" (1995) 69 *Am. Bankr. L. J.* 439.

67 Donald R. Korobkin, "Rehabilitating Values: A Jurisprudence of Bankruptcy" (1991) 91 *Colum. L. Rev.* 717, 722.

68 Karen Gross, *Failure and Forgiveness: Rebalancing the Bankruptcy System*, (New Haven, Yale University Press, 1997) 238.

69 Christopher W. Frost, "Bankruptcy Redistributive Policies and the Limits of the Judicial Process" (1995) 74 *N. C. L. Rev.* 75.

overlapping stakeholders as group. Moreover, other stakeholders, such as employees lack bargaining powers pre-insolvency and post-insolvency, and they cannot easily absorb loss.

In addition, proceduralist perspectives on issues, such as the role of judges in an insolvency setting, and the judicial use of discretion further support the contention that this theoretical school prescribes approaches that are not inclusive to the interests of all stakeholders as a group during corporate insolvency. For example, proceduralist perspectives of equating a judge's role to that of a disinterested arbiter[70] during insolvency proceedings, and the contention that judges should allow creditors to make their own decisions and destinies,[71] would be seen as an unsatisfactory way of dealing with the interests of overlapping stakeholders as a group.

In addition, it may be argued that proceduralists' insistence that insolvency should aim to solve debt collection and coordination issues amongst creditors, rather than rehabilitating insolvent but viable companies, may limit bankruptcy law to being a debt collection tool or a remedial tool for mitigating bad investment decisions. Where this is the case, it may echo the administrative receivership era in the UK that the Enterprise Act 2002 sought to remedy through the virtual abolition of administrative receivership and the improvement of the administration process, as administrative receivership was essentially, a debt collection procedure.[72] It was considered inappropriate for insolvency law to be dominated by a debt collection device like administrative receivership, rather than the collective administration process.

In the US, this approach would also echo the state of affairs of the US bankruptcy law pre-Bankruptcy Code era – the Railroad receivership era. It should be remembered that bankruptcy law in the US is deeply rooted in equity and common law. This may be evidenced in the overwhelming use of equity receiverships in the pre-Bankruptcy Code era. The use of equity receiverships arose because the insolvency laws that regulated the debtor-creditor relationships during the Railroad era predominantly focused on liquidation rather than rehabilitation of financially struggling companies.[73]

Creditors used equity receivership as a model of preserving Railroads as they underwent restructuring.[74] However, receivership is essentially a debt collection device and creditors used it for personal and selfish goals rather than the reorganisation of the debtor's business. A secured creditor of a Railroad would seek court approval to obtain control of the debtor company's assets. Receivership would then act as an automatic stay to competing creditor actions against the Railroad's assets but usually at the detriment of other creditors.[75] This was one

70 Baird, (n 64) 578.

71 Ibid., 580.

72 J. Armour and S. Frisby, "Rethinking Receivership" (2001) 21 *Oxford J. Legal Stud.* 73, 90.

73 David A. Skeel Jr, "Debt's Dominion: A History of Bankruptcy Law in America" (2003) 41 *Osgoode Hall L. J.* 711, 740.

74 Charles J. Tabb, "The History of Bankruptcy Law in the United Stated" (1995) 3 *Am. Bankr. Inst. L. Rev.* 5, 22–23.

75 Ibid., 22, 23.

of the key factors that led to the enactment of the Bankruptcy Reform Act of 1978, laying grounds for the enactment of the Bankruptcy Code in 1978.

However, traditionalist perspectives on insolvency law in a legal system may be seen as more inclusive in approach than those of the proceduralists. Traditionalists consider the interests of stakeholders as a whole and they support mechanisms that may ensure fairness in distributive imperatives in insolvency. The traditionalist approach is therefore, flexible and can be adopted for different circumstances. However, traditionalists do not provide how these factors or perspectives may be balanced despite the fact that they are identified. The approach fails to provide clear answers and this may be regarded as a weakness to this theoretical school's perspectives and approaches.

For instance, Prof. Warren concedes that:

> [w]hile I hope that it is useful to have distinguished the policymaking thrust of state collection law from that of bankruptcy and to have identified the distributional rationale of bankruptcy,... I have not offered a single-rationale policy that compels solutions in particular cases. I have not given any answers to specific statutory issues.[76]

Therefore, the lack of clear answers from the traditionalist approach as discussed above and the fact that the proceduralist approach would create unfairness towards stakeholders creates a form of limitation on both theoretical schools' perspectives on the role of insolvency law and how insolvency law ought to be applied during corporate insolvencies. This form of limitation may arguably be remedied through interpretation, that is, by adopting Ronald Dworkin's interpretative approach to law as posited in his Interpretative Theory of Law.[77]

The interpretative theory of law – Ronald Dworkin – an introduction

There have existed many normative theories from various theoretical perspectives. However, in the field of legal theory and jurisprudence, there have existed mainly two dominant schools of thought. These are the natural law theorists and the legal positivists. The difference in these approaches is best illustrated by the famous debate between Prof. Lon Fuller (on the natural law side) and H.L.A Hart (on the positivist legal side).[78] However, it is worth noting that since this debate, most legal theorists have continued to identify their theories as either being on the natural law side or the positivist legal side of this theoretical divide.

76 Warren, "Bankruptcy Policy" (n 1) 795.

77 R. Dworkin, *Law's Empire* (Cambridge, MA, HUP, 1986).

78 Regrettably, this debate is not discussed in this chapter, and book in general as it is outside its intended normative justification. However, see, H.L.A Hart, "Positivism and the Separation of Law and Morals" (1958) 71 *Harv. L. Rev.* 593; L. Fuller, "Positivism and the Fidelity of Law – A Response to Professor Hart" (1958) 71 *Harv. L. Rev.* 630.

There are mainly two particular versions of legal positivist ideals that natural law theorists argue against that have greatly contributed to this theoretical divide. Legal positivists see law as entirely comprising of rules.[79] To them, law is the law as posited. Second, legal positivists, believe in the concept of judicial discretion. That is, during the course of their adjudication, if faced with legal questions (sometimes referred to as hard case thesis) that cannot be decided on existing laws and precedents, judges must be able to draw on their discretion to fill the gap.[80]

Among the most famous critics of these legal positivist ideals, is Prof. Ronald Dworkin through his Interpretative Theory of Law.[81] Through this theory, Dworkin is seen as creating a sophisticated theory of law that can be termed as an alternative to legal positivism and natural law theories.[82] However, it should be noted that, occasionally Dworkin has referred to his theory as a natural law theory. Moreover, viewed from the lens of the famous Fuller – Hart debate, Dworkin's theory seems to be on the natural law side of the theoretical divide.

Throughout this theory, Dworkin bases his arguments on three main ideals, which if analysed, support his interpretative approach to law as they offer normative perspectives on how law ought to be seen and interpreted in a given legal system or society. These ideals comprise of the right answer thesis (that centres upon his dissent to judicial discretion and Judge Hercules), law as integrity and constructive interpretation (law as principles and rules).[83]

Dworkin's Interpretative approach to law considers social factors, such as fairness, equality and justice that may be useful in analysing extant stakeholder interests during corporate insolvency proceedings. The Interpretative approach would be used as a balancing tool to remedy the limitations presented by both the traditionalist and proceduralist perspectives on corporate insolvency, such that the policy objectives of employment protection law and those of corporate rescue law may be balanced.

Through his Interpretative Theory of Law, Dworkin posits that law as practice and law as legal theory are best understood as a process of interpretation. Dworkin opines that constructiveness and integrity in interpretation leads to a right answer to the question before the judge.[84] Dworkin states that

> every time a judge is confronted with a legal problem, that judge should construct a theory of what the law is, that is, a theory that must adequately fit the past relevant governmental actions, such as the policies underlying the passing of that law to make the law the best it can be.[85]

79 H.L.A Hart, *The Concept of Law* (3rd edn, Oxford, Clarendon Law Series, 2012) Ch. 5.

80 Ibid., Ch.6.

81 R. Dworkin, *Law's Empire* (Cambridge, MA, HUP, 1986) pgs. 46–48.

82 Brian Bix, "On the Dividing Line between Natural Law Theory and Legal Positivism" (2000) 75 *Notre Dame L. Rev.* 1613.

83 R. Dworkin, *Law's Empire* (Cambridge, MA, HUP, 1986), pgs. 46–48.

84 R. Dworkin, "Pragmatism, Right Answers and True Benality" in M. Brint and W. Weaver (eds.) *Pragmatism in Law and Society*, (Boulder, CO, Westview Press, 1991) 365.

85 See R. Dworkin, *Law's Empire* (Cambridge, MA, HUP, 1986) 52.

Therefore, the judge must interpret the law in a manner that fits the legal context at hand because constructiveness in interpretation is the proper approach to artistic and literal interpretation as it coheres with the need to make the law the best it can be, carrying with it, the principles of moral value.[86]

Where constructiveness and integrity are applied in the interpretation of laws, policies and practices, it makes the laws of that society more like a product of a single moral vision. After all, a judge who accepts the interpretative ideal of integrity decides cases by trying to find in some coherent set of principles, about peoples' rights and duties. This is by drawing on the political and legal doctrines embedded in that community or field[87] to find a unique right answer to the legal question before him. This is opposed to a judge using his discretion to fill the gap – a legal positivist notion that Dworkin greatly criticises.

Through his right answer thesis, Dworkin claims that all or almost all legal questions have a unique right answer, even the hardest of cases. To achieve that unique right answer, Dworkin devises the idea of a model judge in Hercules who is seen as super judge that can find an answer to every legal question before him.[88]

However, the idea of Hercules has been seen as one of the most controversial propositions by Dworkin in his writings on legal theory and has therefore attracted more criticism.[89] Among the criticisms is the question as to whether such a judge may ever exist in reality and execute the duties put before him diligently as Dworkin posits. Criticisms put aside, the idea of judge Hercules may be useful in the quest for novel interpretation of laws and policies in our society. This is, especially, where there are no existing legal precedents from which a judge and other legal practitioners may seek guidance and direction.

Conclusion

In conclusion, it may be submitted that the tension between corporate rescue policy objectives inherent in insolvency laws and employment protection policy objectives inherent in employment laws both in the US and the UK has existed for decades. This tension is to a large extent, influenced by the traditionalist and proceduralist perspectives and ideologies on what the role or ultimate aim of insolvency is or ought to be in a legal system. This is because these theoretical perspectives influence the policies and practices underlying the passing of the law that govern the debtor-creditor relationships during corporate insolvency. This tension further transcends into judicial interpretation and application of the law

86 The principle of moral value highlight the importance of the role of principles in judicial interpretation in that, the Judge may weigh up principles to establish which principles have better weight over the others as some principles may be applied in different dimensions.

87 R. Dworkin, *Law's Empire* (Cambridge, MA, HUP, 1986) 255.

88 R. Dworkin, *Taking Rights Seriously* (London, G. Duckworth, 1977) 85.

89 H.L.A Hart, *The Concept of Law* (2nd edn, Oxford, Clarendon Press, 1994) Postscript, 248, 249; David Plunkett and Timothy Sundell, "Dworkin's Interpretivism and the Pragmatics of Legal Disputes" (2013) 19 *Legal Theory* 242.

during corporate insolvency proceedings. In the US, the tension between provisions in the Bankruptcy Code that seek to support bankruptcy reorganisation[90] and the provisions in labour laws that seek to protect employees and their rights during corporate insolvency[91] has not gone unnoticed.[92] In the UK, the tension between corporate rescue objectives within the IA 1986 and employment protection policy objectives of ERA 1996 and TUPE provisions, has also attracted varied debates.[93]

However, despite the existence of the tension between the two policies' objectives, and the various debates around this notion, neither of the theoretical schools' perspectives arguably prescribe a satisfactory solution to this tension. Therefore, a remedy has yet to be established that would remedy this tension and balance both policies' objectives such that both policies' objectives may be pursued simultaneously.

As discussed above, it is the notion that while traditionalists identify factors that should be taken into account during corporate insolvency, they do not say how these factors ought to be applied. The proceduralists on the other hand, provide clear answers to the factors to be taken into account during corporate insolvency, however, these perspectives if applied to insolvencies, would cause unfair outcomes for all stakeholders with interests in the debtor company. There is therefore, a lack of clear answers from the traditionalists and a degree of potential unfairness in the proceduralist perspectives which present a form of limitation on the adoption and application of both theoretical schools' perspectives to corporate insolvencies.

This is the form of limitation that Dworkin's Interpretative theory of law, if adopted, may remedy such that a fair and balanced approach is adopted. Otherwise, without a balanced interpretative approach, judges may continue to give inconsistent decisions during corporate insolvency proceedings which may further exacerbate the tension between insolvency law policy objectives and employment law policy objectives.

According to Dworkin, a judge guided by the legal principles and the policies underlying the passing of that law, would constructively achieve a right answer that would not only conform to fairness, but would also uphold the integrity of the law. This would help to remedy the tension between insolvency law policy objectives and employment law policy objectives. It would also help remedy the lack of clarity from the traditionalist perspectives on corporate insolvency law and the potential unfairness in the proceduralist theoretical perspectives.

90 See generally, provisions such as s.362, s.363, s.1113, s.1114 among other provisions.

91 For example, see, NLRA (1935) s.8 (a) (5) and s.8 (a) (1).

92 See for example, Clyde W. Summers, "The Rights of Individual Workers: The Contract of Employment and the Rights of Individual Employees: Fair Representation and Employment at Will" (1984) 52 *Fordham L. Rev.* 1082, 1085; S.F. Befort, "Labour and Employment Law at the Millennium: A Historical Review and Critical Assessment" (2001) 43 *B. C. L Rev.* 460, 355–375.

93 F. Toube and G. Todd, "The Proper Treatment of Employees' Claims in Administration" (2005) 18 *Insolvency Intelligence* 109.

Bibliography

Books

Bix, H Brian, *Jurisprudence: Theory and Context* (6th edn., London, Sweet & Maxwell, 2012).

Dworkin, R, *Taking Rights Seriously* (London, G. Duckworth, 1977).

Dworkin, R, *Law's Empire* (Cambridge, MA, HUP, 1986).

Goode, R, *Principles of Corporate Insolvency Law* (3rd edn., London, Sweet & Maxwell, 2005).

Gross, Karen, *Failure and Forgiveness: Rebalancing the Bankruptcy System* (New Haven, Yale University Press, 1997).

Hart, HLA, *The Concept of Law* (3rd edn., Oxford, Clarendon Law Series, 2012).

Posner, R, *The Economics of Justice* (Cambridge, MA, HUP, 1983).

Book chapters

Dworkin, R, "Pragmatism, Right Answers and True Benality" in M. Brint and W. Weaver (eds.) *Pragmatism in Law and Society*, (Boulder, CO, Westview Press, 1991).

Cases

United Kingdom

Re Huddersfield Fine Worsteds Ltd and Re Ferrotech Ltd and Granville Technology Ltd [2005] EWCA Civ. 1072.

United States

Butner v United States, 440 U.S. 48 (1978).

Journal articles

Adler, E Barry, "Financial and Political Theories of American Corporate Bankruptcy" (1993) 45 Stan. L. Rev. 311.

Adler, E Barry, "Finance's Theoretical Divide and the Proper Role of Insolvency Rules" (1994) 67 S. Cal. L. Rev. 1107.

Andrade, G, and Kaplan, Steven, "How Costly is Financial (Not Economic) Distress? Evidence from Highly Leverage Transactions that Became Distressed" (1998) 53 J. Fin. 1443, 1444.

Anzari, R Ziad, "Bankruptcy Policy, Legal Heritage and Financial Development: An Agenda for Further Research" (2008) 24(2) Emory Bankr. Dev. J. 382.

Armour, J, and Frisby, S, "Rethinking Receivership" (2001) 21 Oxford J. Legal Stud. 73, 90.

Baird, D, and Jackson, TH, "Corporate Reorganizations and the Treatment of Diverse Ownership Interests: A Comment on Adequate Protection of Secured Creditors in Bankruptcy" (1984) 51 U Chicago L. Rev. 97.

Baird, DG, "The Uneasy Case for Corporate Reorganisations" (1986) 15 J. Legal Stud. 127.

Baird, DG, "Bankruptcy's Uncontested Axioms" (1998) 108 Yale L. J. 573, 578.

Befort, SF, "Labour and Employment Law at the Millennium: A Historical Review and Critical Assessment" (2001) 43 B. C. L. Rev. 460, 355–375.
Bix, Brian, "On the Dividing Line between Natural Law Theory and Legal Positivism" (2000) 75 Notre Dame L. Rev. 1613.
Bufford, L Samuel, "What is Right About Bankruptcy Law and Wrong About Its Critics" (1994) 72 Wash. U. L. Quart. 829.
Frost, WC, "Bankruptcy Redistributive Policies and the Limits of the Judicial Process" (1995) 74 N. C. L. Rev. 75.
Fuller, L, "Positivism and the Fidelity of Law – A Response to Professor Hart" (1958) 71 Harv. L. Rev. 630.
Gross, K, "Taking Community Interests into Account in Bankruptcy: An Essay" (1994) 72 Wash. Univ. L. Quart. 1031.
Hart, HLA, "Positivism and the Separation of Law and Morals" (1958) 71 Harv. L. Rev. 593.
Jackson, TH, "Bankruptcy, Non-Bankruptcy Entitlements and the Creditors" Bargain' (1982) 91 Yale L. J. 857.
Jackson, TH, "Avoiding Powers in Bankruptcy" (1984) 36 Stan. L. Rev. 725.
Janger, E, "Crystals and Mud in Bankruptcy Law: Judicial Competence and Statutory Design" (2001) 43 Ariz. L. Rev. 559, 566.
Kimhi, O, and Doebert, A, "Bankruptcy Law as a Balancing System: Lessons from a Comparative Analysis of the Intersection between Labor and Bankruptcy Law" (2015) 23 Am. Bankr. Inst. L. Rev. 491, 529.
Kirgis, P, "Arbitration, Bankruptcy, and Public Policy: A Contractarian Analysis" (2009) 17 Am. Bankr. Inst. L. Rev. 503, 544.
Korobkin, R Donald, "Rehabilitating Values: A Jurisprudence of Bankruptcy" (1991) 91 Colum. L. Rev. 717.
Korobkin, DR, "Contractarianism and the Normative Foundations of Bankruptcy Law" (1993) 71 Tex. L. Rev. 554.
Mann, J Donald, "Bankruptcy and the Entitlements of the Government: Whose Money is it Anyway" (1995) 70(5) New York U. L. Rev. 1040.
Miller, R Harvey, "The Changing Face of Chapter 11: A Re-emergence of the Bankruptcy Judge as the Producer, Director, and Sometimes Star of the Reorganization Passion Play" (1995) 69 Am. Bankr. L. J. 431.
Modigliani, F, and Miller, M, "The Cost of Capital, Corporation Finance and the Theory of Investment" (1958) 48 Am. Econ. Rev. 261.
Mooney, W Charles Jr, "A Normative Theory of Bankruptcy Law: Bankruptcy as (Is) Civil Procedure" (2004) 61 Wash. & Lee L. Rev. 931.
Nsubuga, HJ, "Corporate Insolvency and Employment Protection: A Theoretical Perspective" (2016) 4(1) NIBLeJ 4.
Plunkett, D, and Sundell, T, "Dworkin's Interpretivism and the Pragmatics of Legal Disputes" (2013) 19 Legal Theory 242.
Rasmussen, K Robert, "An Essay on Optimal Bankruptcy Rules and Social Justice" (1994) U. Ill. L. Rev. 1, 43.
Saint-Paul, G, "The Political Economy of Employment Protection" (2002) 110 J. Pol. Econ. 672, 673.
Schwartz, Alan, "A Contract Theory Approach to Business Bankruptcy" (1998) 107 Yale L. J. 1807, 1851.
Skeel, David. Jr, "Debt's Dominion: A History of Bankruptcy Law in America" (2003) 41 Osgoode Hall L. J. 711, 740.

Summers, W Clyde, "The Rights of Individual Workers: The Contract of Employment and the Rights of Individual Employees: Fair Representation and Employment at Will" (1984) 52 Fordham L. Rev. 1082, 1085.

Tabb, CJ, "The History of Bankruptcy Law in the United Stated" (1995) 3 Am. Bankr. Inst. L. Rev. 5.

Toube, F, and Todd, G, "The Proper Treatment of Employees' Claims in Administration" (2005) 18 Insolvency Intelligence 109.

Warren, E, "Bankruptcy Policy" (1987) 54 U. Chi. L. Rev. 775.

Warren, E, "Bankruptcy Policymaking in an Imperfect World" (1993) 92 Mich. L. Rev. 336, 387.

3 Employee rights under US Chapter 11 bankruptcy reorganisations

Introduction

Bankruptcy reorganisation proceedings in the US are governed by Chapter 11 of the US Bankruptcy Code that was enacted in 1978 as Title 11 of the US Code.[1] The US Bankruptcy Code prescribes a traditional Chapter 11 filing process through which outcomes, such as s.363 business sale or a pre-pack plan may be achieved by a US debtor company during bankruptcy reorganisation proceedings.

In the US, employee claims during bankruptcy reorganisations are either categorised as pre-petition or post-petition claims. The commencement of a Chapter 11 bankruptcy case creates a bankruptcy estate,[2] from which employee pre-petition and post-petition claims may be settled. However, during bankruptcy reorganisations in the US, the main area of concern to employees is likely to centre on job security and whether they will be paid what they are owed. Moreover, job security during bankruptcy reorganisations depends on the employer's decision, subject to court approval, to either adopt or reject executory contracts such as employment contracts and collectively bargained agreements,[3] which is a major concern under the US social policy.

The US social policy – employment at will, collective bargaining and labour unionism

(i) Employment-at-will

The term 'social policy' may be termed as an approach through which social aspirations such as income, wealth, infrastructure, security (in terms of protection to the vulnerable or those who cannot defend themselves) et cetera, are distributed and monitored in a state or society.[4] In the US, the employment relationship in

1 11 U.S.C. ss. 101 – 1330 (2012) Enacted by the Bankruptcy Reform Act 1978 (Pub. L. No.95 – 598, 92 Stat. 2549).

2 11 U.S.C. s.541 (a).

3 See, 11 U.S.C. s. 365.

4 Bryan Warde, *Inequality in U.S Social Policy – An Historical Analysis* (New York, Routledge 2016).

the private labour sector which is arguably, the main source of social income and livelihood is mainly dominated by the employment-at-will practice.[5] The term 'employment at will' is a term used in US labour law contractual relationships to refer to an employment relationship under which an employer possesses the legal authority to determine unilaterally the terms of an employment relationship.

The 'employment at will' practice does not only allow employers to hire and fire employees at will, but is also a justified practice arising from the mutual freedom in the employment relationship. This is because as well as employers having the power to hire and fire employees at will, employees can also terminate their jobs at will at any time. However, these mutual powers can work to the disadvantage of employees, as the employment-at-will practice allows the imbalance in the bargaining powers between employers and employees to operate without restriction which in turn, creates a lack of uniform protection to all employees in the private sector workforce.[6]

With the exception of only a few talented and skilled employees who may be able to negotiate certain provisions of their employment contracts with their employers and employees who are members of labour union who can acquire union representation, a majority of employees rely on their employers for the continuity of employment.[7]

The main form of protection to employees in the private sector workforce in the US is through collective bargaining and the labour union movement (as discussed below in the next section). Statutory protection against employee discharge is substantially low. The National Conference of Commissioners on Uniform State Laws (ULC) adopted The Model Employment Termination Act (META) in 1991[8] as a measure to remedy the imbalance between employers' and employees' concerns in an equitable manner within the US upstream labour market.

This statute was to regulate issues that may affect the employment relationship, such as unfair dismissals (discharge) and employment security and continuity. However, since its enactment, the only US state that has adopted it is the US state of Delaware, which is a further indication of the relaxed approach from several US states to adopting uniform laws that would enhance employment protection.

There have been some legislative attempts by the US Congress to address the employment at will culture within the US. For example, the National Labour Relations Act (1935)[9] mandates collective bargaining rights between employers and employees. The statute makes it an unfair labour practice for employers to

5 Stephen F. Befort, "Labor and Employment Law at the Millennium: A Historical Review and Critical Assessment" (2001) 43 *B. C. L. Rev.* 351, 460.

6 Jennifer L. L. Gant, "Studies in Convergence? Post-Crisis Effects on Corporate Rescue and the Influence of Social Policy: The EU and the US" (2006) 25 *Int. I. Rev.* 72–96.

7 Ibid.

8 Available at < www.uniformlaws.org/shared/docs/Employment%20Termination/META_final_91.pdf> (accessed May 2019).

9 29 U.S.C ss. 151 – 169 (1935).

fail to comply with the collective bargaining requirements.[10] The Fair Labour Standards Act (1994)[11] mandates the minimum wage and the 40-hour working week. The Genetic Information and Non-Discrimination Act 2008[12] mandates a prohibition on discrimination based on genetic information in relation to health insurance and employment, et cetera. However, despite the legislative attempts above to curb the employment at will culture, it is still in place and it is still a widely accepted practice within the US private sector labour market.[13]

(ii) Collective bargaining and labour unionism

Employer power plays a significant role in the way employment relationships are handled in the US. Collective bargaining also plays an important role in some instances in balancing and moderating the employer-employee relationship through a representational approach. Collective bargaining is a means of ensuring that employee participation centres on the duty to consult in good faith and in the performance of mutual obligations.[14]

The most significant role of a collective bargaining agreement (CBA) is the provision that an employee who is part of a CBA may not be discharged by the employer, except for 'just cause'. Just cause' dismissal is where an employer dismisses an employee without fulfilling the statutory dismissal requirements, such as providing reasonable notice of termination or payment in lieu of notice to the employee. For a 'just cause' dismissal, the employer has to prove that an employee has done something contrary to his or her employment contract capable of undermining the employment relationship, such as an employee breaching a key term of an employment contract, insolence or insubordination, conflict of interest, et cetera.

Moreover, an employee covered by a CBA is exempt from the operation of the common law rule on employee discharge by the employer. This common law rule stipulates that employers may discharge their employees at will, for good cause, no cause, or even for a cause morally wrong, without being held guilty of a legal wrong.[15] The National Labour Relations Act (NLRA) 1935[16] grants employees the right to bargain collectively over wages, hours of work and other terms and conditions of employment.[17] Failure by the employer to engage in collective bargaining with respective unions or representatives of its employees in good faith is considered an unfair labour practice.[18]

10 Especially, under NLRA (1935), s.8 (a) (5) and s.158 respectively.

11 29 U.S.C ss. 201 - 209 (1994).

12 42 U.S.C. ss.110 -233, (2008) (Pub. L. 110 -233, 122 Stat. 881).

13 Stephen F. Befort, "Labor Law and the Double-Breasted Employer: A Critique of the Single Employer and Alter Ego Doctrines and a Proposed Reformulation" (1987) *Wis. L. Rev.* 67, 101.

14 Clyde W. Summers, "The Contract of Employment and the Rights of Individual Employees: Fair Representation and Employment at Will" (1984) 52 *Fordham L. Rev.* 1082, 1085.

15 Per the ruling in *Payne v Western & A.R.R.* 81 Tenn. 507, 519 – 20 (1884); *Hutton v Watters*, 132 Tenn.527, 179 S.W 134 (1915).

16 29 U.S.C. ss.151 - 169 (2017) Pub. L. 74–198, 49 Stat. 449.

17 29 U.S.C. s.158 (d).

18 29 U.S.C. ss.8 (a) (5) and 158(a) (5).

Chapter 11 of the Bankruptcy Code further protects this provision by making it difficult for the employer to modify or reject agreed CBAs, in s.1113.[19] This provision imposes both procedural and substantive conditions that a debtor employer has to navigate before rejecting or modifying a CBA. The provision requires the debtor to make proposals to the union that provide for necessary modifications before initiating negotiations to either modify or reject a CBA. The employer also has to ensure that all creditors, the debtor and all affected parties are treated fairly and equitably.[20]

Labour unions empower employees through collective actions, providing a voice and platform through which their employer can listen to their concerns and make endeavours to address those concerns.[21] As a result, employees who are part of labour unions tend to enjoy better wages, benefits and usually have a better degree of representation over non-unionised employees in the US private work sector.

However, it is worth noting that, although these legislative provisions recognise the need to give employees a voice and a right to participate in issues pertaining to their employment relationships with their employer, the threat employees face as a result of Chapter 11 reorganisations remains huge and plays a big role in the balancing of the employee-employer relationships during bankruptcy reorganisation proceedings.

It is the concern that the framework within which unions work with respective employers, limits the level of input from unions as they are excluded from meaningful decision-making processes. These include, for example, corporate investment decisions and decisions regarding the future direction of the employer's business which may affect member employees' interests.[22] The law affords the employer broader corporate decision making powers while employees, apart from a few in higher management positions, and their unions are not afforded the same participation rights in this respect.

This may affect the union's ability to protect their members' employment related interests, as they may find it difficult to deal with issues, such as the ever-changing labour market, capital mobility and corporate structural changes, especially, in situations where the employer has other affiliates in other US states or international subsidiaries.[23]

19 11 U.S.C s.1113.

20 11 U.S.C. s.1113 (b) (I) (A). However, see, Christopher D. Cameron, "How 'Necessary' Became the Mother of Rejection: An Empirical Look at the Fate of Collective Bargaining Agreements on the Tenth Anniversary of Bankruptcy Code Section 1113" (1994) 34 *Santa Clara L. Rev.* 841, 869.

21 M. Finkin, "Directions in Labor Law – Concerns for the Dignity of the Worker: Revisionism in Labor Law" (1984) 43 *Md. L. Rev.* 23.

22 J. Melone, "Union Blues: Why Collective Bargaining Agreements that are Neither Rejected nor Modified Pursuant to 11 U.S.C. 1113 are Not Granted Administrative Expense Priority in a Chapter 11 Bankruptcy Reorganization by S. 1113 of the Bankruptcy Code" (2006) 32 *Ohio N.U. L. Rev.* 429, 442.

23 D. Bordewieck and V. Countryman, "The Rejection of Collective Bargaining Agreements by Chapter 11 Debtors" (1983) 57 *Am. Bankr. L. J.* 293, 294.

Where this is the case, it further shifts the balance of power on the side of the employer and against the union and its employee members which is a shift away from the notion of industrial democracy, that the NLRA sought to implement as a central rationale for the protection of employees and the regulation of the employer-employee relationships in general.[24]

The diminishing role of labour union movement in the US

An employer who is under a CBA with its employees' union is restrained from making alterations to the terms and conditions of its employees' contracts of employment without first negotiating with the relevant union.[25] The employer is also restrained from unilaterally making alterations to specific terms of an already existing CBA without the respective union's consent. This is a move to afford employees a voice through representation to avoid arbitrary managerial decisions that may infringe on employees' rights.[26]

On occasion, labour unions have negotiated successfully for provisions restricting employee dismissals to those for just cause. Successor and assignment clauses have also been negotiated successfully, requiring the new buyer or successor employer to adopt collective bargaining agreements following a business transfer.[27] However, labour unions still face challenges in that they lack power to influence or effect the transfer or business sale. This is because the decision to sell or transfer the business is termed as a permissible subject of bargaining out of the union and their member employees' control.[28] The employer has exclusive choice as to whom to sell and when to sell or transfer the business. The employer is only required to bargain with unions and employees on how employee interests are to be treated where jobs are to be terminated.

Moreover, the success of the labour union movement in the US, even in the former strongholds, such as in the Steel, Aircraft and Automobile industries, has substantially declined over the years. For example, a 2017 Economic News Release by the Bureau of Labor Statistics, United States Department of Labor on 26 January 2017 reported that the percentage of wage and salary workers that were members of unions in 2016 was at 10.7 percent, down 0.4 percent from the overall membership in 2016.[29]

24 A. Cox, "The Duty to Bargain in Good Faith" (1958) 71 *Harv. L. Rev.* 1407.

25 NLRA, s.158 (a) (5).

26 NLRA, s.158 (d).

27 See cases, such as *John Wiley & Sons, Inc. v Livingston* 376, U.S. 543 (1963); *NLRB v Burns Int'l Sec. Serv.*, 406 U.S. 272 (1972); *Fall River Dyeing & Fishing Corp. v NLRB*, 482 U.S. 27 (1987).

28 G M. Roberts, "Bankruptcy and the Union's Bargain: Equitable Treatment of Collective Bargaining Agreements" (1987) 39 *Stan. L. Rev.* 1015, 1047; B. A. Ceccotti, "Lost in Transformation: The Disappearance of Labor Policies in Applying Section 1113 of the Bankruptcy Code" (2007) 15 *Am. Bankr. Inst. L. Rev.* 415, 431.

29 Full report / news release at <<U> www.bls.gov/news.release/union2.nr0.htm></U> (accessed 22 May 2019).

In 1980 when these statistics were first published, the percentage of unionised workers was at 20 percent. Even this represents a proportionately low level of union representation which leaves a majority of employees lacking protection. This has weakened the political influence in both advocacy and representation to its members. The decline may be attributed to the changing nature of the US market economy with both capital mobility and technological advancement having shaped and changed the private sector labour industry.[30]

For example, in the 1970s and the 1980s, mobility of capital and labour was very limited. Technology was still in its early stages of influence. Therefore, if an employer made irrational proposals to a labour union and member employees to modify or reject collectively bargained agreements and those proposals were rejected by the union, the employer would be inclined to consider those proposals. Threats of potential strike actions or walkouts by union employees would be costly to that employer. An employer would not easily obtain immediate substitute labour providers to continue running the business during the standoff period.

However, today, labour and capital mobility is very fast-paced due to technological advancements. Moreover, companies may now have subsidiaries and affiliates in other US states which may provide substitute labour cover at shorter notice periods. In addition to the above, some employers incorporate mobility clauses[31] in labour contracts with terms and conditions that give them the leverage to change them, as per the need of the service.[32]

Moreover, the policy underpinnings of the need to provide unionised employees with a voice through union representation in the NLRA, have on occasion, been found to be in conflict with the provision of Chapter 11 of the Bankruptcy Code. It is the notion that during the build up to the confirmation of a Chapter 11 reorganisation plan, a debtor may assume or reject an existing CBA, with court approval[33] provided the debtor employer shows that a rejection of that CBA is in the best interests of bankruptcy estate.[34] This is a move that conflicts with the ethos of s.158 (a) of the NLRA[35] in its mandate for negotiation and representation for employees through collective bargaining.

30 D. Keating, "The Continuing Puzzle of Collective Bargaining Agreements in Bankruptcy" (1994) 35 *Wm. & Mary L. Rev.* 503, 526.

31 'Mobility Clauses' are terms or conditions that may be incorporated into an employment contract by an employer affording that employer power and flexibility to change employees' place of work. This is, especially, where the employer has not identified a specific place as the principal place of work in the employees' terms and condition of employment. See cases, such as *Horst v High Tables Ltd* [1997] EWCA Civ. 2000; *Home Office v Evans* [2007] EWCA Civ. 1089 (CA).

32 Laura N. Coordes, "The Geography of Bankruptcy" (2015) 68 *Vand. L. Rev.* 381–439.

33 11 U.S.C. s.365 (a).

34 See *In re Del Grosso*, 115 B.R 136, 138 (Bankr. N.D 111 1990); *In re Tres – Ark Inc.*, 09 -12589 (Bankr. W.D Texas 2012).

35 This provision provides that '[I]t shall be an unfair labour practice for an employer to interfere with, restrain or coerce employees in the exercise of the rights guaranteed in section 157 of this title. For full provisions under s.158 (a), please see, NLRA (1935), s.158 (a) (1) – (5).

A paradigmatic shift in collective bargaining – NLRB v Bildisco & Bildisco

The influence of labour union movement and collective bargaining movement as a concerted model of employee protection in the US was largely affected by employers' ability to reject collective bargaining agreements. The question of an employer's ability to reject or assume a CBA was at the central point of deliberation in the case of *NLRB v Bildisco & Bildisco*.[36] The court in this case had to decide whether a CBA like any other contract of the debtor, could be rejected by the debtor, by showing that its rejection would be to the benefit of the bankruptcy estate.

The respondent debtor (Bildisco), a building supplies distributor, filed a voluntary petition in bankruptcy for reorganisation under Chapter 11 of the Bankruptcy Code and was subsequently authorised by the bankruptcy court to operate the business on a debtor-in-possession basis in 1980. At the time the petition was filed, approximately 45 percent of Bildisco's workers were represented by the Local 408 of the International Brotherhood of Teamsters, Chauffeurs, Warehousemen and Helpers of America (the Union). Bildisco had negotiated a three-year collective bargaining agreement that was to expire in April 1982. The CBA expressly provided that it was binding on the parties and their successors even though bankruptcy should supervene.

By early 1980, Bildisco had failed to meet some of its obligations under the CBA including the payment of health and pension benefits and the remittance to the Union, of the dues collected. Bildisco had also refused to pay wage increases called for in the agreement by the Union. Bildisco then filed a motion with the bankruptcy court requesting permission to reject the CBA on the ground that rejection of the CBA would save the company approximately $100,000 that was granted in 1981.

The Union filed unfair labour practice charges with the National Labour Relations Board (NLRB). The NLRB found that Bildisco had violated ss. 8(a) (5) and 8(a) (1) of the (NLRA 1935) by unilaterally changing the terms of the CBA and by refusing to negotiate with the Union. The NLRB ordered Bildisco to make the pension and health contributions, and to remit dues to the Union and petitioned the Court to enforce its order. The Court rejected NLRB's request to enforce its order and held that a collective bargaining agreement is an executory contract subject to rejection by a debtor-in-possession under s. 365(a) of the Bankruptcy Code.[37]

The decision by the Court was that a debtor can reject a CBA only in circumstances where the court finds that 'equities balance in favour of rejecting such a contract.'[38] In addition, the Court also held that a debtor can unilaterally alter the terms of a collectively bargained agreement during the interim period that runs between the period of filing of the bankruptcy petition, and the time during which the order authorising rejection is entered.[39]

36 *NLRB v Bildisco & Bildisco*, 465 U.S. 523 (1984). (Hereafter *Bildisco*).
37 *NLRB v Bildisco & Bildisco*, 465 U.S. 523 (1984), para. 516.
38 Ibid., para. 526.
39 Ibid., paras. 532, 533.

However, the Court recognised the fact that as a result of this decision, the incentive to bargain collectively on the side of the employees and their unions may be lost, which might lead to increased abuse of employees' rights to bargain collectively and to be represented. Consequently, the Court placed a pre-condition that for the debtor employer to benefit from the above provisions, and therefore, reject a CBA, or make changes to its specific provisions, that employer should have made reasonable efforts to renegotiate the terms and conditions contested with unions. The employer must also show that such efforts of renegotiation are not likely to produce a prompt and satisfactory outcome before rejecting that CBA effectively.[40]

However, the concern is that this pre-condition may be vulnerable to misinterpretation and application by the debtor employer as it affords a certain degree of indirect advantage to the debtor employer. The debtor employer has an upper hand in determining the likelihood of the ongoing negotiations with the union to produce a satisfactory outcome.[41] This is to the advantage of the debtor employer in that, the length (in terms of duration) and, mode of negotiation may make it difficult for the unions to reach a satisfactory outcome.[42]

Moreover, the debtor employer has an added advantage in that, during the negotiation to modify or reject a CBA, a court may authorise interim alterations to employees' benefits, such as wages and other employment related benefits where doing so is essential to continuation of the debtor employer's business. The court may also authorise interim alteration to a CBA where doing so would help prevent irreparable damage to the bankruptcy estate.[43] Although this may turn out to be advantageous to employees in the long run where the survival of the bankruptcy estate preserves jobs and ensure continuity of employment, the overall effect still remains that the debtor employer retains an upper hand over the union and its employee members whenever these provisions are applied.[44]

Legislative response post-Bildisco – failure in ascendancy?

As a form of mitigating the effect originating from the *Bildisco* decision above, the US Congress enacted s.1113 of the Bankruptcy Code,[45] as a move to restrict the debtor's ability to reject or modify CBAs strategically. Following the Supreme Court's ruling in *Bildisco*, there were numerous bankruptcy reorganisation proceedings that mainly targeted CBAs and labour costs.[46]

40 *Bildisco*, paras. 525, 526.

41 M. West, "Life After Bildisco: Section 1113 and the Duty to Bargain in Good Faith" (1986) 47 *Ohio St. L. J.* 65, 103; Ann J. McClain, "Bankruptcy Code Section 1113 and the Simple Rejection of Collective Bargaining Agreements: Labor Loses Again" (1991) 80 *Geo. L. J.* 191, 206.

42 Clyde W. Summers, "The Contract of Employment and the Rights of Individual Employees: Fair Representation and Employment at Will" (1984) 52(6) *Fordham L. Rev.* 1082, 1085.

43 11 U.S.C. s.1113 (e).

44 For example, *see In re WorldCom Inc.*, 346 F. 2d 628 (Bankr. S.D.N.Y 2004).

45 11 U.S.C. s.1113.

46 See, for example, *In re Chateaugay Corp.*, 64 B.R 990 (Bankr. S.D.N.Y. 1986); *In re Continental Airlines*, 64 B.R. 858 (*Bankr.* S.D Texas 1984*); In re Wilson Foods Corp.*, 31 B.R. 269 (Bankr. Okl. 1983).

Moreover, preceded by a tight split of a five-to-four majority in the decision in *Bildisco*, the dissenting judges gave opinions that raised some concerns about the majority ruling. Most notably, the dissenting judges (Justices White, Marshall and Blackmun) led by Justice Brennan, expressed dissatisfaction by the majority's opinion (led by Justice Rehnquist) that the power by the employer to reject or modify CBAs included the power to reject or modify employment contract terms and conditions under s.365 immediately upon filing for bankruptcy without bargaining with the labour union.[47]

Justice Rehnquist was of the opinion that:

> ...[t]he debtor was empowered by virtue of the Bankruptcy Code to deal with its contracts and property in a manner it could not have employed absent the bankruptcy filing.[48]

However, Justice Brennan was of the opinion that:

> ...[f]or both policies of bankruptcy (allowing rejection or modification of CBA by the employer) and the NLRA (1935) (of ensuring the continuation of collective bargaining) in the interim period between filing for bankruptcy and rejection, the requirement on the debtor (DIP) under the NLRA (1935) s.8 (d) 'to bargain collectively and to confer in good faith with employees in respect to wages, hours and other terms and conditions of employment or the negotiation of an agreement or any questions arising their under' should remain effective and enforceable on the DIP until rejection is approved by the bankruptcy court.[49]

However, the Supreme Court was of the view that from the filing of the bankruptcy petition until formal acceptance, a CBA is not an enforceable contract. The requirement on the debtor employer under s.8 (d) of the NLRA 1935 would be in conflict with the Bankruptcy Code's overall objective of allowing a DIP some flexibility and breathing space.[50] Therefore, it would undermine the debtor's rejection or modification rights.[51]

The difference in opinions by the Supreme Court judges attracted both Congressional and Senate debates in relation to the effects that the *Bildisco* ruling was having on collective bargaining and labour union movement during bankruptcy reorganisations in the US. For example, in Congress, Congressman Peter Rodino Jr introduced a bill to amend title 11 of the United States Code to clarify the circumstances under which CBAs may be rejected in cases under Chapter 11 of such title and for other purposes.

47 *NLRB v Bildisco & Bildisco*, 465 U.S. 523 (1984), para. 528 – 529.
48 Ibid., para. 528.
49 *Bildisco*, para. 550 – 553.
50 Ibid., para. 532.
51 Ibid., para. 529.

This bill lobbied for a stringent standard to be applied to CBA rejection cases and a prohibition on unilateral modification of CBAs. Rodino's bill was incorporated into the Omnibus Bankruptcy Bill (H.R. 5174)[52] that was later passed into legislation by the 98th US Congress as the Bankruptcy Amendments and Federal Judgeship Act 1984.[53]

In the Senate, Senator James Strom Thurmond introduced a bill that required a 30 days' notice by the debtor to labour unions before unilateral modifications to CBAs and the balancing of equities test.[54] Senator Thurmond's bill was followed by Senator Robert William Parkwood tabling a bill before the Senate with proposals to permit CBA rejection where the debtor had shown that minimum modification to employees' benefits and protection would also permit the reorganisation of the debtor taking into consideration the sacrifices to be made by all affected parties.[55] However, the debates continued in both Congress and Senate on the subject of collective bargaining post *Bildisco*.[56]

It should be noted that at the time the Supreme Court gave its opinion in *Bildisco*, the US Congress was undergoing a period of 'jurisdictional crisis' following the Supreme Court's ruling in *Northern Pipeline Construction Co. v Marathon Pipe Line Corporation*.[57] The Supreme Court had held in this case that the 1978 Congressional jurisdiction grant to bankruptcy courts was unconstitutional as the bankruptcy judges created by the 1978 Bankruptcy Code were not article III judges who could exercise the broad jurisdiction created by the Bankruptcy Code.

However, in order to reach the agreement on the treatment of collective bargaining post *Bildisco*, both Congress and Senate reached a general consensus by adopting an amendment bill H.R. 5174[58] on the jurisdictional amendment to the Bankruptcy Code. Therefore, a joint House of Congress and Senate conference committee was held on 28 June 1984 and a compromise was passed by the US Congress on 29 June 1984 and signed into legislation by the President on 10 July 1984 as the Bankruptcy Amendments and Federal Judgeship Act 1984[59] that led to the enactment of s.1113 to the bankruptcy Code.

52 H.R. 5174, 98th Cong. 2d Sess., 130 CONG. REC. H1832 – 43 (daily ed. March 21, 1984).
53 Bankruptcy Amendments and Federal Judgeship Act (1984) (Pub. L. No. 98 – 353, 98 Stat. 333, 392 (1984).
54 130 CONG. REC. 10, 13061 (1984). See also, Daniel S. Ehrenberg, "Collective Bargaining Agreements under Section 1113 of Chapter 11 of the 1984 Bankruptcy Code: Resolving the Tension Between Labor Law and Bankruptcy Law" (1994) 2 *J. L. & Policy* 55, 68 where Senator Thurmond's proposals are broadly analysed.
55 130 CONG. REC. S8988 (daily ed. June 29 1984).
56 R. Rosenberg, "Bankruptcy and the Collective Bargaining Agreement – A Brief Lesson in the Use of the Constitutional System of Checks and Balances" (1984) 58 *Am. Bankr. L. J.* 293, 312 – 321.
57 *Northern Pipeline Construction Co. v Marathon Pipe Line Co.* 458 U.S. 50 (1982).
58 H.R. 5174, 98th Cong. 2d Sess., 130 CONG. REC. H1832 – 43 (daily ed. March 21, 1984.
59 Bankruptcy Amendments and Federal Judgeship Act (1984) (Pub. L. No. 98 – 353, 98 Stat. 333, 392 (1984).

Section 1113(a) of the US Bankruptcy Code provides that:

> [T]he debtor in possession, or the trustee if one has been appointed under the provisions of this chapter, other than a trustee in a case covered by subchapter IV of this chapter and by title I of the Railway Labor Act, may assume or reject a collective bargaining agreement only in accordance with the provisions of this section.

This provision requires the debtor company to make proposals to the union that provide for necessary modifications before initiating negotiations and to ensure that all creditors, the debtor and all affected parties are treated fairly and equitably.[60] Therefore, this provision provides a protective shield to employees as it imposes a parallel obligation on the debtor employer to bargain in good faith like the obligation imposed under s.158 of the NLRA.[61]

To employees, this may be viewed as an elevation to the participation and consultation rights on the issues that may affect their interests and benefits during bankruptcy reorganisations. This is because for employees and their unions to fully evaluate the proposals on offer from the debtor employer, the employer would have to supply them with information that is relevant enough for them to make informed decisions. The information must also be conferred in good faith in order to reach mutually satisfactory decisions.[62]

In addition to the above, the employees' authorised unions or representatives may reject such proposals but rejection must be born out of good causes.[63] Otherwise, the court may authorise a rejection of a CBA where it is satisfied that employees or representative unions have rejected the proposals without good cause or where, the balance of equities favours rejection.[64]

However, despite the legislative attempts to mitigate the effects of *Bildisco* above, employee protection through labour union movement and collective bargaining has not gained the balance that the US Congress sought to implement through the enactment of s.1113. This is because the provisions in s.1113 protect unionised employees as opposed to non-unionised employees who are not parties to CBAs. This leaves non-unionised employees with no formal legislative protection under s.1113 and therefore, vulnerable to unfair and unjustifiable modifications to wages, benefits, and other employment-related interests.[65]

60 11 U.S.C. s.1113 (b) (I) (A).

61 Particularly, see, NLRA (1935), s.158 (a) (1) – (5).

62 11 U.S.C. s.1113 (b) (2).

63 11 U.S.C. s.1113(c)(2).

64 11 U.S.C. s.1113(c). See also, E. Warren and J. L. Westbrook, "The Success of Chapter 11: A Challenge to the Critics" (2009) 107 *Mich. L. Rev.* 603, 609.

65 M. Efthimiou, "State Legislative Attempts to Mandate Continuation of Collective Bargaining Agreements during Business Change: The Unfulfilled Expectations and the Pre-empted Results" (1992) 77 *Cornell L. Rev.* 47, 51.

Proposals for reform of s.1113 – The American Bankruptcy Institute Recommendations

In 2012, the American Bankruptcy Institute (ABI) commissioned a study into the operation of Chapter 11 of the US Bankruptcy Code and provided a report and recommendations for reform of Chapter 11 of the US Bankruptcy Code in March 2013.[66] Among the major areas explored by the ABI Commission, and therefore, part of the recommendations for reform in the ABI report was the operation of s.1113 of the US Bankruptcy Code during bankruptcy reorganisations proceedings in the US.

In its Report, the ABI Commission acknowledged that the use of s.1113 during bankruptcy reorganisation proceedings by the debtor to reject or modify a CBA creates disputes that can be time-consuming, emotionally charged and disruptive to employees who are critical to a company's successful restructuring.[67] On the same point, Stephen S. Mitchell, a retired US bankruptcy judge in his statement on the ABI Report referred to Chapter 11 as being largely about breaking economic promises such as collective bargaining agreements, pension plans and retiree health plans that have historically been judged of special importance in the interest of promoting the rehabilitation of financially troubled businesses.[68]

The ABI Commission recommended that s.1113 should be amended to further the objectives of negotiation and consensual resolution underlying the collective bargaining process under s.1113.[69] To achieve this, the ABI Report recommended that in addition to provisions in s.1113(b)(1), the trustee (DIP) should provide notice to the applicable labour organisation that modifications to the CBA are being proposed along with an initial proposal and description of the information to be made available for the labour organisation to evaluate the proposal. The trustee (DIP) should also file a notice of intent to initiate proceedings under s.1113 (b) and schedule an initial conference with the court regarding such proceedings.[70]

With notice from the trustee and (served to the authorised employees' representatives), the court would schedule a status conference with the trustee (DIP) and authorised representatives or labour organisation to review the notice and discuss the initial proposal, proposed information disclosure, timetable for conducting negotiations and to decide whether a mediator may be required to assist

66 American Bankruptcy Institute, "Commission to Study the Reform of Chapter 11 – Final Report and Recommendations" < www.insol.org/emailer/Dec_2014_downloads/ABI%20Commission%20Report_9%20December%202014.pdf > accessed 12 May 2019. (Hereafter ABI Report).

67 ABI Report, para.156.

68 See, Stephen S. Mitchell, "Statement on American Bankruptcy Institute Commission to Study Reform of Chapter 11" (ABI Commission, 14 March 2014 <http://commission.abi.org/sites/default/files/statements/14mar2013/Stephen_Mitchell.pdf> (accessed 12 May 2019).

69 ABI Report, para. 156.

70 ABI Report, paras. 156, 157.

in the negotiations. These arrangements are aimed at facilitating consensual and mutually agreed modifications to the CBA between the trustee (DIP) and the labour organisation or representatives.

In the absence of mutually consensual agreement between the trustee and labour organisation in the first conference, the court may schedule another conference for further negotiations and the trustee may also request for a case management process for a motion to reject or modify the CBA.[71] In view of these proposals, it may be submitted that the proposals aim to improve the industrial relations through negotiations between debtors and employees where s.1113 rejections to CBA are initiated. These recommendations, if adopted by the US Congress and changes made to the provisions under s.1113, a balance in bargaining power and control in the CBA rejection process may be achieved between the debtor and its employees.

However, it may be noted that these recommendations are subject to certain limitations. The ABI Report recommended that the above recommendations should not be read to and intended to alter the current law under s.1113 (e).

Section 1113 (e) provides that:

> If during a period when the collective bargaining agreement continues in effect, and if essential to the continuation of the debtor's business, or in order to avoid irreparable damage to the estate, the court, after notice and a hearing, may authorize the trustee to implement interim changes in the terms, conditions, wages, benefits, or work rules provided by a collective bargaining agreement. Any hearing under this paragraph shall be scheduled in accordance with the needs of the trustee. The implementation of such interim changes shall not render the application for rejection moot.

In light of the above provision, it may be argued that although the recommendations above, if adopted by Congress, and other policy makers, would improve the CBA rejection process, the debtor would still have a broader scope and flexibility than employees in the CBA rejection process. By leaving the provisions under s.1113 (e) intact (not subject to reform proposals) the balance is tipped towards augmenting the reorganisation prospects of the debtor rather than favouring employee protection.

It is therefore the contention that although the ABI Recommendations aim to improve the negotiation, participation and transparency imperatives in the employer-employee relationships during s.1113 CBA rejection proceedings that have been the subject of academic and judicial critical analysis for decades,[72] it remains a moot point whether, if adopted and incorporated into the Bankruptcy Code, the industrial relations between employers, employees and labour union movement in the US, would be improved as originally sought by the NLRA (1935).

71 ABI Report, para. 158.

72 Daniel Keating, "Transforming a Non-Claim into a Claim: s. 1114 and the Curious Case of *In re Visteon*" (2011) 85 *Am. Bankr. L.J.* 1.

Pre-petition and post-petition employee claims under Chapter 11

In the event that the company is liquidated and therefore, employment security is no longer guaranteed, the treatment of employee claims such as for accrued wages and salaries, is cast into the spotlight. The allocation of the company's assets for the payment of unsecured claims of the debtor company on liquidation is based on statutory priorities.[73] Where assets of the debtor company are insufficient to pay in full all unsecured claims, it would mean that payments of unsecured claims will be dictated by their priority status. Pre-petition employee claims, such as claims for wages, salaries and commissions earned in the 180 days prior to bankruptcy filing that remain unpaid rank fourth in priority under Chapter 11 of the Bankruptcy Code.[74] Pre-petition pension and welfare benefit claims, such as a defined benefit plan claims also rank fourth in priority.[75]

Pre-petition employee claims

Employee pre-petition debts are benefits and interests that arise out of employee contractual arrangements with their employer that remain unpaid at the time when the debtor employer files for bankruptcy. These may include claims for wages, salaries and commissions that remain unpaid. Pension contributions arising out of pension plans, outstanding damage claims, such as for wrongful discharge arising in breach of employment contract, accrued welfare benefit claims for sick leave and holiday pay are among such claims. Some of these claims, such as claims for wages and salaries, take the form of direct compensation and, therefore, are paid ahead of other claims subject to a statutory limit.[76]

It may be noted that although the Bankruptcy Code accords some employee pre-petition claims with priority status, this priority protection only covers a small percentage of employees that are members of unions as a significant majority of employees in the private sector workforce in the US are non-unionised.[77]

In addition to the above, the priority statutory protection in s.507 (a) (3) and (4) of the Bankruptcy Code is not guaranteed. The protection is dependent

73 11 U.S.C. s. 507 (a) (3), (4) and (5).

74 11 U.S.C. s.507 (a) (4) (A) and (B). However, wages and salaries, and sales commission claims (only where an employee worked as an independent contractor to the debtor company and 75 percent of his earnings were earned as an independent contractor in the last 12 months prior to bankruptcy filing) are subject to a statutory limit of $10,000 per each individual employee as of February 2017.

75 11 U.S.C. s. 507(a) (5) (A) and (B). Please note that pension income refers to retirement income while welfare benefits may include severance pay, training, medical, health, accident, death benefits, pre-paid legal services, et cetera.

76 11 U.S.C. s. 507(a) (3), (4).

77 For example, see the economic news release by the by the Bureau of Labor Statistics, United States Department of Labor, on 26 January 2017 highlighting the decline in labour union membership in the US private sector workforce <<U> www.bls.gov/news.release/union2.nr0.htm></U> (accessed 12 May 2019).

on whether the debtor employer adopts or rejects employee contracts following bankruptcy filing.[78] This is because Chapter 11 of the Bankruptcy Code grants a debtor company power to free itself from pre-petition executory contractual agreements and liabilities by either amendment or rejection. These contracts include employment contracts and collective bargaining agreements. Trade and supply contractual agreements may also be affected.

If the debtor employer chooses to adopt employee contracts of employment, then employment protection and continuity may be maintained. This also comes with an inherent advantage in that it is a requirement on formal adoption of executory contracts that the debtor employer adopting such contracts cures any outstanding pre-petition defaults and payment of outstanding damages. As part of confirming a Chapter 11 reorganisation plan, it is a requirement that such a plan provides for payment of priority claims as a pre-condition for a reorganisation plan confirmation.[79]

However, in the event that employee contracts of employment are rejected, the debtor employer is under no obligation to honour claims for damages and other related claims immediately. They would be categorised as general unsecured claims which may not be paid until the time of formal distribution,[80] which has no definitive timescale. Although there have been instances where the debtor employer has made immediate payment of employee pre-petition claims on a court's authorisation,[81] this is not a common practice and on other occasions, judges have turned down requests for such payments.[82] This leaves employees' fate to the mercy of bankruptcy judges to exercise their equitable powers[83] to authorise expenditure outside the ordinary course of business to meet such claims.[84]

Employee pension and retirement benefits

Like any other legal contract existing at the time of a bankruptcy filing under Chapter 11, a pension plan is one form of contract that the debtor employer may contemplate modifying or rejecting after filing for a Chapter 11 bankruptcy petition. However, pension plans existing at the time of filing for bankruptcy, are protected by the provisions of s.1113 of Chapter 11 Bankruptcy Code, provided such a pension plan is part of a collective bargaining agreement.

If covered by a CBA, for a debtor employer to reject or modify such a pension plan, procedural and substantive provisions of s.1113 have to be satisfied.

78 Via 11 U.S.C. s.365(a).

79 11 U.S.C. s.1129 (a) (9).

80 11 U.S.C s.549 (a).

81 See, for example, *In re Gulf Air Inc.*, 112 B.R 152, 154 (Bankr. W.D. La 1989); *In re Chateagay Corp.*, 80 B.R 279, 286 –87 (Bankr. S.D.N.Y. 1987).

82 For example, *In re FCX Inc.*, 60 B.R 405, 411 -12 (Bankr. E.D.N.C. 1986); *In re Structurlite Plastics Corp.*, 86 B.R 922, 932. (Bankr. S.D. Ohio 1988).

83 11 U.S.C. s.105.

84 11 U.S.C. s.363 (b).

The debtor employer has to show that proposals have been made to unions or employee representatives that provide for necessary modifications to the pension plan, and that all creditors, the debtor and all affected parties are treated fairly and equitably.[85] The negotiations must also be conducted in good faith, in order to reach a mutually satisfactory agreement.[86]

However, if existing employee pension plans are not covered by a CBA and the debtor employer seeks to modify or terminate such pension plans, the debtor employer is restrained by the provision of the Employment Retirement Income Security Act (ERISA) 1974,[87] which governs the treatment of employee pension plans during corporate bankruptcy reorganisations in the private sector workforce in the U.S.

This statute protects two categories of pension plans namely; defined benefit plans and defined contribution plans.[88] The difference between these two categories is that, in a defined contribution pension plan, employees make payments into the plan during their employment and their level of benefit depends on the amount of money paid into the plan. However, a defined benefit pension plan is one where employee members are promised a certain level of income or payment upon retirement arising from their employment relationship. This may be in a form of a lump sum or an annuity, payable on retirement which accrues over the years of service.

Defined benefit plans are guaranteed[89] while defined contribution plans are not. Because of this difference in terms of guarantee, ERISA, as a means of protection, requires that promised pension benefits are adequately protected to ensure that in situations such as the bankruptcy of the employer company, employee members, especially retirees do not fall victims since they rely on such payments for their livelihood upon retirement.[90]

Therefore, ERISA established a Pension Benefit Guaranty Corporation (PBGC), a federal government corporation which insures defined benefit plans against defaults by employers.[91] PBGC is beneficial to employees in that, where a debtor employer files for bankruptcy and does not have enough funds to pay for defined benefit payments, PBGC steps in and assumes responsibility for payments to employees, subject to a statutory limit.[92] PBGC then initiates a statutory claim over the debtor employer for the amount paid.[93]

85 11 U.S.C. s.1113 (b) (1) (A).
86 11 U.S.C. s.1113 (b) (2).
87 29 U.S.C. ss. 1001 – 1461 (2016).
88 See, 29 U.S.C. s.1002 (34).
89 29 U.S.C. s.1332.
90 Please note that retiree benefits are protected by the Bankruptcy Code under s.1114 as they are afforded administrative expenses status under s.1114 (e) (1), (2). Therefore, the employer is restrained from making modification or termination of such benefits unless agreed by respective unions, employee representative or court. (s.1114 (e) (1).
91 29 U.S.C. s.1302 (a).
92 For example, the statutory limit to employees retiring at the age of 65 years, as of 2015, was $5,512.50, per month, on annuity basis. See, 29 U.S.C. ss. 1341, 1342.
93 29 U.S.C. ss.1362 (a) and (b) (1) (A).

However, it should be noted that although defined benefit plans are insured by the PBGC, defined contribution plans are not. ERISA requires employers to adequately protect defined contribution plans. For example, the employer is required to keep defined contribution plan assets in a separate trust, away from the corporate assets of the employer company. However, most defined contribution plans are attached to and tied into company assets which comes with a risk of depreciation in value, especially, where the company drifts into financial difficulties. However, the company or its benefit plan trustees may be subjected to civil enforcement for liability arising out of breach of fiduciary duty.[94]

Where this is the case, employees may not be able to obtain all the benefits to which they are entitled where their employer opts to terminate such benefit plans on bankruptcy. However, the termination would be subject to distress termination rules under ERISA which requires the provision of a written notice of intention to terminate by the employer company to all affected employees.[95]

Moreover, in a multi-employer defined benefit plan, the level of benefit assumed by the PBGC is substantially lower than the amount assumed in a single employer defined benefit plan. Multi-employer defined benefit plans usually arise out of CBAs which may involve employee members of more than one employer. The risk is that, in a multi-employer defined benefit plan, a single employer who is part of a multi-employer plan may file for bankruptcy with insufficient or no funds to meet guaranteed benefit payments which may lead to distress termination of the benefit plan.[96]

Although the PBGC may provide financial assistance for the continued functionality of the plan, this may not be enough to sustain the running of the plan in the long run. This may negatively affect other employer members to the plan who may also terminate the defined benefit plans of their employees, which would be a threat to employee benefits and protection.[97]

In addition to the above, other employee benefit plans, such as health care plans, medical and accidental care plans et cetera, are not covered by ERISA per se. These benefits arise out of non-bankruptcy legislation such as contract law and labour law. This has the effect that the employer, through contractual terms and conditions and company policies and procedures, may vary these benefit plans as they see fit. Where this is the case, the employer is not required to adhere to the requirements on employee consultation and participation rights in relation to these benefit plans under ERISA.[98] Moreover, where such benefit plans are terminated due to bankruptcy, the employer is under no obligation to honour claims arising out of such terminations as such claims are not covered by the PBGC.

94 29 U.S.C. 1132 and 29 U.S.C. s.1109.
95 29 U.S.C.s.1341(C).
96 29 U.S.C. s.1362.
97 29 U.S.C. ss.1332(a) and 1341(a).
98 29 U.S.C. s.1051 (1).

Retiree benefits protection under Section 1114 of the US bankruptcy code

Following the *Bildisco* decision that an employer may reject or modify executory contracts upon filing for bankruptcy, CBAs and retiree benefits became increasingly targeted by debtors for strategic modification or rejection upon filing for bankruptcy as they were deemed to fall under executory contracts.[99]

For example, in 1986, a Dallas-based Corporation, LTV Steel Corporation, filed for a Chapter 11 bankruptcy proceedings and subsequently terminated the retiree benefits of 78,000 former LTV employees.[100] This led to a strike by the union workers, attracting a strong reaction from the US Congress which condemned the actions of LTV Steel Corp., by branding the termination 'irresponsible, unfair and unwelcome'.[101] The US Congress followed their condemnation of LTV's termination of retiree benefits by extending temporary retiree benefits to the former LTV employees and enacted the Retiree Benefits Bankruptcy Protection Act (RBBPA) (1998)[102] which became codified as section 1114 of the Bankruptcy Code.[103]

Retiree benefits under s.1114 are defined as follows:

> a payments made "to any entity or person for the purpose of providing or reimbursing payments for retired employees and their spouses and dependents, for medical, surgical, or hospital care benefits, or benefits in the event of sickness, accident, disability, or death" through fund established at least in part by debtor prior to filing for Chapter 11 bankruptcy.[104]

The enactment of s.1114 provided additional protection in respect of retiree benefits during Chapter 11 bankruptcy reorganisations. This section mandates the continuation of retiree benefits by a corporation upon filing for bankruptcy and also limits a debtor from modifying retiree benefits except where such modifications are permitted by statute.[105] The provisions under s.1114 state that:

> Notwithstanding any other provision of this title, the debtor in possession, or the trustee if one has been appointed under the provisions of this chapter

99 Susan J. Stabile, "Protecting Retiree Medical Benefits: The Scope of Section 1114 of the Bankruptcy Code" (1993) 14 *Cardozo L. Rev.* 1911.

100 *LTV Steel Corp., v United Mineworkers of America* (*In re Chateaugay*, 922 F.2d 86, 88 (2nd Cir. 1990).

101 See, '66,000 LTV Retirees' Benefits Revived by Bankruptcy Judge', *New York. Times* (1 August 1986) at < www.nytimes.com/1986/08/01/us/66000-ltv-retirees-benefits-revived-by-bankruptcy-judge.html> (accessed 12 May 2019).

102 Retiree Benefits Bankruptcy Protection Act 1988 (Pub. L. No. 100 – 334, 102 Stat. 610), An Act passed by the US Congress to halt the suspension of retiree medical, life and disability benefits in pending bankruptcy cases that later became codified as s.1114 of the US Bankruptcy Code.

103 11 U.S.C. s.1114 (2017).

104 11 U.S.C. s. 1114 (a).

105 11 U.S.C. s. 1114 (e).

(hereinafter in this section "trustee" shall include a debtor in possession), shall timely pay and shall not modify any retiree benefits, except that –

A the court, on motion of the trustee or authorized representative, and after notice and a hearing, may order modification of such payments, pursuant to the provisions of subsections (g) and (h) of this section, or
B the trustee and the authorized representative of the recipients of those benefits may agree to modification of such payments, after which such benefits as modified shall continue to be paid by the trustee'.[106]

From this provision, it may be submitted that s.1114 sets out to protect retirees from having their benefits modified upon their former employer filing for bankruptcy. Retirees are a particularly vulnerable class of creditors during Chapter 11 bankruptcy because a debtor may decide to modify or terminate retiree benefits based on economic pressures present in the bankruptcy context, yet retirees may lack a voice to protect their benefits.[107] Retirees may rely on such benefits as a source of livelihood upon retirement and where such benefits are easily targeted by debtors to achieve their reorganisation plans, retirees' livelihoods may be heavily impacted.[108]

Retiree benefits are not guaranteed protection under s.1114 during bankruptcy reorganisations. Retiree benefits may be either modified or rejected by a debtor upon fulfilling the procedural and substantive requirements under s.1114 (f).[109] Under s.1114(e)(1)(A) and (B), a debtor may modify retiree benefits upon filing a request to the court and following hearing processes, a court may permit modification provided the debtor and retiree representatives agree to the proposed modifications.[110] However, the procedural and substantive requirements for modification of retiree benefits have to be exhausted. The debtor must initiate negotiation proposals with the retiree representatives, detailing the desired modifications of the retiree benefits and the proposals must be necessary to permit the reorganisation of the debtor.[111]

In other words, the debtor must provide retiree representatives with sufficient information regarding the proposed modification of retiree benefits for the retiree representatives to make informed decisions.[112] Otherwise, the court may grant modifications of the retiree benefits where retiree representatives fail to agree to the proposed modifications without good cause. Moreover, the court may also grant permission to the debtor where the court is satisfied that modification of retiree benefits is essential to the successful reorganisation imperatives of the debtor.[113]

106 11. U.S.C. s.1114.
107 Ashleigh K. Reibach, "Amplifying the Voice of Retirees: The Third Circuit's Broad Interpretation of Bankruptcy Code Section 1114 in re Visiteon Corp" (2014) 58 (6) *Vill. L. Rev.* 120.
108 Daniel Keating, "Good Intentions, Bad Economics: Retiree Insurance Benefits in Bankruptcy" (1990) 43 *Vand. L. Rev.* 161, 174.
109 11 U.S.C. s. 1114 (f) (1).
110 11 U.S.C s. 1114 (e) (1) (A) and (B).
111 11 U.S.C. s. 1114 (f) (1) (A) – (B).
112 Ibid.
113 11 U.S.C. s. 1114 (g) (1) – (3).

Therefore, it is contention that although the US Congress sought to afford retirees a chance to have their benefits protected from strategic modification by their former employers upon filing for bankruptcy, this protection may not be fully utilised by retirees as it would require time and money to challenge former employers where retiree benefits subject to modification.

Moreover, the judicial approach to s.1114 is still a point of concern in relation to jurisdictional imperatives. While some courts have accepted that s.1114 applies to all debtors in Chapter 11 bankruptcy proceedings,[114] a majority of courts are of the view that s.1114 does not apply to retiree benefits that can be terminated or modified unilaterally outside bankruptcy.[115] In this perspective, it may be submitted that the protection to retiree benefits under s.1114 that the US Congress sought to achieve is yet to be fully realised.

Worker adjustment and retraining notification (WARN) Act 1988 protection

The Worker Adjustment and Retraining Notification Act 1988 (WARN Act)[116] offers some additional protection to employees in the US where their employer is contemplating a sale of the business or part of it, or a business unit or plant closure that would lead to mass loss of employment during any 30-day period.

The WARN Act was enacted by the US Congress on 4 August 1988 and took effect on 4 February 1989. The WARN Act requires employers who employ over 100 employees or more including wage and salaried workers, hourly paid workers, managers and supervisors, to give a 60-day notice to employees to be affected by job losses.[117] Employees' representatives or labour unions (where employees are covered by a CBA),[118] state or chief elected official of the local government at locations where the layoffs are expected also have to be notified.[119] However, employees with less than six months' employment in the last 12 months are not covered by this requirement on the employer.

The requirement on employers to offer the 60 days' notice to affected employees is a form of a process to give affected employees a transition period within

114 *In re Farmland Industries, Inc.*, 294 B.R. 903, 914, 919 (W.D. Mo. 2003) (where it was held that debtors are obligated to follow procedure set forth in Section 1114 despite fact that benefits may be unilaterally modified or terminated outside bankruptcy).

115 *See In re Delphi Corp.*, No. 05-44481 WL 637315 (Bankr. S.D.N.Y. Mar. 10, 2009) where it was held that debtors have a right to modify retiree benefits if benefits can be unilaterally modified outside bankruptcy); *In re Visteon Corp.*, 612 F.3d 210, 218 (3rd Cir. 2010) (where it was held that Section 1114 applies to retiree benefits that can be unilaterally modified outside bankruptcy).

116 29 U.S.C. s.2101 – 2109 Pub. L. 100 -379, 101 Stat. 890 (Hereafter WARN Act).

117 29 U.S.C. s.2101 (a) (2). A plant closure under the WARN Act is defined as a shutdown of a single site of employment or one or more facilities or operating units within a single site of employment.

118 29 U.S.C. s.2102 (1).

119 29 U.S.C. s. 2102 (2).

which they may prepare and plan ahead of potential layoffs or transfers. The notice would include a description of the planned actions, a statement on whether the planned actions are short term or permanent, dates and duration of the process and contact details of the officials undertaking the planned actions. Affected employees may use this period to seek alternative employment or seek retraining to acquire skills that would enable them to compete in the job market.[120]

However, these notification and information requirements on employers are not applicable to employees who are actively engaged in a labour dispute or lockout with their employer or taking part in a strike action at the time when the employer is contemplating a business sale or plant closures.[121] In addition, workers employed on a temporary basis, business partners, consultants and regular federal, state and local government employees are exempted from the notification from the employer as long as they are aware that their employment was limited in duration.[122]

In addition to the above exceptions, the employer may be exempted from fulfilling the 60 days' notification and information requirements with employees where the reasons for the contemplated business sale, transfer or plant closures are caused by unforeseeable business circumstance such as a deep economic recession or loss of key contract of the business that were beyond the employer's control.[123] Capital liquidity issues, such as a drive to raise capital or investment for the faltering business may also be a justifiable reason for an employer not fulfil the 60 days' notice and information requirement.[124]

The employer may be convinced in good faith that there is a potential of raising key investment or capital to sustain the faltering business and invoking the notification requirement may jeopardise that prospect. Natural disasters such as flooding, hurricanes or earthquakes are other causes that may render an employer exempted from fulfilling the 60 days' notification requirements.[125]

Notwithstanding the above exceptions, the WARN Act affords individual or collective actions for employees or their representative labour unions or local government units power to initiate civil actions against an employer who has not fulfilled the notification requirement in federal district courts with a view of obtaining monetary compensation. The employees may be awarded back dated pay and benefits for each working day the notice was not provided to a maximum of 60 days.[126]

Moreover, the sale of the business or part of it in itself does not constitute a job loss but may lead to a job transfer from the seller to the buyer. Therefore, the 60 days' notification and information requirement on the employer may enable

120 Christopher P. Yost, "The Worker Adjustment and Retraining Notification Act of 1988: Advance Notice Required?" (1989) 38(3) *Cath. U. L. Rev. 675*.

121 29 U.S.C. s.2103 (1) + (2).

122 29 U.S.C. s.2103 (1).

123 29 U.S.C. s.2102 (b) (2) (a).

124 29 U.S.C. s.2102 (b) (1).

125 29 U.S.C. s.2102 (b).

126 29 U.S.C. s.2104 (1) (a).

the employee subject to the transfer to make an informed decision about new job arrangements, including (where applicable), the new place and location of the business or plant.[127] In addition, where a business sale has led to an automatic transfer, WARN Act still places a duty on the buyer to comply with the 60 days' notification requirement which is a form protection to employees.[128]

Post-petition employee claims

The treatment of post-petition employee claims is however different from the treatment of pre-petition claims during bankruptcy reorganisations under Chapter 11. Employee post-petition claims for wages and salaries are afforded priority status in payment, as they are deemed administrative expenses of the bankruptcy estate.[129] This is a direct form of protection to employee claims in that employees are assured that they will be paid wages and salaries for services rendered during the reorganisation process.

The DIP is permitted to enter into contracts and transactions, such as for wages and salary payments, without notice or hearings during the ordinary course of business.[130] Other post-petition employee claims, such as for severance in lieu of notice or termination of employment by the debtor employer are afforded administrative expense status and therefore, endorsed by bankruptcy courts.[131] However, although employees' wages and salaries may be guaranteed post-petition, employees' participation in their debtor employer's reorganisation proceedings is not guaranteed, nor contemplated. Formal participation in post-petition bankruptcy proceedings is mainly controlled by the DIP and post-petition secured creditors to a certain extent.

General employees have no participation in the business affairs of their employer yet they have interests and benefits that may be affected by their employer's decisions.[132] Therefore, apart from having claims for wages and salaries assured and afforded priority in payment, employee participation in the affairs of their debtor employer's reorganisation process post-petition is substantially low, if non-existent. Moreover, after filing for bankruptcy, employees' hopes of participation are further curtailed as by the time a petition for bankruptcy is filed, decisions on the next course of their employer's business are often already taken. This, arguably, leaves the employees' hopes of participation in the hands of the creditors' committee as established by the Bankruptcy Code.[133]

127 Yost, (n 20) 123.
128 29 U.S.C. s.2101 (b) (1).
129 11 U.S.C. s.503 (b) (1) (A).
130 11 U.S.C. s.363(c) (1).
131 See cases such as *In re Mammoth Mart Inc.*, 536 F. 2d 955, (1st Cir. 1976); *In re W.T Grant Co.*, 620 F. 2d 319,321 (2nd Cir. 1980).
132 L. Ponoroff, "Enlarging the Bargaining Table: Some Implications of the Corporate Stakeholder Model for Federal Bankruptcy Proceedings" (1994) 23 *Capital U. L. Rev.* 441; Janis Sarra "Widening the Insolvency Lens: The Treatment of Employee Claims" in Paul J. Omar (ed.) *International Insolvency Law: Themes and Perspectives* (Hampshire, Ashgate Publishing, 2008).
133 11 U.S.C. s.1102 (b) (1).

In contrast, creditors' committees have a great deal of influence over the debtor's business affairs during reorganisation proceedings. These include investigating the financial conditions of the debtor[134] and access to information regarding the reorganisation proceedings. However, this does not mean that employees will be given a real voice and protection. This is because the established creditors' committee represent creditors' interests as a group and different creditors may have different interests. This comes with a risk that employee interests may be overridden or overshadowed by the divergent group interests. Although on occasion a court may appoint a special creditors' committee where it has discovered that a certain group of creditors is not adequately represented by the existing creditors' committee,[135] this has been rarely the case as judges have often not supported it whenever the need for it arose.[136]

Conclusion

As highlighted in this chapter, the lack of uniform protection to all employees in the US private sector workforce is still a major concern to employment protection and the move towards balancing employment protection objectives with business reorganisation during bankruptcy proceedings in the US. The federal laws that govern the treatment of stakeholder interests during bankruptcy reorganisations in the US, such as Title 11 of the US Bankruptcy Code and The National Labour Relations Act (1935) give primacy of protection to employees who are members of labour unions and CBAs. The employment at will practice is another area that is need of addressing at federal level.

In light of these concerns, there is a need to harmonise the level of protection to all employees in the US labour industry as a measure of uniform protection. However, to achieve this, the US Congress would need to enact legislation at federal level that is less dependent or preferably, non-dependent on trade unionism and collective bargaining philosophical underpinnings[137] that is applicable and protective of all employees.

In the US, employee claims in bankruptcy are usually in respect of wages, salaries and other benefits attached to their employment relationships with their employers, which are usually of small amounts compared to interests of other big and secured creditors. In view of this limitation, doubt has been cast as to whether employees' involvement in the bankruptcy process would be of any significance in terms of advantages to employees.[138] However, the counter argument to this assertion is that participation rights of affected stakeholders in

134 11 U.S.C. s.1103(c).

135 11 U.S.C. s.1102 (a)(b).

136 See cases such *as In re Salant Corp.*, 53 B.R158, 161. (Bankr. S.D.N.Y. 1985); *In re Mansfield Ferrous Castings Inc.*, 96 B.R 779,781. (Bankr. N.D. Ohio).

137 Daniel Keating, "The Fruits of Labour: Workers Priorities in Bankruptcy" (1993) 35 *Ariz. L. Rev.* 905, 907.

138 See, for example, comment by David. A. Skeel Jr, "What is So Bad about Delaware?" (2001) 54 *Vand. L. Rev.* 310.

bankruptcy, irrespective of the size or value of their claims ought to be based on the principles of fairness, equality and justice. This is because employee claims would have greater significance, if we look at creditors by headcount, rather than by value.

The economic rationale for this argument is implicit in the contention that at the beginning of their employment, employees are usually paid low wages but as they continue with the employment relationship, their skills and dependency on their employer grows, together with mutual expectations, such as continuity of employment in the form of job security. As a result of continued longer service and better skills, employee salaries tend to increase towards the end of their careers.[139] However, during bankruptcy reorganisations or business transfers, these accrued benefits are less protected and employees stand to lose out the most, as the skills developed over the years may be firm-specific skills, which may not readily add weight to their search for alternative employment. Moreover, the minimal protection that is afforded employees is further limited by institutional challenges precipitated by the diffusion of power between federal and state law jurisdictional challenges as discussed in the next chapter.

Bibliography

Books

Warde, Bryan, *Inequality in U.S Social Policy – An Historical Analysis* (New York, Routledge 2016).

Book chapters

Sarra, J, "Widening the Insolvency Lens: The Treatment of Employee Claims" in Paul J. Omar (ed.) *International Insolvency Law: Themes and Perspectives* (Hampshire, Ashgate Publishing, 2008).

Cases

United Kingdom

Home Office v Evans [2007] EWCA Civ. 1089 (CA).
Horst v High Tables Ltd [1997] EWCA Civ. 2000.

United States

Fall River Dyeing & Fishing Corp. v NLRB, 482 U.S. 27 (1987).
Hutton v Watters, 132 Tenn.527, 179 S.W 134 (1915).
In re Chateaugay Corp., 64 B.R 990 (Bankr. S.D.N.Y. 1986).
In re Chateagay Corp., 80 B.R 279, 286–87 (Bankr. S.D.N.Y. 1987).

139 See, Marleen A. O'Connor, "Restructuring the Corporation's Nexus of Contracts: Recognizing a Fiduciary Duty to Protect Displaced Workers" (1991) 69 *N.C. L. Rev.* 1189, 1197.

In re Continental Airlines, 64 B.R. 858 (Bankr. S.D Texas 1984).
In re Del Grosso, 115 B.R 136, 138 (Bankr. N.D 111 1990).
In re Delphi Corp., No. 05-44481 WL 637315 (Bankr. S.D.N.Y. Mar. 10, 2009).
In re Farmland Industries, Inc., 294 B.R. 903, 914, 919 (W.D. Mo. 2003).
In re FCX Inc., 60 B.R 405, 411–12 (Bankr. E.D.N.C. 1986).
In re Gulf Air Inc., 112 B.R 152, 154 (Bankr. W.D. La 1989).
In re Mammoth Mart Inc., 536 F. 2d 955, (1st Cir. 1976)
In re Mansfield Ferrous Castings Inc., 96 B.R 779,781. (Bankr. N.D. Ohio).
In re Salant Corp., 53 B.R158, 161. (Bankr. S.D.N.Y. 1985).
In re Structurlite Plastics Corp., 86 B.R 922, 932. (Bankr. S.D. Ohio 1988).
In re Tres – Ark Inc., 09-12589 (Bankr. W.D Texas 2012).
In re Visteon Corp., 612 F.3d 210, 218 (3rd Cir. 2010).
In re W.T Grant Co., 620 F. 2d 319,321 (2nd Cir. 1980).
In re Wilson Foods Corp., 31 B.R. 269 (Bankr. Okl. 1983).
In re WorldCom Inc., 346 F. 2d 628 (Bankr. S.D.N.Y 2004).
John Wiley & Sons, Inc. v Livingston 376, U.S. 543 (1963).
NLRB v Burns Int'l Sec. Serv., 406 U.S. 272 (1972).
NLRB v Bildisco & Bildisco, 465 U.S. 523 (1984).
Northern Pipeline Construction Co. v Marathon Pipe Line Co. 458 U.S. 50 (1982).
Payne v Western & A.R.R. 81 Tenn. 507, 519 – 20 (1884).

Journal articles

Befort, F Stephen, "Labor Law and the Double-Breasted Employer: A Critique of the Single Employer and Alter Ego Doctrines and a Proposed Reformulation" (1987) Wis. L. Rev. 67, 101.

Befort, F Stephen, "Labor and Employment Law at the Millennium: A Historical Review and Critical Assessment" (2001) 43 B. C. L. Rev. 351, 460.

Bordewieck, D, and Countryman, V, "The Rejection of Collective Bargaining Agreements by Chapter 11 Debtors" (1983) 57 Am. Bankr. L. J. 293, 294.

Cameron, D Christopher, "How 'Necessary' Became the Mother of Rejection: An Empirical Look at the Fate of Collective Bargaining Agreements on the Tenth Anniversary of Bankruptcy Code Section 1113" (1994) 34 Santa Clara L. Rev. 841, 869.

Ceccotti, BA, "Lost in Transformation: The Disappearance of Labor Policies in Applying Section 1113 of the Bankruptcy Code" (2007) 15 Am. Bankr. Inst. L. Rev. 415, 431.

Coordes, NLaura, "The Geography of Bankruptcy" (2015) 68 Vand. L. Rev. 381–439.

Cox, A, "The Duty to Bargain in Good Faith" (1958) 71 Harv. L. Rev. 1407.

Efthimiou, M, "State Legislative Attempts to Mandate Continuation of Collective Bargaining Agreements during Business Change: The Unfulfilled Expectations and the Pre-empted Results" (1992) 77 Cornell L. Rev. 47, 51.

Ehrenberg, D, "Collective Bargaining Agreements under Section 1113 of Chapter 11 of the 1984 Bankruptcy Code: Resolving the Tension Between Labor Law and Bankruptcy Law" (1994) 2 J. L. & Policy 55, 68.

Finkin, M, "Directions in Labor Law – Concerns for the Dignity of the Worker: Revisionism in Labor Law" (1984) 43 Md. L. Rev. 23.

Gant, JLL, "Studies in Convergence? Post-Crisis Effects on Corporate Rescue and the Influence of Social Policy: The EU and the US" (2006) 25 Int. I. Rev. 72–96.

Keating, D, "Good Intentions, Bad Economics: Retiree Insurance Benefits in Bankruptcy" (1990) 43 Vand. L. Rev. 161, 174.

Keating, D, "The Continuing Puzzle of Collective Bargaining Agreements in Bankruptcy" (1994) 35 Wm. & Mary L. Rev. 503, 526.

Keating, D, "Transforming a Non-Claim into a Claim: s. 1114 and the Curious Case of *In re Visteon*" (2011) 85 Am. Bankr. L.J. 1.

McClain, JA, "Bankruptcy Code Section 1113 and the Simple Rejection of Collective Bargaining Agreements: Labor Loses Again" (1991) 80 Geo. L. J. 191, 206.

Melone, J, "Union Blues: Why Collective Bargaining Agreements that are Neither Rejected nor Modified Pursuant to 11 U.S.C. 1113 are Not Granted Administrative Expense Priority in a Chapter 11 Bankruptcy Reorganization by S. 1113 of the Bankruptcy Code" (2006) 32 Ohio N.U. L. Rev. 429, 442.

O'Connor, M, "Restructuring the Corporation's Nexus of Contracts: Recognizing a Fiduciary Duty to Protect Displaced Workers" (1991) 69 N.C. L. Rev. 1189, 1197.

Ponoroff, L, "Enlarging the Bargaining Table: Some Implications of the Corporate Stakeholder Model for Federal Bankruptcy Proceedings" (1994) 23 Capital U. L. Rev. 441.

Reibach, KA, "Amplifying the Voice of Retirees: The Third Circuit's Broad Interpretation of Bankruptcy Code Section 1114 in re Visiteon Corp" (2014) 58(6) Vill. L. Rev. 120.

Roberts, GM, "Bankruptcy and the Union's Bargain: Equitable Treatment of Collective Bargaining Agreements" (1987) 39 Stan. L. Rev. 1015, 1047.

Rosenberg, R, "Bankruptcy and the Collective Bargaining Agreement – A Brief Lesson in the Use of the Constitutional System of Checks and Balances" (1984) 58 Am. Bankr. L. J. 293, 312 – 321.

Skeel, DA. Jr, "What is So Bad About Delaware?" (2001) 54 Vand. L. Rev. 310.

Stabile, SJ, "Protecting Retiree Medical Benefits: The Scope of Section 1114 of the Bankruptcy Code" (1993) 14 Cardozo L. Rev. 1911.

Summers, W Clyde, "The Contract of Employment and the Rights of Individual Employees: Fair Representation and Employment at Will" (1984) 52 Fordham L. Rev. 1082, 1085.

Warren, E, and Westbrook, JL, "The Success of Chapter 11: A Challenge to the Critics" (2009) 107 Mich. L. Rev. 603, 609.

West, M, "Life After Bildisco: Section 1113 and the Duty to Bargain in Good Faith" (1986) 47 Ohio St. L. J. 65, 103.

Yost, P. C, "The Worker Adjustment and Retraining Notification Act of 1988: Advance Notice Required?" (1989) 38(3) Cath. U. L. Rev. 675.

Legislation

Bankruptcy Amendments and Federal Judgeship Act (1984) (Pub. L. No. 98-353, 98 Stat. 333, 392 (1984).

Bankruptcy Reform Act 1978 (Pub. L. No.95–598, 92 Stat. 2549).

National Labour Relations Act 1935 (29 U.S.C ss. 151–169).(Pub. L. 74–198, 49 Stat. 449).

Retiree Benefits Bankruptcy Protection Act 1988 (Pub. L. No. 100–334, 102 Stat. 610).

The Genetic Information and Non-Discrimination Act 2008. U.S.C. ss.110–233, (Pub. L. 110–233, 122 Stat. 881).

4 Institutional challenges – the federal vs state law conundrum

Introduction

The US has a federal system of government.[1] The US constitution has seven original articles and twenty-seven amendments that govern the political, social and economic structures, such as bankruptcy and other institutions. Bankruptcy law is under the control of the federal government.[2] However, while bankruptcy law and its structures are a matter of federal concern, and therefore guided by federal law, other areas of law, such as labour law and contract law that establish certain employment rights and protections, such as a right to a minimum wage, right to equal pay, et cetera, are state law and are covered by the Commerce Clause,[3] not the bankruptcy law.

The Commerce Clause affords the federal government duty to regulate business activities conducted at state level across the US. Although the diffusion of power between federal and state jurisdictions has had the effect that some labour law statutes, such as the National Labour Relations Act (NLRA) 1935[4] are federal laws, labour law in the US is not the subject of federal jurisdiction. It is the subject of state jurisdiction.

The Bankruptcy Code was enacted by the US Congress on a federal level to regulate the debtor-creditor relationships during bankruptcy reorganisation proceedings. However, although the Bankruptcy Code seeks to regulate these relationships, it does not create these relationships. It is the non-bankruptcy laws, at state level, such as contract law and labour law that create these relationships.[5]

1 M. H. Redish, "Doing it with Mirrors: *New York v. US* and Constitutional Limitations on Federal Power to Require State Law Legislation" (1993) 21 *Hastings Const. L. Q.* 593, 604.
2 Article 1, Section 8, Clause 4 of the US Constitution affords the US Congress power to establish a uniform rule on naturalisation and uniform laws on the subject of bankruptcies throughout the US.
3 Article 1, Section 8 of the Preamble to the US Constitution.
4 29 U.S.C. ss.151 – 169 (2017) (Hereafter NLRA). Enacted by the 74th United States Congress on 6 July 1935, Pub. L. 74–198, 49 Stat. 449 to create a National Labor Relations Board and to regulate labour disputes between employers and employees that may burden or obstruct interstate and foreign commerce. This statute is also known as the Wagner Act.
5 Daniel A. Austin, "Bankruptcy and the Myth of 'Uniform Law'" (2012) 42 *Seton Hall L. Rev.* 1081, 1168.

Consequently, bankruptcy creates tensions between state law and federal law provisions on employee protection and bankruptcy reorganisations. This tension is reflected in the level of protection that both federal law and state law afford employees during bankruptcy reorganisations.[6] For instance, employment protection concerns that arise out of bankruptcy but are beyond the scope of the Bankruptcy Code may create tensions between state law provisions and federal law provisions mandating employment protection during bankruptcy reorganisations.

Substantive provision in state labour laws, such as provisions defining what constitutes a right, an interest, or benefit to an employee that are not specifically defined or established by the Bankruptcy Code but covered and well controlled by state laws and state courts may be affected by federal bankruptcy laws, such as the Bankruptcy Code.[7] This is because in certain instances, provisions of the Bankruptcy Code make references that invoke state laws to determine whether certain debtor-creditor arrangements were breached pre-bankruptcy.[8] However, a majority of the provisions in the Bankruptcy Code override state law[9] under the jurisprudence of the Supremacy Clause in the US Constitution. The Supremacy Clause is enshrined in Article VI, Paragraph 2 of the US Constitution. This clause establishes federal law supremacy over state law. It provides that the federal constitution and federal laws of the US take precedence over state constitutions and state laws.

The federal -v- state division: the US State of Delaware

Different states may interpret the provisions of the Bankruptcy Code differently. This may be influenced by the provisions of their non-bankruptcy State laws, such as contract law, property law and labour law during bankruptcy reorganisations. This is in addition to different judicial attitudes.[10] Where this is the case, it creates a certain degree of deviation from the intended uniform application of the federal Bankruptcy Code. A deviation from a uniform application of the Bankruptcy Code in various US states creates an inconsistency born out of inter alia, the interaction between bankruptcy laws and state non-bankruptcy laws which may be detrimental to employee protection during bankruptcy reorganisations.

In a bid to bring greater consistency to the protection to employees in the Bankruptcy Code, some US states have enacted legislation to regulate the

6 Thomas E. Plank, "Bankruptcy and Federalism" (2002) 71 *Fordham L. Rev.* 1063.

7 Ralph Brubacker, "The Erie Doctrine, Code Common Law, and Choice-of-Law Rules in Bankruptcy (Part 1)". 32 *Bankr. L. Letter Online* (Thompson Reuters) 4.

8 For example, 11 U.S.C. s.365(C).

9 See, for example, Bankruptcy Code provisions such as; 11 U.S.C. s. 362 – mandating moratoria on creditor actions against the debtor, after filing for bankruptcy, 11 U.S.C s.365 – allowing a debtor to assume or reject executory contracts upon bankruptcy filing, 11 U.S.C. s.1113 – allowing a debtor to assume or reject collectively bargained agreements, et cetera. The provision if invoked, would override any state law provisions that arise out of contract law and labour law bestowed upon stakeholders by state law.

10 Lynn M. LoPucki, *Courting Failure: How Competition for Big Cases is Corrupting the Bankruptcy Courts* (Michigan, University of Michigan Press, 2006).

employer-employee relationships during bankruptcy reorganisation. Among these states is the state of Delaware. Delaware is my choice of a state case study in this book because its state labour laws are comparatively friendly to employees' protection among other US states.

Delaware's state labour laws have provisions that provide for employee protection on issues such as collective bargaining, continuity of the employment relationship through the successorship doctrine and protection from termination or impairment of a labour contract because of a business sale, transfer or merger. These provisions are discussed in the paragraphs below. The interplay between Delaware's non-bankruptcy state laws and the provisions for dealing with employee claims during bankruptcy reorganisations in Chapter 11 of the Bankruptcy Code would provide a good platform for analysing the treatment of employee interests and benefits during bankruptcy reorganisations in a form of a federal-state comparison.

Delaware is one of the smallest states in the US[11] but it is well known for its business-friendly incorporation laws for businesses all over the US and the world at large. Delaware has in fact been crowned a haven for its handling of corporate businesses, establishing a market like the sort handled in other known havens, such as Bermuda, the Cayman Islands and Mauritius.[12]

Due to its friendly incorporation laws, a majority of large publicly traded corporations in the US have been incorporated in Delaware, with the inherent advantages of this being partly, due to the 'internal affairs' doctrine. The 'internal affairs doctrine' is a choice of law term in the Law of Corporations which provides that the law of a corporation's state of incorporation governs that corporation's issues, such as shareholders' voting rights, distribution of dividends, tax issues, et cetera.

The overall effect of the internal affairs doctrine is that the internal affairs of a corporation are governed by the laws of the state or country of incorporation. Therefore, companies incorporated in Delaware are protected from restrictions from other US states or countries on issues like taxes, and other corporate disclosure requirements. Delaware's record of being one of the most used US states for business incorporations is further supplemented by its record as one of the most used states for filing for bankruptcy in the US in recent years.[13]

Employment protection provisions under Delaware state law: The Delaware Code

The state of Delaware has legislation that places a mandatory obligation on a debtor employer and a prospective successor employer to protect employee interests and benefits attached to an employment contract during a business sale, merger or changes in the identity of the employer. This is a form of ensuring employment protection and continuity.

11 Ibid., 52.
12 Ibid., 53.
13 Ibid., 49, 54.

As a measure of employee protection, it is mandated in the Delaware Code that:

> [n]o merger, consolidation or sale of assets shall result in the termination or impairment of the provisions of any labour contract covering persons engaged in employment in this state and negotiated by a labour organisation or by a collective bargaining agent or other representative.[14]

The Delaware Code also provides employees with remedies, such as a right to initiate a civil action against the employer or a successor in interest, where employee claims such as for wages or salaries, remain unpaid following restructuring, business sales or transfers.[15] The Delaware Code further imposes notification, posting and records obligations on employers to ensure that an employer, who employs more than three employees, notifies each employee, at the time of hiring, the hourly or daily rate of pay and place of payment in writing, or through a posted notice, maintained and accessible to all employees.[16] Although this protection is outside bankruptcy, it highlights how Delaware as a state protects employees at state level.

The Delaware Code recognises and emphasises the need for employees to bargain collectively with their employers as a measure of participation and inclusion in regulating and moderating the employer-employee relationship.[17] It is the notion that through collective bargaining, issues such as successorship obligations on the new owner of the debtor's business (in case of a business sale or transfer) may be imposed on the employer.

The successorship doctrine, although not specifically prescribed by the Bankruptcy Code, has been developed by federal bankruptcy courts, on a case by case basis, where provisions for such obligations have been incorporated into a CBA and are therefore binding on the new owner.[18] Where successorship obligations are imposed on the buyer / new owner of the business, it leads to automatic continuity of the rights and obligations attached to the employment relationship between the employer and the employees.

State laws are enacted by state legislators who are locally situated and well acquainted with local state issues affecting both business owners and employees. State legislators know what the state needs. Very often, these state legislators would have witnessed the effects that corporate reorganisations may have on employees and other stakeholders, such as local state revenue and community development.

The inherent advantage of state laws regulating the employer-employee relationship is that state law is usually broader than federal law in scope of

14 DEL. CODE ANN. tit. 19, s.706 (a).
15 DEL. CODE ANN. tit. 19, s.911.
16 DEL. CODE ANN. tit. 19, s.1108.
17 DEL. CODE ANN. tit. 19, s.913.
18 See cases such as *John Wiley & Sons, Inc. v Livingston* 376, U.S. 543 (1963); *NLRB v Burns Int'l Sec. Serv.*, 406 U.S. 272 (1972); *Fall River Dyeing & Fishing Corp. v NLRB*, 482 U.S. 27 (1987).

application and protection to stakeholders, such as employees.[19] For instance, The Delaware Code extends collective bargaining and successorship obligations to employers in all aspects that affect employee interests and benefits, such as on business sales, business transfers, mergers, or changes in the identity of the employer. This is in contrast to federal laws, such as the Bankruptcy Code or, the NLRA that are invoked during bankruptcy proceedings.[20]

For instance, under the federal Bankruptcy Code, for employees to enjoy the benefits of successorship obligations discussed above, a CBA that mandates its existence and effectiveness, is dependent on whether, it is adopted, amended or rejected during reorganisation proceedings or business sales by the debtor employer, subject to exceptions.[21]

The Supreme Court in *John Wiley & Sons, Inc. v Livingston*[22] recommended that:

> ...[t]he objectives of national labor policy, reflected in established principles of federal law require that the rightful prerogatives of owners independently to rearrange their businesses and even eliminate themselves as employers be balanced by some protection to employees from a sudden change in the employment relationship.[23]

This was following a merger of a small publishing company (with 40 employees) with John Wiley & Sons Inc., (John Wiley & Sons) represented by District 65 of the Retail, Wholesale and Department Store Union (District 65). Following the merger, District 65 intended to continue to represent the merged employees, requesting that all seniority rights, vacation pay, severance pay and union pension fund contributions be recognised and continued by John Wiley & Sons. However, John Wiley & Sons declined to recognise these rights, asserting that, the merger terminated the CBA and any form of employee rights and benefits pertinent to it.[24]

Following its deliberation, the Supreme Court held that:

> ...[T]he disappearance by merger of a corporate employer which has entered into a collective bargaining agreement with the union does not automatically terminate all rights of employees covered by the agreement...... the successor employer may be required to arbitrate with union under the agreement.[25]

19 Austin, (n 5) 1088.
20 DEL. CODE ANN. tit. 19, s.706(a).
21 See provisions such as; 11 U.S.C. s.365 and 11 U.S.C. s.1113 respectively.
22 *John Wiley & Sons, Inc. v Livingston*, 376 U.S. 543 (1964).
23 Ibid., 549.
24 Ibid., paras. 544–545.
25 Ibid., para. 548.

However, in *Howard Johnson Co. v Detroit Local Joint Executive Board*,[26] the Supreme Court stated that:

> ...[T]he real question in each of these 'successorship' cases is, on the particular facts, what are the legal obligations of the new employer to the employees of the former owner or their representative? The answer to this inquiry requires analysis of the interests of the new employer and employees and of the policies of the labor laws in light of the facts of each case and the particular legal obligation that is at issue, whether it be the duty to recognize and bargain with the union, the duty to remedy unfair labor practices, the duty to arbitrate, etc.[27]

Therefore, from the observations above, it may be submitted that establishing whether a collective agreement survives the restructuring process and it is therefore, adopted by the new employer is determined on a case by case basis, but not guaranteed. It is dependent on the nature of the obligations the new employer is assuming and the interplay between labour law policies on the continuity of the employment relationships and federal bankruptcy law's policy for the continuity and survival of the financially struggling business undergoing bankruptcy reorganisations.[28] Where state labour law objectives conflict with those of federal bankruptcy law, the courts have often tipped the balance towards the survival of the company undergoing reorganisation rather than the continuity of inherited obligations arising out of collectively bargained agreements.[29]

Moreover, under the successorship doctrine, the successor employer's main responsibility to the predecessor's union and collectively bargained agreements is maintaining the duty to bargain but not a mandatory adoption of the agreements entered into by the predecessor. Where the successor employer adopts the predecessor's collectively bargained agreements, the successor employer does so voluntarily.

Therefore, as a result of the Supremacy Clause,[30] it would not only be difficult for a state court in Delaware to mandate for the continuity of collective bargaining following a business sale or transfer, but would be deemed unconstitutional, as such a mandate would be contrary to the policies and objectives inherent in the US Congress' enactment of the NLRA.

The US Congress' enactment of the NLRA in 1935 was to mainly implement a form of industrial democracy between employer companies and employees through collective bargaining at federal level. It would imply that although state

26 *Howard Johnson v Detroit Local Joint Exec. Bd.*, 417 U.S. 249, 264 (1974).

27 Ibid., para.9.

28 Marcus Efthimiou, "State Legislative Attempts to Mandate Continuation of Collective Bargaining Agreements during Business Change: The Unfulfilled Expectations and the Pre-empted Results" (1992) 77 *Cornell L. Rev.* 47, 51.

29 *Howard Johnson v Detroit Local Joint Exec. Bd.*, 417 U.S. 249, 264 (1974) and *John Wiley & Sons, Inc. v Livingston 376*, U.S. 543 (1963). See further, *NLRB v Burns Int'l Sec. Serv.*, 406 U.S. 272 (1972); *Fall River Dyeing & Fishing Corp. v NLRB*, 482 U.S. 27 (1987).

30 See, Article VI, Paragraph 2 of the US Constitution.

laws may have provisions mandating collective bargaining between employer companies and employees at state level, provisions on collective bargaining under NLRA (1935) if invoked, would take precedence as the NLRA is a federal legislation. Therefore, provisions under the NLRA would be at federal (national level) not state level.[31]

A bankruptcy filing, however small, presents its own problems which may not only affect immediately attached stakeholders like employees, but may also cause significant local disruptions, especially to a particularly small community in a state, such as Delaware. It is however notable that not all Delaware incorporated companies are active in Delaware, as such a state might have provided some incentives for companies to be incorporated in anticipation of benefits such as job creation and generation of local revenue.[32] However, the state may not enjoy such benefits because while the company is incorporated in Delaware, it operates elsewhere, maintaining only some kind of administrative office in the state. Therefore, the impact of failures of companies registered in a state may not be great in many cases and it may be that greater impacts are on communities in states other than the state of incorporation.

Bankruptcy venue forum shopping – an impediment to employee participation

The Bankruptcy Venue Statute[33] and the Bankruptcy Code[34] afford a large debtor[35] with almost unlimited choice as to where to file a petition for bankruptcy. Under the Bankruptcy Venue Statute, a debtor may file for bankruptcy where it is incorporated, where its principal place of business or assets is located, or, in a state where there is a pending case against its affiliate, general partner or partnership. This virtually unlimited choice may be viewed as an encouragement to debtor companies to choose a bankruptcy court or state where they would project a better outcome than in other states which may be termed as bankruptcy venue forum shopping.[36]

Bankruptcy venue forum shopping may sometimes, be seen as an impediment to employees during bankruptcy reorganisation proceedings as it not only affects employee participation in the bankruptcy proceedings of their debtor employer,

31 Omari S. Simmons, "Delaware's Global Threat" (2015) 41 *J. Corp. L.* 217.

32 Austin, (n 5).

33 28 U.S.C. s.1408 (2016).

34 11. U.S.C. s.109 – defining who may be a debtor for purposes of bankruptcy.

35 According to the Bankruptcy Code, an entity that has an aggregate non-contingent liquidated, secured and unsecured debts, as of the date of filing for bankruptcy, in an amount not more than $2,490,225 is considered a small business debtor. A debtor with debts exceeding this amount, is considered a large debtor- (11 U.S.C. s.101 (51D) (A) (2012). Please note that this amount is subject to periodic adjustment by the Judicial Committee of the United States.

36 The term forum shopping is used here, to denote the fact that unless in an involuntary bankruptcy filing, the debtor company that chooses to file for bankruptcy has a choice as to venue and state of filing.

but also undermines employee protection. Bankruptcy forum shopping encourages cross-state filing which, if analysed, may benefit the filing debtor company more than other stakeholders such as employees. The effect of this cross-state filing is that, access to information regarding the debtor employer's case which would enable meaningful participation for employees, may be compromised.

Because of the cross-state filing, employees may not be able to gain first-hand information about the state and the court of filing by their debtor employer. It may also be the case that by the time affected employees track down the location of the state and court of filing, most decisions regarding the debtor company's debts and claims may have been taken.[37] This may leave employees in a compromised position compared to other stakeholders and key players in the bankruptcy process, such as the debtor company, its lawyers and post-petition secured lenders.

In addition, even where employees locate the state and court of filing, the distance from their state of domicile and the state of filing may hinder meaningful participation due to costs and time (duration) of the petition hearing. Some Chapter 11 bankruptcy petitions involve long and protracted negotiations which may turn out to be costly to an average employee to pursue compared to other stakeholders such as trade creditors with huge claims to pursue. This may turn out to be a form of employee shut out, which casts doubt as to whether cross state filing is contemplated by the debtor employer to escape the problems at home.

The almost unlimited choice of venue of filing by the debtor employer may be challenged under the principles of 'justice and convenience' of all stakeholders upon request by a stakeholder with an interest in the debtor company's bankruptcy case.[38] However, the stakeholder must prove to the bankruptcy court with evidence that a better venue which would serve the interests of all stakeholders is available, if the judge is to consider the request.[39] This is because venue choice discussions are not part of the bankruptcy hearing process. Provided the debtor company's choice of venue meets the threshold encapsulated in the Bankruptcy Venue Statute above, a presumption usually arises in favour of the debtor company's venue choice.[40] Moreover, research on this issue indicates that it is only in small bankruptcy cases[41] as opposed to big cases that venue choices have been changed by bankruptcy courts.[42]

37 Lynn. M. LoPucki and J. W. Doherty, "Delaware Bankruptcy: Failure in the Ascendancy" (2006) 73 *U. Chi. L. Rev.* 1387.

38 28 U.S.C. s.1412.

39 Thomas M. Horan and E. F. Johnson, "Basics of Bankruptcy Venue, Transfer of Cases" (2012) 30 (10) *Am. Bankr. Inst. J.* 40, 43. See also; *In re Patriot Coal Corp.*, 482 B.R 718, 739 (Bankr. S.D.N.Y 2012); *In re Caesers Entertainment Operating Company Inc.*, 134 S. Ct 1188, 1194 (Bankr. D. Delaware 2015).

40 Laura N. Coordes, "The Geography of Bankruptcy" (2015) 68 *Vand. L. Rev.* 381, 439.

41 A small bankruptcy case refers to an entity that has filed for bankruptcy where its aggregate non contingent liquidated, secured and unsecured debts, as of the date of filing for bankruptcy is not more than $2,490,225. A debtor with debts exceeding this amount, is considered a large debtor-(11 U.S.C. s.101 (51D) (A) (2012).

42 See, for example, a research study on this issue on Lynn LoPucki's Bankruptcy Research database at, <http://lopucki.law.ucla.edu/sample_download.htm> which indicates that only 26 big

Most largely traded corporations in the US that have filed for bankruptcy have indulged in some form of forum shopping practices, either as to venue or state of choice. For example, General Motors (GM)[43] that was incorporated in Delaware with headquarters in Detroit-Michigan filed for bankruptcy in New York. New York is a state that is about six hundred and fifty miles from Detroit, Michigan. Although GM's choice of filing for bankruptcy in New York might have been inspired by the Southern District of New York bankruptcy court's expertise in handling large bankruptcy cases,[44] GM had almost 200 branches all over the US with only one affiliate in New York. This was a Harlem dealership that it used to initiate one of the largest bankruptcies in the US bankruptcy history.[45]

General Motors' choice of venue for filing met the threshold in the Bankruptcy Venue Statute above, and was therefore legal. However, to an ordinary employee, it may turn out to be unfair and inequitable, as filing for bankruptcy in New York, would make it difficult for employees left in Detroit, to pursue their claims as bankruptcy proceedings are opened in a different state. It would not only be costly for employees to meet commuting and accommodation costs if they chose to attend the court hearing in New York but their voices and access to information would be interrupted due to the level of inconveniences involved.

Bankruptcy venue forum shopping – a disregarded SOS call? In *re* WorldCom Inc.,

The effect of bankruptcy venue forum shopping as an impediment to employee participation and involvement in bankruptcy reorganisations had earlier been witnessed in *In re* WorldCom Inc.[46] WorldCom was one of the largest communications companies in the US. Its headquarters were in Mississippi although it relocated to Virginia after being bought by MCI in 2003. Faced with financial difficulties, WorldCom filed for bankruptcy in the Southern District of New York bankruptcy court in 2002. It emerged from bankruptcy with $5 billion in debt and $6 billion in cash. However, most of its stakeholder claims, especially, those of employees who had been dismissed shortly before filing for bankruptcy, remained unpaid.

Employee claims, such as for pre-petition wages, severance pay, and other employment related benefits and interests remained unsettled, despite the fact that a huge sum of money was set aside to settle various claims arising from WorldCom's bankruptcy filing. While pre-petition bondholder claims were paid $0.36 on the dollar and stocks in the new company, employee claims were largely left

bankruptcy cases have had venue changes by bankruptcy courts out of the 991 cases studied. (accessed 20 May 2019).

43 *In re General Motors Corp., 407 B.R 463, 505 (Bankr. S.D.N.Y. 2009).*

44 LoPucki and Doherty, (n 37).

45 Benjamin A. Berringer, "It's just a Little Bit of History Repeating: An Examination of the Chrysler and GM Bankruptcies and their Implications for Future Chapter 11 Reorganizations" (2010) 7 *N.Y.U. J. L.* & Bus. 361, 391.

46 *In re WorldCom Inc., 346 F. 2d 628 (Bankr. S.D.N.Y 2004).*

unsettled and employees felt hugely shut out of the bankruptcy proceedings. This prompted WorldCom's dismissed employees to seek avenues to voice their concerns in pursuit of their claims.

With limited options of getting involved in the bankruptcy proceedings, the employees set up an advocacy group – "ex WorldCom5100"[47] that represented a majority of ex-employees. The group used an internet website to serve as an online meeting venue to mobilise, organise and devise informal ideas on how best to pursue their claims successfully or seek representation in New York.[48]

From an analytical point of view, WorldCom's decision to file for bankruptcy in New York, would arguably, make it difficult for employees (in Mississippi) to meaningfully pursue their claims against their debtor employer in New York. This is one of the bankruptcy cases that highlighted the effect of bankruptcy venue forum shopping to employees in pursuing their interest against the debtor during bankruptcy proceedings in the US.

It may be noted that one of the most important procedural rights in adjudication is the right to either be represented or to present evidence on one's own behalf, where the subject matter of adjudication is of concern to that individual, class or group.[49] However, venue forum shopping in bankruptcy reorganisations often silences employee voices and their ability to meaningfully pursue their claims against their debtor employer.

Moreover, bankruptcy venue forum shopping is usually to the benefit of the debtor employer. This is because the debtor employer's bankruptcy proceedings may not be interrupted or slowed down by overlapping employee interests, as would be the case, where bankruptcy proceedings were heard in the local bankruptcy court.[50] The effect of such practices is that, certain legal principles, such as "proximity" to key parties involved in the case and "equality" of treatment of all stakeholders involved in the case which would lead to "fairness" and "justice" are, not only disrupted, but usually sidestepped.[51]

Conclusion

It has been noted that the US Congress is aware of the problems faced by employees during bankruptcy reorganisations, especially, employees' lack of equal participation, inclusion, and adequate access to information on their employer's bankruptcy process in contrast to other stakeholders involved in the process such

47 See Martin Kady II, "Ex-WorldCom Workers Unite, Fight Back" *Wash. Bus. J. Online* (Washington, 12 August 2002) www.bizjournals.com/washington/stories/2002/08/12/story5.html?page=all. (accessed 21 May 2019).

48 Ibid.

49 Samuel L. Bufford, "International Insolvency Case Venue in the European Union: The Parmalat and Daisytek Controversies" (2006) 12 *Columb. J. Eur. L.* 429, 483.

50 M. Curriden, "Playing on Home Court: New York and Delaware May Loose Their Grip on Bankruptcy Cases" (2012) 98 *A.B.A. J.* 16, 17.

51 E. Warren and J. L. Westbrook, "Financial Characteristics of Businesses in Bankruptcy" (1999) 73 *Am. Bankr. L. J.* 499, 553.

as the DIP.[52] There is also a lack of new legislation from the US Congress that would aim to provide a federal-state uniform model of employee involvement during bankruptcy reorganisations. The current bankruptcy venue statutes and procedures tend to create a system that often fails to recognise or involve employees in their debtor employer's bankruptcy proceedings.

There is a need to balance the federal-state law division, bridge the widening gap between these two jurisdictions and reward stakeholders, such as employees who contribute to the going concern value of their employer's business. Very often employees find themselves less protected by state laws when bankruptcies strike. Their interests are treated under generalised federal bankruptcy laws yet the business culture and practice in their local states may be different from other states. For instance, the business culture and practices, in light of the lending market and mobility of capital in New York, might be completely different from that in Delaware.[53]

The concern is that even a few US states that have slightly stronger legislation mandating employee protection during business sales, mergers or transfers, such as Delaware, restrict the level of protection to unionised employees or employees that are members of collective bargaining agreements. This further leaves non-unionised employees without consolidated legislative protection.[54]

In view of these challenges, the task is on US bankruptcy judges to bridge this disparity in employment protection and achieve the balance needed through interpretation. However, judges cannot remedy the whole problem of course as the fault lies in legislation but they can aim towards optimal decision making in the cases that come before them. The next chapter analyses the interpretative challenges to bankruptcy judges during Chapter 11 reorganisation proceedings and how Dworkin's approach may arguably provide a remedy.

Bibliography

Books

LoPucki, M Lynn, *Courting Failure: How Competition for Big Cases is Corrupting the Bankruptcy Courts* (Michigan, University of Michigan Press, 2006).

Cases

Fall River Dyeing & Fishing Corp. v NLRB, 482 U.S. 27 (1987).
Howard Johnson v Detroit Local Joint Exec. Bd., 417 U.S. 249, 264 (1974).

52 C. E. Vance and P. Barr, "The Facts and Fictions of Bankruptcy Reform" (2003) 1 *De Paul Bus. & Com. L. J.* 361, 410.

53 For a similar point of discourse, see, M. Bradley and M. Rosenzweig, "The Untenable Case for Chapter 11" (1992) 101 *Yale L. J.* 1043, 1078.

54 For example, Delaware and Massachusetts have state legislations that provide for mandatory assumption of successorship obligations upon corporate mergers, takeover or transfers but those obligations have to be arising out of collectively bargained agreements. See, DEL. CODE ANN. tit. 19, s.706 (a) (Supp. 1992) and MASS. ANN. LAWS Ch.149, s.20 (E) (Law. Co-op. Supp. 1993) respectively.

In re Caesers Entertainment Operating Company Inc., 134 S. Ct 1188, 1194 (Bankr. D. Delaware 2015).
In re General Motors Corp., 407 B.R 463, 505 (Bankr. S.D.N.Y. 2009).
In re Patriot Coal Corp., 482 B.R 718, 739 (Bankr. S.D.N.Y 2012).
In re WorldCom Inc., 346 F. 2d 628 (Bankr. S.D.N.Y 2004).
John Wiley & Sons, Inc. v Livingston 376, U.S. 543 (1963).
NLRB v Burns Int'l Sec. Serv., 406 U.S. 272 (1972).

Journal articles

Austin, A Daniel, "Bankruptcy and the Myth of 'Uniform Law'" (2012) 42 Seton Hall L. Rev. 1081, 1168.
Berringer, A Benjamin, "It's Just a Little Bit of History Repeating: An Examination of the Chrysler and GM Bankruptcies and their Implications for Future Chapter 11 Reorganizations" (2010) 7 N.Y.U. J. L. & Bus. 361, 391.
Bradley, M, and Rosenzweig, M, "The Untenable Case for Chapter 11" (1992) 101 Yale L. J. 1043, 1078.
Brubacker, Ralph, "The Erie Doctrine, Code Common Law, and Choice-of-Law Rules in Bankruptcy (Part 1)" (2012) 32 Bankr. L. Letter Online (Thompson Reuters) 4.
Bufford, L Samuel, "International Insolvency Case Venue in the European Union: The Parmalat and Daisytek Controversies" (2006) 12 Columb. J. Eur. L. 429, 483.
Coordes, N Laura, "The Geography of Bankruptcy" (2015) 68 Vand. L. Rev. 381, 439.
Curriden, M, "Playing on Home Court: New York and Delaware May Loose their Grip on Bankruptcy Cases" (2012) 98 A.B.A. J. 16, 17.
Efthimiou, Marcus, "State Legislative Attempts to Mandate Continuation of Collective Bargaining Agreements during Business Change: The Unfulfilled Expectations and the Pre-empted Results" (1992) 77 Cornell L. Rev. 47, 51.
Horan, M Thomas, and Johnson, EF, "Basics of Bankruptcy Venue, Transfer of Cases" (2012) 30(10) Am. Bankr. Inst. J. 40, 43.
Kady, Martin II, "Ex-WorldCom Workers Unite, Fight Back" Wash. Bus. J. Online (Washington, 12 August 2002) < www.bizjournals.com/washington/stories/2002/08/12/story5.html?page=all> (accessed 21 May 2019).
LoPucki, M Lynn, and Doherty, JW, "Delaware Bankruptcy: Failure in the Ascendancy" (2006) 73 U. Chi. L. Rev. 1387.
Plank, E Thomas, "Bankruptcy and Federalism" (2002) 71 Fordham L. Rev. 1063.
Redish, MH, "Doing it with Mirrors: *New York v. US* and Constitutional Limitations on Federal Power to Require State Law Legislation" (1993) 21 Hastings Const. L. Q. 593, 604.
Simmons, S Omari, "Delaware's Global Threat" (2015) 41 J. Corp. L. 217.
Vance, CE, and Barr, P, "The Facts and Fictions of Bankruptcy Reform" (2003) 1 De Paul Bus. & Com. L. J. 361, 410.
Warren, E, and Westbrook, JL, "Financial Characteristics of Businesses in Bankruptcy" (1999) 73 Am. Bankr. L. J. 499, 553.

Legislation

Massachusetts Code (MASS. ANN. LAWS Ch.149, Law. Co-op. Supp. 1993).
National Labour Relations Act 1935 (29 U.S.C ss. 151–169). (Pub. L. 74–198, 49 Stat. 449).
The Delaware Code (DEL. CODE ANN. tit. 19, Supp. 1992).

5 Interpretation as a balancing tool in the US – applying Dworkin

Introduction

When the US Congress passes legislation that is intended to address a particular aspect in the US legal system, that legislation is usually non-prescriptive. That legislation is passed and brought into effect but the legislature does not provide how such legislation should be interpreted. This task is left to the judiciary to interpret and apply that legislation to the relevant legal questions before the courts.[1]

The non-prescriptive character of the legislation would imply that judges have to apply the linguistic, systematic or purposive analyses to their interpretative approaches to interpreting and applying legislation to the legal questions before the courts.[2] The linguistic analysis may involve judges drawing on the legislative language and the criteria of reasoning to enable the understanding of specific statutory terms to be applied to the facts before them. Systematic analysis may involve judicial analysis of the conceptual or logical reasoning in past precedents or policy reasoning while the purposive analysis would involve analysing substantive legal and policy reasons behind the passing of such laws.[3]

Judicial interpretation can play an integral part in addressing the debtor-creditor concerns during bankruptcy reorganisation proceedings in the US. Bankruptcy proceedings are presided over by specialist bankruptcy judges in specialist bankruptcy courts in the US. Therefore, when the debtor employer and the employees (often with their affiliated labour unions or representatives) fail to resolve their concerns and seek judicial intervention, judges are tasked with interpreting the laws and policies underlying the specific areas of dispute between the two parties to reach a fair and equitable decision.

1 N. MacCormick and R. S. Summers, *Interpreting Statutes: A Comparative Study* (Aldershot, Dartmouth Publishing, 1991).

2 H. Van Schooten, "Law as Fact, Law as Fiction: A Tripartite Model of Legal Communication" in Ann Wagner, Wouter G. Werner and Deborah Cao (eds.) *Interpretation, Law and the Construction of Meaning: Collected Papers on Legal Interpretation in Theory, Adjudication and Political Practice* (The Netherlands, Springer, 2007).

3 Ibid.

However, during bankruptcy proceedings in the US, the policy objectives of business rescue, that is, the need to support insolvent but viable businesses to successfully reorganise their businesses and continue operating as going concerns, usually conflict with the policy objectives of employment protection and continuity. Therefore, the conflict between these two policy objectives creates an interpretative dilemma on the bankruptcy judges that is analogous to the 'hard case' thesis that is posited by Dworkin in the Interpretative Theory of Law.[4]

In order to achieve a balanced approach that would enable a simultaneous pursuit of both policy objectives of successful business reorganisations and employment protection during bankruptcy reorganisation proceedings without compromising the other, a balance ought to be made. However, this balance would, arguably, best be archived through interpretation.

According to Professor Dworkin in his Interpretative Theory of Law, law as practice and law as legal theory are best understood as a process of interpretation.[5] Therefore, when faced with a legal question, a judge must interpret the law in a manner that fits the legal context at hand because constructiveness in interpretation is the proper approach to artistic and literal interpretation.[6] Constructive interpretation coheres with the need to make the law the best it can be, carrying with it the principles of moral value. Therefore, every time a judge is confronted with a legal question, that judge should construct a theory of what the law is, that adequately fits into past relevant governmental policies underlying the passing of that law to make the law the best it can be.[7]

However, the interpretation and application of s.1113 of the US Bankruptcy Code[8] during bankruptcy reorganisation proceedings in the US has been the subject of inconsistent approaches from different bankruptcy courts.[9] These inconsistent approaches have failed to provide the balance needed to fairly balance the policy objectives of successful business reorganisations and the policy objectives of employment protection during bankruptcy reorganisation proceeding in the US.

Interpretation as a balancing tool

When the debtor employer files for bankruptcy in the US, one area of concern to employees is whether their employment contracts and collectively bargained

4 R. Dworkin, *Taking Rights Seriously* (London, Duckworth, 1977) 85.

5 R. Dworkin, *Law's Empire* (Cambridge, MA, HUP, 1986) 46–48.

6 R. Dworkin, "Pragmatism, Right Answers and True Benality" in M. Brint and W. Weaver (eds.) *Pragmatism in Law and Society*, (Boulder, CO, Westview Press, 1991) 365.

7 R. Dworkin, *Law's Empire* (Cambridge, MA, HUP, 1986) 52.

8 11 U.S.C s.1113.

9 See, for instance, the different interpretative approaches adopted by different courts in the cases of *Brotherhood of Railways, Airline and Steamship Clerks v REA Express, Inc.*, 523 F. 2d 164 (2nd Cir. 1975); *Wheeling-Pittsburgh Steel Corp. v United Steel Workers of Am.*, 791 F. 2d 1074, 1091 (3rd Cir. 1986) and *Truck Drivers Local 807 v Carey Transportation*, 816 F. 2d 82 (2nd Cir.1987).

agreements would be either, modified, adopted or rejected by their debtor employer. After filing for bankruptcy, a US debtor employer is afforded powers to modify, assume or reject employment contracts or collective bargaining agreements.[10] However, the modification, rejection or adoption of employment contracts or CBA may create adverse consequences between the objectives of corporate rescue and employment protection if not balanced to meet both policy objectives simultaneously without constricting the other.

Dworkin argues that where a judge adopts the interpretative ideals of integrity and constructiveness, that judge finds a unique right answer to the legal question before him, rather than using judicial discretion to fill the gap.[11] It may be noted that judicial use of discretion is one of the forms of legal positivism mainly posited by H.L.A. Hart[12] that Dworkin strongly criticises and formed one of the famous debates in modern legal theory and jurisprudence between legal positivists and natural law theorists.[13]

Dworkin opines that by applying the ideals of constructiveness and integrity in interpretation, a judge may be able to interpret the law based on legal principles that may fit perfectly into the legal context before the court to achieve a right answer to the legal question.[14] This is as opposed to interpreting the law based on rules, which may be static in application and may not fit perfectly into the legal scenario at hand.[15]

This is because, legal principles have been described as being flexible in application and having better weight than legal rules in terms of relevance to their application to legal scenarios before court.[16] On the other hand, legal rules have been described as having an 'open texture'.[17] Legal rules are usually, expressed in general terms and they may be interpreted in different contexts and cannot be weighed against each other, which may lead to different outcomes.[18]

Therefore, it is the notion that, to fairly adopt an approach that would balance the tension between employment protection policy objectives and business reorganisation policy objectives, the judge has to understand the rules and principles, inherent in the laws before the court in order to construct a theory of the law that is required to balance both policies' objectives, and how to apply such law to the factual situations before the court.

In addition to legal principles and rules, legal precedents may also be useful to the judge in that, they may provide the context within which past legal conflicts

10 Via 11 U.S.C. s.365 and 11 U.S.C. s.1113 respectively.

11 R Dworkin, *Law's Empire* (Cambridge, MA, HUP, 1986) 255.

12 H.L.A Hart, "Positivism and the Separation of Law and Morals" (1958) 71 *Harv. L. Rev.* 593.

13 L. Fuller, "Positivism and the Fidelity of Law – A Response to Professor Hart" (1958) *71 Harv. L. Rev.* 630; R. Dworkin, *Taking Rights Seriously* (London, Duckworth, 1977); R. Dworkin, *Law's Empire* (Cambridge, MA, HUP, 1986).

14 Dworkin, (n 7) 365.

15 R. Dworkin, *Law's Empire* (Cambridge, MA, HUP, 1986) 255.

16 K. Kress, "Legal Indeterminacy" (1989) 77 *Calif. L. Rev.* 235.

17 H. L. A. Hart, *The Concept of Law* (Oxford, Clarendon Press, 1961).

18 Kress, (n 17).

or concerns between parties were resolved. This may aid the judge to inform context on how competing legal questions before the court may be resolved by drawing on those legal precedents' relative importance to the present legal disputes.[19] However, sometimes the legal precedents that are available to the judge may not fit into the context of the present legal questions before the judge and therefore, they may be considered distinguishable.

Therefore, in the absence of compatible legal precedents, statutory interpretation may require that the judges revert to legal rules and principles to find a suitable approach to solving the legal questions before the court. This may involve, for example, identifying legal rules and principles which would fit into the legal questions before the court that would not only fit into the policies underlying the passing of the law that is the subject of interpretation, but would also inform the judge's reason for the decision taken.[20] According to Dworkin, the judge is able to achieve this by adopting the principles of constructiveness and integrity in interpretation and the right answer thesis as argued in the Interpretative Theory of Law.

Judicial interpretation approaches to U.S.C. s.1113

Section 1113 of the US Bankruptcy Code[21] was enacted by the US Congress as a form of mitigating the effects of the Supreme Court's ruling in *NLRB v Bildisco & Bildisco.*[22] In this case, the Supreme Court held that a debtor employer may reject a CBA in circumstances where, the court finds that 'equities balance in favour of rejecting such a contract'.[23] The Supreme Court also held that a debtor employer can unilaterally alter the terms of a collectively bargained agreement, during the interim period that runs between the period of filing of the bankruptcy petition, and the time during which the order authorising rejection is entered.[24]

Following this decision by the Supreme Court, there were growing concerns that employees' rights to bargain collectively with their employers that are bestowed upon them by the NLRA 1935[25] would be affected and rendered meaningless, if the debtor employer could reject collective agreements where rejection would augment the reorganisation plans of the debtor company during bankruptcy. Therefore, the US Congress enacted s.1113 of the Bankruptcy Code, as a move that would restrict the debtor employer's ability and flexibility to reject or modify collective bargaining agreements.[26]

19 R. Cross, *Precedent in English Law* (4th edn, Oxford, Clarendon Press, 1991).

20 Richard A. Posner, *How Judges Think* (Cambridge, MA, HUP, 2008); William M. Landes and Richard Posner, "Rational Judicial Behaviour: A Statistical Study" (2009) 1 *J. Legal Anal.* 775–831.

21 11 U.S.C. s.1113.

22 *NLRB v Bildisco & Bildisco*, 465 U.S. 523 (1984).

23 Ibid., para. 526.

24 Ibid., paras. 532, 533.

25 NLRA (1935) s.8(a)(5) and s.8(a)(1).

26 D. Rosenberg, "Bankruptcy and the Collective Bargaining Agreement – A Brief Lesson in the Use of the Constitutional System of Checks and Balances" (1984) 58 *Am. Bankr. L. J.* 293,

This provision imposes both procedural and substantive conditions that a debtor employer must meet before rejecting or modifying a CBA. The provision requires the debtor to make proposals to the union that provide for necessary modifications before initiating negotiations and to ensure that all creditors, the debtor and all affected parties are treated fairly and equitably.[27] However, the judicial approach to the interpretation and application of this provision during CBA rejection petitions filed under s.1113 has been met with differing standards and approaches from different judges.[28]

It should be remembered that the policies underpinning the US Congress' enactment of s.1113 were mainly to remedy the effects of the *Bildisco* decision. This was achieved by placing limitations on the debtor employer's ability and flexibility towards CBA rejection and modifications. However, it is through the same provision that Congress left the door open to a debtor employer to apply to court to seek court approved rejection or modifications to CBAs courtesy of s.1113 (e).

Per s.1113 (e), a CBA rejection motion may be approved by the court where its rejection is essential to the continuation of the debtor's business, or where rejection and unilateral changes to the terms and conditions of a CBA would prevent irreparable damage to the debtor's bankruptcy estate. Moreover, after notice and hearing processes, a court may authorise interim changes to employee's employment terms, wages, benefits or working conditions covered by a CBA under the 'business judgement rule'.

The business judgement rule was developed by the courts in recognition that that judges are not better positioned than business owners or business managers to make subjective business decisions for insolvent businesses. They therefore keep faith in the business expertise of the debtor / DIP to make decisions that are in the best interests of the business. Therefore, a debtor may reject an executory contract such as a CBA provided that the debtor shows that the rejection of such executory contract is to benefit the bankruptcy estate in its reorganisation endeavours. However, the debtor is required to obtain court approval before rejection under s.365 or s.1113 respectively.[29]

Under the business judgement rule, bankruptcy courts presume that the debtor has acted prudently on an informed basis, in good faith and in honest belief that the action taken is in the best interest of the bankruptcy estate. The question of whether rejection of CBA or employment contracts satisfies the business judgement rule is one to be decided by the bankruptcy court. Therefore, where the debtor employer adduces credible evidence to support the submission

312–321; Daniel S. Ehrenberg, "Collective Bargaining Agreements under Section 1113 of Chapter 11 of the 1984 Bankruptcy Code: Resolving the Tension Between Labor Law and Bankruptcy Law" (1994) 2 *J. L. & Policy* 55, 68.

27 11 U.S.C. s.1113 (b) (I) (A).

28 For instance, compare and contrast *Brotherhood of Railways, Airline and Steamship Clerks v REA Express, Inc.*, 523 F. 2d 164 (2nd Cir. 1975) and *Wheeling-Pittsburgh Steel Corp. v United Steel Workers of Am.*, 791 F. 2d 1074, 1091 (3rd Cir. 1986).

29 See, for example, the decision of the Ninth Circuit court in *In re Pomona Valley Medical Group, Inc.*, 476 F.3d 665, 670 (9th Cir. 2007).

that a rejection would benefit the bankruptcy estate and lead to successful reorganisation,[30] bankruptcy courts would generally approve such CBA rejection motions unless the court finds the debtor's application not to be reasonably based on sound business judgement, but on bad faith, whim or caprice.[31]

However, cognisance has to be given to the potential that the business judgement rule may be vulnerable to abuse or misapplication. For example, through the business judgement rule, employers may seek strategic use of bankruptcy filing by using Bankruptcy Code specific provisions such as s.362 automatic stay provisions, rejection powers in s.1113 (e), s.363 business sales et cetera, to achieve business strategies that they may have failed to achieve outside bankruptcy.[32] This may include, for example, use of labour transformational policies and strategies such as labour cost reduction through rejection of employment contracts, moratoria on creditor enforcements or modification and termination of defined benefit pension plans.[33]

For instance, in *re Delta Airlines Inc.*,[34] *Delta's* 'Transformational Plan' included initiatives to use bankruptcy to obtain cost savings in respect of pension funding, labour costs and retiree health cost savings. In this case, *Delta's* affiliate, *Comair* initiated plans to reject pilots' and flight attendants' labour agreements and CBAs on the grounds that these agreements affected *Delta's* longer-term economic ability to compete in the market place.

In granting *Delta's* rejection application the court concluded that the debtor employer could not be expected to make commitments to the pilots and flight attendants' job security that would erode the debtor's ability to compete.[35] It may be argued that this judgement and the judicial application of the business judgement rule may be seen as a move away from the Congressional policies underlying the enactment of s.1113 in the first place which was to preclude debtor employers from using bankruptcy as a strategic weapon in dealing with labour cost reduction through rejection or modification of CBAs.[36]

The 'necessary' and the 'fair and equitable' standards

During s.1113 rejection proceedings, bankruptcy courts apply two standards in analysing whether the debtor employer has fulfilled the procedural

30 *In re Sun City Investments, Inc.*, 89 B.R. 245, 249 (Bankr. M.D. Fla. 1988).

31 *In re Prime Motor Inns*, 124, B.R. 378, 381 (Bankr. S.D. Fla. 1991).

32 Kevin J. Delaney, *Strategic Bankruptcy: How Corporations and Creditors Use Chapter 11 to their Advantage* (Berkeley, University of California Press, 1999). William T. Bodoh and Beth Buchanan, "The Future of Labour through the Prism of Bankruptcy: Ignored Consequences – The Conflicting Policies of Labor Law and Business Reorganization and Its Impact on Organized Labor" (2007) 15 *Am. Bankr. Inst. L. Rev.* 395, 413.

33 See for example, *In re UAL Corporation*, 428 F. 3d 677, 684 (7th Cir. 2005).

34 *In re Delta Air Lines*, 359 B.R 468, 473 (Bankr. S.D.N.Y. 2006).

35 Ibid., para. 488.

36 See, *In re Century Brass Prods. Inc.*, 795, F. 2d 265, 272 (2nd Cir. 1986); *Adventure Res., Inc. v Holland*, 137 F. 3d 786, 798 (4th Cir. 1998).

and substantive requirements under s.1113 before deciding whether or not to grant a debtor company's rejection petition. These standards are the 'necessary' and the 'fair and equitable' standards. Through the 'necessary' standard, judges base their examination of the debtor employer's rejection application on whether the proposed rejections to employee contracts of employment or CBAs are necessary for the successful reorganisation of the debtor company to avoid liquidation.

However, where bankruptcy courts apply the 'necessary' and 'fair and equitable' standards, they analyse whether the debtor employer's rejection application is not only necessary for the successful reorganisation of the debtor employer, but whether the rejection proposals are also fair and equitable to all affected parties with interests in the debtor company.[37]

The 'necessary' and 'fair and equitable' standards are better analysed by examining how these standards were applied by both the Second and Third Circuit Courts of Appeal in the cases of *Wheeling-Pittsburgh Steel Corp. v United Steelworkers of America*[38] and *Truck Drivers Local 807 v Carey Transportation Inc.*,.[39] In both cases, each court gave a conflicting ruling on how both the 'necessary' and the 'fair and equitable' standard ought to be applied in bankruptcy proceedings involving motions by debtor employees to reject employee collective bargaining agreements.

Wheeling-Pittsburgh Steel Corp. v United Steelworkers of America

In *Wheeling-Pittsburgh*, the debtor employer sought authorisation from the bankruptcy court to reject all of its CBAs with United Steelworkers of America on the ground that the rejection was necessary to achieving its five-year reorganisation plan. The court was to deliberate on whether the proposed rejections were necessary for Wheeling-Pittsburgh's reorganisation success.

After examining Wheeling-Pittsburgh's submissions, the court found that Wheeling-Pittsburgh had satisfied the requirements and conditions in s.1113 and in light of the then critical state of the US Steel industry and the company's deep financial difficulties, the rejections were necessary for Wheeling-Pittsburgh to maintain its labour stability during the proposed five-year reorganisation plan.[40] The court further found that although Wheeling-Pittsburgh did not provide clauses to upward labour rate adjustment in case it rebounded financially during the reorganisation period, all parties were, treated fairly and equitably.[41]

37 Martha West, "Life after Bildisco: Section 1113 and the Duty to Bargain in Good Faith" (1986) 47 *Ohio St. L. J.* 65, 103.

38 *Wheeling-Pittsburgh Steel Corp. v United Steelworkers of Am.*, 791 F.2d 1074 (3rd Cir. 1986). (*Wheeling-Pittsburgh*).

39 *Truck Drivers Local 807 v Carey Transportation., Inc.*, 816 F.2d 82, 89 (2d Cir. 1987) (*Carey Transportation*).

40 *Wheeling-Pittsburgh*, at 977–979.

41 Ibid., paras. 979–980.

More notably, in reaching its conclusion, the court drew significantly on the legislative history, the language of the statute and the sequence of events leading to the final version of the statute. This included examining the statements from the legislators that were most involved in the passing of the statute with regard to the meaning of the term 'fair and equitable'.[42] For example, the court analysed Congressman Morrison's views on the meaning of 'fair and equitable'. Congressman Morrison was of the view that:

> Language that requires assurance that "all creditors, the debtor and other affected parties are treated fairly and equitable", ... would ensure that where the trustee seeks to repudiate a collective bargaining agreement would ensure covered employees do not bear either the entire financial burden ... or a disproportionate share of that burden...[43]

The court also explore Senator Parkwood's statement[44] where he was of the view that:

> ...[t]o ensure fairness and equitableness for all creditors, the debtor and other affected parties, the focus for cost cutting must not be directed exclusively at unionised workers.[45]

This was to prohibit the rejection of CBAs merely because the court deemed the rejection to be equitable to other affected parties, particularly creditors.[46] The court therefore defined the term 'necessary' during the proceedings to mean that the proposed rejections were 'essential' to preventing the debtor company from requiring liquidation.[47]

The court concluded that the 'necessary' element of the standard was 'conjunctive' with the requirement that the proposals for CBA rejection treated all of the affected parties fairly and equitably, otherwise it would defeat the Congressional policy of remedying the *Bildisco* standard which was not sensitive to the national policy goals of favouring collective bargaining between employers and employees.

Truck drivers Local 807 v Carey Transportation Inc.,

In *Truck Drivers Local 807 v Carey Transportation Inc.,*[48] Carey Transportation filed a proposal to modify its collective bargaining agreements pursuant to

42 *Wheeling-Pittsburgh*, paras. 1086, 1089.
43 Ibid., paras. 1087–1088.
44 130 CONG. REC. H7496 (daily ed. June 29 1984).
45 *Wheeling-Pittsburgh*, paras. 1087, 1089.
46 Ibid., para. 1081.
47 Ibid., para. 1089.
48 *Truck Drivers Local 807 v Carey Transportation Inc.*, 816 F.2d 82, 89 (2d Cir. 1987). (*Carey Transportation*).

11 U.S.C. 1113(b)(1)(A) post-petition. The proposal was designed to achieve annual savings of $1.8 million for each of the next three fiscal years in light of its reorganisation plan. However, the central issue in the Court of Appeal was whether the proposed modifications were necessary to Carey Transportation's reorganisation success.

In addition, the court had to deliberate as to whether the proposed modifications treated all parties fairly and equitably, and whether the balancing of the equities clearly favoured rejection of the collective bargaining agreements. The court approved Carey Transportation's application to reject the CBAs by holding that Carey Transportation had met its burden of proving compliance with the procedural and substantive standards set forth in the statute.[49]

On appeal to the Court of Appeal, the Second Circuit Court of Appeal affirmed the Southern District of New York bankruptcy court's ruling that all parties were participating "fairly and equitably" in the attempt to save the debtor company from liquidation. Interestingly, is the fact that the Second Circuit Court of Appeal departed from applying the 'necessary' element of the rejection standard on its own and instead, adopted the 'necessary' and the 'fair and equitable' standards conjunctively. The court did not support the view of interpreting the term 'necessary' as in *Wheeling-Pittsburgh* where it was construed to mean that the proposed rejections were 'essential' to preventing the liquidation of the debtor company.

The court based the interpretation of the term 'necessary' on the statutory text itself and interpreted the terms 'necessary' and 'fair and equitable' separately. The court's reasoning was that the requirement that the rejection proposals were necessary to prevent the debtor company from facing liquidation placed on the debtor company the burden of proving that its proposals for rejection were made in good faith and contained necessary but not minimal changes that would enable the debtor company to complete the reorganisation process successfully.[50]

In light of Dworkin's interpretative approach

From the discussion above, it may be concluded that there exists no definitive and binding standard to guide bankruptcy judges in applying the required standard in s.1113 rejection proceedings. Judges in s.1113 rejection proceedings may be guided by the evidence adduced by the parties to the litigation beforehand in deciding whether to apply the 'necessary' standard on its own as was the case in *Carey Transportation* by the Second Circuit Court of Appeal, or to apply the 'necessary' and the 'fair and equitable' standards conjunctively as the Third Circuit Court of Appeal did in *Wheeling-Pittsburgh*.

It should be remembered that prior to the decision in *Bildisco*, the courts applied a strict standard test in deciding CBA rejection cases. This was the decision

49 *In re Carey Transportation, Inc.*, 50 B.R. 203 (Bankr. S.D.N.Y. 1985).
50 Ibid., para. 90.

from the Court of Appeal in *Brotherhood of Railways, Airline and Steamship Clerks v REA Express, Inc.*,[51] where the court held that;

> [I]n view of the serious effect which rejection has on the carrier's employees, rejection should be authorised only where it clearly appears to be the lesser of the two evils and that unless the agreement is rejected, the carrier will collapse and employees will no longer have their jobs.[52]

This was the standard test that was supported by the National Labour Relations Board (NLRB) as it balanced both the interests of the debtor employer and the employees. However in *Bildisco*, this standard was rejected by the Supreme Court holding that the standard was unacceptably narrow and fundamentally at odds with the policies of 'flexibility and equity' of Chapter 11 of the US Bankruptcy Code.[53] The effect of this new approach, as adopted in *Bildisco* is that bankruptcy courts are not guided by a single binding model or approach in applying the rejection standards. This has arguably led to inconsistent approaches adopted by bankruptcy judges in applying the rejection standards as discussed above.

By analysing the court's application of the 'necessary' test on its own as was the case in *Carey Transportation*, it could be concluded that decisions on whether a proposal for rejection is 'necessary' to the successful reorganisation of the debtor employer may be determined by the court without considering whether it is 'fair and equitable' to employees and their affiliated labour unions.

In *Wheeling-Pittsburgh* above, the court interpreted the term 'necessary' as being conjunctive with the requirement that the proposal for rejection treated all of the affected parties fairly and equitably.[54] The court drew significantly on the legislative history, the language of the statute and the sequence of events leading to the final version of s.1113. It may be noted that this approach by the Third Circuit Court of Appeal would fit into Dworkin's ideals of constructiveness and integrity in interpretation to reach the right answer. By the court interpreting the term 'necessary' as 'essential', it was to ensure that the rejection was not only necessary but essential to its successful reorganisation otherwise the debtor employer would be liquidated and apart from having the CBA rejected, employee jobs would also be lost permanently.

However, in *Carey Transportation*, the court departed from this standard on the ground that the term 'necessary' should not be construed as essential by adding elements of fairness and equity as established in *Wheeling-Pittsburgh*. The court based its interpretation of the term 'necessary' on the statutory text itself and interpreted the terms 'necessary' and 'fair and equitable' separately.[55]

51 *Brotherhood of Railways, Airline and Steamship Clerks v REA Express, Inc.*, 523 F. 2d 164 (2nd Cir. 1975).

52 Ibid., para. 172.

53 *NLRB v Bildisco & Bildisco*, 465 U.S. 523 (1984) para. 525.

54 *Wheeling-Pittsburgh*, para. 1089.

55 *Carey Transportation*, paras. 88–90.

The court's reasoning was that the requirement that the rejection proposals were necessary to prevent the debtor employer from liquidation placed on the debtor company the burden of proving that its proposals for rejection were made in good faith and contained necessary but not minimal changes that would enable the debtor company to complete the reorganisation process successfully.[56] However, it should be remembered that this is the very essence of the policy underlying the enactment of s.1113. Part of the requirement of the debtor employer's rejection application is to show that negotiations have been held with employee representatives and unions in a fair and equitable manner.[57]

This would arguably, be seen as a move away from the policy of ensuring fairness in the treatment of the diverse stakeholder interests. The court in *Carey Transportation* may be construed as paying more regard to the debtor employer's reorganisation prospects than the effect such proposed rejections would have on employees such as changes to their expected compensations already negotiated with their labour unions.

The difference between interpreting the term 'necessary' in conjunction with the elements of 'fairness and equity' as articulated in *Wheeling-Pittsburgh* may mean both the debtor employer's interests and the employees' interests are balanced on the principles of fairness and equity which may be seen as a form of a balanced approach – an approach that would be achieved through applying constructiveness and integrity to the judicial approaches in interpreting rejection motions.

Conclusion

In conclusion, it may be submitted that the tension between corporate rescue policy objectives inherent in insolvency laws and employment protection policy objectives inherent in employment laws in the US has existed for decades but it has yet to be remedied. This tension is to a large extent, influenced by the inconsistencies in the interpretative approaches adopted by bankruptcy judges as highlighted above. However, the same tension may be remedied through interpretation.

The tension between the provisions in the Bankruptcy Code that seek to support bankruptcy reorganisation[58] and the provisions in labour laws that seek to protect employees and their rights during corporate insolvency[59] has not gone unnoticed.[60] The US Congress is still silent on the interpretation and application of s.1113 to

56 Ibid., para. 90.

57 See 11 U.S.C. s.1113 (b) (1) (A).

58 See generally, provisions such as s.362, s.363, s.1113, s.1114 among other provisions.

59 For example, see, NLRA (1935) s.8 (a) (5) and s.8 (a) (1).

60 Clyde W. Summers, "The Rights of Individual Workers: The Contract of Employment and the Rights of Individual Employees: Fair Representation and Employment at Will" (1984) 52 *Fordham L. Rev.* 1082, 1085; S. F. Befort, "Labour and Employment Law at the Millennium: A Historical Review and Critical Assessment" (2001) 43 *B. C. L Rev.* 460, 355–375.

bankruptcy reorganisation proceedings. To date, there has been no new legislation passed on the interpretation and application of s.1113 despite a significant number of inconsistent judgements from bankruptcy courts on its interpretation and application to bankruptcy proceedings. In the absence of new legislation from the US Congress, the onus is on the bankruptcy judges, to find the right approach and balance both labour policies and bankruptcy policies through interpretation.

However, the interpretative inconsistencies as exemplified by the Second and Third Circuit Courts discussed above do not help to remedy the imbalances in the legislative provisions that aim to support employment protection and business rescue during bankruptcy proceedings.

Therefore, it is the argument that to achieve the balance needed in the interpretative approaches to address both employees' and employers' interests fairly during bankruptcy proceedings, Dworkin's interpretative approach to law would provide the remedy. As discussed above, Dworkin's ideals such as constructive interpretation of the laws, rules and principles, coupled with the need to maintain the integrity of the law, would inform a balanced approach for a judge to adopt while interpreting s.1113 rejection applications by debtor employers.

As posited by Dworkin, a judge guided by legal principles and policies underlying the passing of that law, would constructively achieve a right answer that would not only conform to fairness but would also uphold the integrity of the law. This would help to remedy the tension between insolvency law policy objectives and employment law policy objectives during bankruptcy proceedings. Therefore, in the absence of a definitive binding approach on the interpretation and application of s.1113 and other relative provision of the Bankruptcy Code such as s.365 (power by the debtor employer to reject executory contracts) and s.362 (power by a debtor employer to restrict employee actions by invoking moratoria protection upon filing for bankruptcy), Dworkin's interpretative approach would provide a better guiding alternative.

Bibliography

Books

Cross, R, *Precedent in English Law* (4th edn., Oxford, Clarendon Press, 1991).

Delaney, JK, *Strategic Bankruptcy: How Corporations and Creditors Use Chapter 11 to Their Advantage* (Berkeley, University of California Press, 1999).

Dworkin, R, *Law's Empire* (Cambridge, MA, HUP, 1986).

Dworkin, R, *Taking Rights Seriously* (London, Duckworth, 1977).

Hart, HLA, *The Concept of Law* (Oxford, Clarendon Press, 1961).

MacCormick, N, and Summers, RS, *Interpreting Statutes: A Comparative Study* (Aldershot, Dartmouth Publishing, 1991).

Posner, A Richard, *How Judges Think* (Cambridge, MA, HUP, 2008).

Book chapters

Dworkin, R, "Pragmatism, Right Answers and True Benality" in M. Brint and W. Weaver (eds.) *Pragmatism in Law and Society*, (Boulder, CO, Westview Press, 1991).

Van Schooten, H, "Law as Fact, Law as Fiction: A Tripartite Model of Legal Communication" in Ann Wagner, Wouter G. Werner and Deborah Cao (eds.) *Interpretation, Law and the Construction of Meaning: Collected Papers on Legal Interpretation in Theory, Adjudication and Political Practice* (The Netherlands, Springer, 2007).

Cases

Adventure Res., Inc. v Holland, 137 F. 3d 786, 798 (4th Cir. 1998).
Brotherhood of Railways, Airline and Steamship Clerks v REA Express, Inc., 523 F. 2d 164 (2nd Cir. 1975).
In re Century Brass Prods. Inc., 795, F. 2d 265, 272 (2nd Cir. 1986).
In re Delta Air Lines, 359 B.R 468, 473 (Bankr. S.D.N.Y. 2006).
In re Delta Air Lines, 359 B.R 468, 473 (Bankr. S.D.N.Y. 2006).
In re Nw. Airlines Corp., 346 B.R 307, 322 (Bankr. S.D.N.Y. 2006).
In re Pomona Valley Medical Group, Inc., 476 F.3d 665, 670 (9th Cir. 2007).
In re Prime Motor Inns, 124, B.R. 378, 381 (Bankr. S.D. Fla. 1991).
In re Sun City Investments, Inc., 89 B.R. 245, 249 (Bankr. M.D. Fla. 1988).
In re UAL Corporation, 428 F. 3d 677, 684 (7th Cir. 2005).
NLRB v Bildisco & Bildisco, 465 U.S. 523 (1984).
Truck Drivers Local 807 v Carey Transportation, 816 F. 2d 82 (2nd Cir.1987).
Wheeling-Pittsburgh Steel Corp. v United Steel Workers of Am., 791 F. 2d 1074, 1091 (3rd Cir. 1986).

Journal articles

Befort, SF, "Labour and Employment Law at the Millennium: A Historical Review and Critical Assessment" (2001) 43 B. C. L. Rev. 460, 355–375.
Bodoh, T. William, and Buchanan, Beth, "The Future of Labour through the Prism of Bankruptcy: Ignored Consequences – The Conflicting Policies of Labor Law and Business Reorganization and its Impact on Organized Labor" (2007) 15 Am. Bankr. Inst. L. Rev. 395, 413.
Ehrenberg, S. Daniel, "Collective Bargaining Agreements under Section 1113 of Chapter 11 of the 1984 Bankruptcy Code: Resolving the Tension between Labor Law and Bankruptcy Law" (1994) 2 J. L. & Policy 55, 68.
Fuller, L, "Positivism and the Fidelity of Law – A Response to Professor Hart" (1958) 71 Harv. L. Rev. 630.
Hart, HLA, "Positivism and the Separation of Law and Morals" (1958) 71 Harv. L. Rev. 593.
Kress, K, "Legal Indeterminacy" (1989) 77 Calif. L. Rev. 235.
Landes, M. William, and Posner, Richard, "Rational Judicial Behaviour: A Statistical Study" (2009) 1 J. Legal Anal. 775–831.
Rosenberg, D, "Bankruptcy and the Collective Bargaining Agreement – A Brief Lesson in the Use of the Constitutional System of Checks and Balances" (1984) 58 Am. Bankr. L. J. 293, 312–321.
Summers, W. Clyde, "The Rights of Individual Workers: The Contract of Employment and the Rights of Individual Employees: Fair Representation and Employment at Will" (1984) 52 Fordham L. Rev. 1082, 1085.
West, Martha, "Life after Bildisco: Section 1113 and the Duty to Bargain in Good Faith" (1986) 47 Ohio St. L. J. 65, 103.

6 Employee rights and protection in the UK – TUPE transfers and business sales

Introduction

The Transfer of Undertakings (Protection of Employments) Regulations[1] were brought into force to implement the Acquired Rights Directives (ARD)[2] in the UK. The purpose and scope of TUPE Regulations is to afford a degree of protection to employees of businesses or undertakings that are the subject of a 'relevant transfer'[3] from their employers (transferors) to new buyers (transferees) in the UK. This is a form of social protection to employees from unfair employer prerogatives that the European Union (EU) sought to mitigate.[4] This is because the ARD did not only seek to safeguard employees' interests and rights during business sales and relevant transfers but also sought to strike a fair balance between the interests of the employees and their employers (business owners) as was affirmed by the Court of Justice of the European Union (CJEU) in *Alermo-Herron and Others v Parkwood Leisure Ltd.*[5]

In *Alermo-Herron and Others v Parkwood Leisure Ltd,*[6] the CJEU held that the ARD required a balance between employee and employer interests and that due weight was to be given to the principle of freedom of contract as a result of Article 16 of the Charter of Fundamental Rights. Article 16 of the Charter

1 Transfer of Undertakings (Protection of Employment) Regulations 1981 (SI 1981/1794), Transfer of Undertakings (Protection of Employment) Regulations 2006 (SI 2006/246), and The Collective Redundancies and the Transfer of Undertakings (Protection of Employment) (Amendment) Regulations 2014.

2 The original ARD to be transposed into UK law was Directive 77/187/EC, followed by Directives 98/50/EC and 2001/23/EC.

3 A 'relevant transfer' is defined under TUPE (2006) Regulations as a transfer of an undertaking, business or part of an undertaking or business situated immediately before the transfer to another person where there is a transfer of an economic entity which retains its identity. See, TUPE (2006), Regulation 3 (1) (a).

4 C. Brewster and P. Teague, *European Social Policy and its Impact on the UK* (London, Institute of Personnel Management, 1989).

5 Case C-499/04 [2006] ECR 1- 2397. See also, J. Prassl, "Freedom of Contract as a General Principle of EU Law? Transfers of Undertakings and the Protection of Employer Rights in EU Labour Law: Case C-426/11 *Alermo-Herron and Others v Parkwood Leisure Ltd*" (2013) 42 ILJ 434.

6 Case C-499/04 [2006] ECR 1- 2397. (*Alermo-Herron*).

of Fundamental Rights of the European Union establishes and recognises the freedom to conduct a business.

In *Alermo-Herron*, the CJEU was of the view that under the freedom of contract, '[t]he transferee must be able to assert its interests effectively in a contractual process to which it is party and to negotiate the aspects determining changes in the working conditions of its employees with a view to its economic activity'.[7] Therefore, the ARD aims to strike a fair balance between the interests of employees and employers by ensuring that the transferee is in a position to make adjustments and changes necessary to carry on its operations.[8]

However, the transposition of the ARD through the TUPE Regulations into UK law altered the way in which employment relations on corporate insolvency, which were hitherto executed based on common law principles, operate in the UK. It should be remembered that under the common law provisions, that is, prior to the TUPE Regulations being implemented in the UK, a business sale or transfer terminated all existing employment contracts.[9] This was because the common law notion of a contract for employment was based on the understanding or agreement between the employer and the employee both of whom agreed on what was expected of each other.[10]

The seminal decision and jurisprudence enacted in *Nokes v Doncaster Amalgamated Collieries*[11] by the House of Lords (HL) constituted the long-standing principle that the employee's right to choose for himself whom he would serve was the main difference between a servant and a serf. Therefore, reversing the Court of Appeal's (CA) decision in *Nokes,* the HL established that:

> [A] free citizen, in the exercise of his freedom, is entitled to choose the employer whom he promises to serve, so that the right to his services cannot be transferred from the employer to another without his assent.[12]

Therefore, at common law, and following the above decision, it was an established rule in practice that whenever there was a sale of a business or transfer of an undertaking, the contracts of employment of affected employees were effectively terminated. This was due to the fact that their contracts of employment could not be transferred to another employer without their consent.[13]

This common law position was however greatly affected by the introduction of TUPE Regulations into UK employment legislation to regulate relevant transfers and also, to protect the rights of employees in such situations. It is therefore, the position in the UK today that where an undertaking is sold or transferred

7 *Alermo-Herron*, at paragraphs, 32–33 and 35.

8 Ibid., para. 25.

9 See *Nokes v Doncaster Amalgamated Collieries Ltd* [1940] AC 1014.

10 J. McMullen, "Atypical Transfers, Atypical Workers and Atypical Employment Structures – A Case for Greater Transparency in Employment Issues" (1996) 25 (4) *Ind. L. J.* 286, 307.

11 [1940] 1014 AC; [1940] 3 All ER 549.

12 [1940] AC 1014 (Viscount Simon LC) 1020.

13 See the Court's reasoning in *Bolwell v Redcliffe Homes Ltd* [1999] IRLR 485.

from one owner to another and falls within the context of a 'relevant transfer', TUPE Provisions would apply and both the transferor (old employer) and the transferee (new employer) would be required to comply with the substantive and procedural provisions of the TUPE Regulations.[14]

Failure by both the transferor and the transferee to comply with the TUPE provisions during relevant transfers may lead to various claims, such as claims for unfair dismissals or unlawful variations to contract terms and conditions of employment being initiated by the affected employees which may in turn lead to financial compensation or other remedies granted to affected employees by employment tribunals or courts.[15]

The scope of employee protection under TUPE regulations

Although the TUPE Regulations seek to protect various aspects of employment protection during relevant transfers in the UK, the main areas of employee protection that impact on corporate rescue policy objectives mainly centre on three major pillars of protection. The first pillar of protection is the automatic transfer provisions enshrined in TUPE regulation 4 which automatically transfers employees' rights, obligations and liabilities to the new buyer (transferee) unless the employee(s) objects to the automatic transfer. The second pillar of protection is the protection from unfair dismissal of employees by their employers because of the transfer. This is enshrined in regulation 7(1). The third pillar of protection is the protection from variations to employees' contract terms and conditions of employment, collective agreements and other employment-related benefits because of the transfer pursuant to regulation 4(4).

These three areas of employee protection are the focal point of analysis in this chapter due to their impact on other TUPE provisions that seek to balance the rights of employers and employees during relevant transfers such as regulation 7(2) (the ETO exceptions), regulation 4(5) (permissible variation) among other provisions.

The automatic transfer provision under regulation 4 of TUPE 2006

The automatic transfer provision under regulation 4 of TUPE 2006 is one of the key pillars of protection that TUPE Regulations bestow onto employees during relevant transfers in the UK. By virtue of regulation 4(1) and (2) of TUPE 2006, in the context of a relevant transfer, all affected employees' contracts of employment, rights and liabilities arising out of their employment are automatically

14 Sandra Frisby, "TUPE or not TUPE? Employee Protection, Corporate Rescue and 'One Unholy Mess'" (2000) *C.F.I.L.* 260; J. McMullen, "Restructuring and TUPE" *Ind. L. J.* (2012) 41(3) 358–362.

15 J. Armour and S. Deakin, "The Rover Case (2): Bargaining in the Shadow of TUPE" (2009) 29 (4) *Ind. L. J.* 395, 402.

transferred to the new buyer (transferee)[16] unless the automatic transfer is objected to by the affected employee.[17]

Therefore, the contracts of all employees that are employed in the business 'immediately before the transfer'[18] are by default, automatically transferred to the transferee with the same terms and conditions of employment as they originally had with their previous employer. The employees' contracts of employment will have effect as if they were originally entered into between them and the transferee.

However, the automatic transfer provision in regulation 4 does not afford transferred employees new contractual benefits that they were not originally entitled to under their original employment contracts with the transferor. This was confirmed by the Court of Appeal (CA) in *Jackson v Computershare Investor Services Plc.*[19] In this case, Mrs Jackson had been transferred to the respondent's company via a TUPE transfer in 2004. When she was made redundant in 2005, Mrs Jackson claimed enhanced severance pay which was only available to employees who had joined the company prior to the TUPE transfer in 2004. The CA held that TUPE Regulations did not give additional rights to an employee, other than the rights that the employee was entitled to prior to the TUPE transfer.[20]

However, despite the language and text of regulation 4 (1) and (2), that is, the mandate to safeguard employees' security and continuity or employment during relevant transfers in the UK, there are a number of concerns that have been raised in relation to the scope and application of regulation 4 to relevant transfers. These concerns, for example, range from a lack of clear specification of the automatically transferrable liabilities to the consequences and effects that such liabilities have on business owners' flexibility to effect business decisions that have an effect on insolvency outcomes.[21]

The automatic transfer of rights and liabilities

A relevant transfer automatically transfers all of the transferor's rights, powers, obligations and liabilities attached to the transferring employees' contracts of employment.[22] The transferee cannot cherry-pick the liabilities to inherit from the transferor.[23] The automatic transfer of the transferor' liabilities is mandatory.[24]

16 TUPE (2006) regulation 4(1) and (2).

17 TUPE (2006) regulation 4(7). Where an employee objects to the automatic transfer, that employee's employment contract would be terminated as a result of the relevant transfer and that employee will not be treated for any purpose as having been dismissed by the transferor courtesy of regulation 4(8) of TUPE (2006).

18 TUPE 2006, regulation 4(3).

19 *Jackson v Computershare Investor Services Plc* [2007] EWCA Civ. 1065 (CA).

20 [2007] EWCA Civ. 1065 (CA), paras. 28, 31.

21 J. McMullen, "An analysis of Transfer of Undertakings (Protection of Employment) Regulations 2006" [2006] *Ind. L. J.* 113.

22 TUPE (2006), Regulation 4(2) (a).

23 This notion was emphasised in *Stirling District Council v Allan* [1995] ICR 1082.

24 C-362/89 *D'Urso v Ercole Marelli Ellectromeccanica Generale SPA* [1991] ECR 1-4105, para. (20).

Therefore, the rights, obligations and liabilities of the transferor existing on the date of the relevant transfer automatically transfer to the transferee.

However, regulation 4(2) does not provide clear categories of the liabilities that should automatically be transferred to the transferee. At EU level, the ECJ through various case law has established that both contractual liabilities and non-contractual liabilities can transfer as long as these existed before the relevant transfer took place.[25] However on the UK national level, the absence of clarity from regulation 4(2) on the nature or categories of the liabilities that should automatically transfer has meant that the task of providing guidance on these categories has been assumed by the UK courts and tribunals. Therefore, through a number of judicial authorities,[26] the courts and tribunals have given rulings indicating that contractual and non-contractual liabilities that precede a relevant transfer are capable of passing to the transferee courtesy of regulation 4(2).

Contractual liabilities are the type of liabilities that may be expressly or impliedly attached to a contract of employment. These may include, for example, liabilities arising from an employment contract, salary and wage liabilities, liabilities arising from CBAs, liabilities for unfair dismissals effected by the transferor before a relevant transfer, etc. These liabilities, if subsisting on the date of the relevant transfer are automatically transferred or inherited by the transferee.[27] Contingent and unknown liabilities such as claims for work related injuries or illnesses such as asbestos related illnesses that are unknown at the time of the TUPE transfer but manifest after the transfer are also capable of passing to the transferee.[28]

Non-contractual liabilities however, are the type of liabilities that are not expressly or impliedly attached to an employment contract. These may include, for example, liabilities arising from tortious claims such as for acts of omission, breach of statutory duties or torts of negligence committed by the transferor prior to the relevant transfer taking place.[29] Liability for injuries is a tortious employers' liability but there is an implied contractual term that the employer will care for the employees' health and safety.

In *Bernadone v Pall Mall Services Group Ltd*,[30] (a conjoined hearing with *Martin v Lancashire County Council*,[31] by the CA) the automatic transfer of tortious liabilities to a transferee following a relevant transfer was considered by the court. The claimant had had an accident and suffered injuries some years before

25 C- 135/83 *Abels v Bedrijfsvereniging voor de Metallindustrie en de Electrotechnische Industrie* [1985] ECR 469; *Arie Botzen and others v Rotterdamsche Droogdok Maatschappij BV* (Case 186/83) [1985] ECR 519, para 16.

26 See cases, such as *Jefferies v Powerhouse Retail Ltd* [UKEAT 1328]; *Whent v T. Cartledge Ltd* [1997] IRLR 153; *Bernadone v Pall Mall Services Group Ltd* [2001] ICR 197.

27 *Celtec Ltd v Astley* [2005] IRLR 647.

28 *Martin & Others v South Bank University* [2004] ICR 1234, ECJ.

29 Per the reasoning of Peter Gibson LJ in *Bernadone v Pall Mall Services Group Ltd* [2001] ICR 197.

30 *Bernadone v Pall Mall Services Group Ltd* [2001] ICR 197, CA.

31 *Martin v Lancashire County Council* [2001] ICR 197, CA.

the relevant transfer of the business took place. Years following the transfer, the claimant filed a claim for negligence and breach of statutory duties that led to the accident and injuries suffered under the Occupiers Liability Act 1957. The court had to give a ruling on whether liabilities in tort were 'under and in connection' to the contract of employment and who would be the correct defendant (the transferor or the transferee) to the claim before the court.

The court held that the duty of care to the employee arose out of the employment contract. The court also held that the transferee was liable and was therefore, the correct defendant as regulation 4 transferred liability for acts, omissions and torts of the transferor to the transferee. Therefore, the transferee was not exempted from personal injury claims of the transferred workforce.

In *Martin v Lancashire County Council*, the claim for a personal injury against the transferee was initiated by the claimant some two years (in 1995) following the relevant transfer (in 1993). Both cases, *Martin* and *Bernadone* may be viewed as typical examples that highlight the impact and effects of TUPE Regulations (in this regard, regulation 4(2)) and how these effects have contributed to the tension between the policies underlying employment protection and the need to boost corporate rescue through the sale of insolvent but viable businesses in the UK.

Where employees have a wider scope of initiating tortious claims against the transferee years following the transfer courtesy of the automatic transfer of contingent and unknown liabilities, potential buyers of the insolvent but viable businesses may be disincentivised from buying such businesses for fear of inheriting expensive unknown claims. However, where the scope for employees' ability to initiate tortious claims against the transferee following a TUPE transfer is narrow, this may be beneficial for business rescue. Hence, the narrower, the scope of employment protection the wider the scope of business rescue.

Impact of the automatic transfer of liabilities on business rescue

Both cases of *Martin* and *Bernadone* highlight the technicalities that the mandatory inheritance of known and unknown liabilities present on both the transferor's and the transferee's flexibility to effect business decisions that would boost corporate rescue prospects to avoid potential liquidations for fear of breaching TUPE provisions. It is the contention that at the time of the relevant TUPE transfer, such contingent and unknown liabilities may not be known to both the transferor and the transferee or even contemplated to occur in the near future following a relevant transfer. However, the automatic transfer provision in regulation 4 (2) places a mandatory inheritance of such liabilities on the transferee.[32]

Moreover, the transferor might have committed such torts, such as a breach of statutory duty or omission (that manifest into liabilities post-relevant transfer) several years before the relevant transfer was in contemplation but the transferee

32 Frisby, (n 14).

has to bear the burden of remedying the breaches in spite of having no complicity. Known contractual liabilities and the risks associated with such liabilities at the time of the transfer may be easier to measure and plan for (financially and economically) by the transferee during negotiations for the sale of the business.[33]

However, the concern is that unknown liabilities may manifest into huge financial liabilities post transfer which may present a huge financial impact on the transferee which may defeat the very purposes the business was acquired in the first place. This is especially where post relevant transfer unknown liabilities are for claims for illnesses that manifest several years after the relevant transfer took place such as asbestos related illnesses. Such illnesses usually affect a large number of workers and can also be initiated at any time.[34]

Therefore, due to the possibility of inheriting unknown liabilities that may present a huge financial burden to the transferee, potential buyers of insolvent but viable businesses may become somewhat risk-averse[35] to buying such businesses. This is especially in high stakes cases such as asbestos related businesses or chemical producing businesses. This may hinder rescue prospects of struggling businesses which may also affect employee jobs where insolvent but viable businesses are liquidated as a result of failing to obtain a buyer.

Employee protection from unfair dismissals under regulation 7

In addition to the automatic transfer provision discussed above, TUPE Regulations also provide for protecting employees from being unfairly dismissed by their employers because of a relevant transfer. Therefore, by virtue of regulation 7(1) of TUPE 2006, where an employee is dismissed either before or after a relevant transfer and the sole or principal reason for the dismissal is the transfer, such a dismissal is deemed to be automatically unfair.[36]

Regulation 7(1) provides that:

> Where either before or after a relevant transfer, any employee of the transferor or transferee is dismissed, that employee shall be treated for the purposes of Part X of the 1996 Act (unfair dismissal) as unfairly dismissed if the sole or principal reason for his dismissal is the transfer.

33 J. McMullen, "Restructuring and TUPE" *Ind. L. J.* (2012) 41(3) 358–362.

34 Under the Limitation Act 1980, a claim or an action for a personal injury or death is subjected to a three-year time frame within which to initiate a claim. However, the provisions of the Limitation Act 1980 may be applied differently where a claim, such as for an illness that manifests itself after a long period of time is initiated. The claimant may not be subjected to a strict time frame of three years. In such instances, the time does not run against such a claim from the time the injury was suffered. Rather, time starts to run against the claimant from the time the illness is discovered. See, Limitation Act 1980, s.33.

35 A 'risk-averse' company is one which chooses to invest in business transactions with known risks that may provide low returns than unknown risks with higher predictable returns.

36 TUPE 2006, regulation 7(1). This point was further affirmed and emphasised by the Court of Appeal in *Spaceright Europe Ltd v Baillavoine and Another* [2011] EWCA Civ. 1565.

Therefore, it may be drawn from the above provision that the overall aim of regulation 7(1) is to restrict employers from unfairly dismissing employees during relevant transfers to either make their insolvent but viable business attractive to potential buyers or dismissing employees and offering to rehire them on arguably new, revised or unfavourable terms.[37] However, a dismissal may be potentially but not automatically unfair where the reasons for the dismissal are either for economic, technical or organisational (ETO) reasons[38] entailing changes in the workforce.[39]

This may have the effect that the restriction on employers not to unfairly dismiss employees because of relevant transfers may be relaxed where the employer dismisses employees for economic, technical or organisational reasons. For example, the employer may carry out staff restructuring so as to comply with the terms of a business, such as a retendering process.[40] Where this is the case, the economic, technical or organisational exception to the unfair dismissal presumption may be balanced against employer's business rescue prospects.

In addition to the above, regulation 7(1) has the mandate of ensuring that employers (transferors) or the appropriate owners of the businesses subject to a relevant transfer accept or assume liability for unfair dismissal because of a relevant transfer. This is especially where the dismissals were not for economic, technical or organisational reasons entailing changes in the workforce but were for strategic reasons such as to make the business on sale attractive to potential buyers.[41]

However, it may be noted that despite the mandate by regulation 7(1) to protect employees from unfair dismissals because of the relevant transfer, the ARD also seeks to strike a balance between the interests of employees and business owners (transferors).[42] Therefore, there is a need to balance the application and operation of regulation 7(1) against its possible consequences or effect on the transferors' ability to effect business decisions that would enable successful sale of their insolvent but viable businesses. This is the need to keep the operation of regulation 7(1) within the bounds contemplated by the ARD. Per Briggs LJ in *Crystal Palace F.C and Another v Kavanagh and Another*:[43]

> [t]he tie-breaker which must be applied to resolve the potential conflict between the Insolvency Code and the TUPE regime for the protection of employees in the UK, is at least, regulation 7 of the 2006 Regulations.

37 See, *Hazel v Manchester College* [2014] EWCA Civ. 72.

38 TUPE Regulations 2006, regulation 7(2).

39 For example, compare and contrast *Spaceright Europe Ltd v Baillavoine and Another* [2011] EWCA Civ. 1565 and *Crystal Palace F.C Ltd v Kavanagh and Others* [2014] IRLR 139, CA.

40 For example, see, *Addison v Community Integrated Care* [UKEAT/250779/11].

41 In *Spaceright*, Mummery LJ held obiter that for an ETO reason to be available, the employer must have had the intention to make changes in the workforce and the continuation of the business as opposed to making the business attractive for sale. Mummery LJ, para. 47.

42 J. Prassl, "Freedom of Contract as a General Principle of EU Law? Transfers of Undertakings and the Protection of Employer Rights in EU Labour Law: Case C-426/11 *Alermo-Herron and Others v Parkwood Leisure Ltd*" (2013) 42 *Ind. L. J.* 434.

43 *Crystal Palace F.C and Another v Kavanagh and Another* [2014] IRLR 139, CA.

> It was designed to implement in the UK, the spirit and intendment of Art. 4.1 of the Directive...[44]

The job of balancing the interests of employees and employers during relevant transfers may therefore, be achieved through TUPE regulation 7(2) as a balancing provision. However, to achieve the balance needed between employees' and employers' interests during relevant transfers, judicial interpretation and application of regulation 7(2) would need to be approached in a manner that sets out to achieve this balance. However, the interpretation and application of regulation 7 during relevant transfers by the UK courts and employment tribunals has been the subject of inconsistent approaches, especially, where regulation 7(2) is used as an exception to regulation 7(1) as analysed below.

Economic, technical and organisational (ETO) reasons

By virtue of regulation 7(2), some employee dismissals before or after a relevant transfer may not be deemed automatically unfair provided the reason for the dismissals is an ETO reason entailing changes in the workforce. While such a dismissal may be potentially unfair, it may not be automatically unfair.[45] In such instances, the dismissal is treated by virtue of s.98 (1) (b) of Employment Rights Act (ERA) 1996 as being carried out for either redundancy or other substantial reasons.

Regulation 7(2) provides that:

> This Paragraph applies where the sole or principal reason for the dismissal is an economic, technical or organisational reason entailing changes in the workforce of either the transferor or transferee before or after a relevant transfer.

Therefore, regulation 7(2) where applicable, may be seen as an exception or a defence to the automatic unfair presumption of employee dismissals enshrined in regulation 7(1) during relevant transfers provided the employer can provide that the reasons for the employees' dismissals were for economic, technical or organisational reasons entailing changes in the workforce.[46]

In this perspective, regulation 7(2) may be seen as a balancing provision that may be used to balance both employees' rights of protection from unfair dismissal and at the same time, balancing the rights of employers. This is by affording employers a 'window of opportunity' to make business decisions that would address their business needs as going concerns without fear of potential consequences or liabilities from employees for breach of regulation 7(1) or regulations 4(4).

44 Ibid., per Briggs LJ. para. 24.

45 Per the reasoning in *Meade & Baxendale v British Fuels Ltd* [1998] ICR 387, CA.

46 J. McMullen, "TUPE, Variation of Employment Terms and the ETO Reason" (2014) 43 (3) *Ind. L. J.* 364.

However, it should be noted that regulation 7(2) may be used by employers strategically to escape liabilities arising from unfair dismissals during relevant transfers.[47] It is the concern that an employer may use regulation 7(2) as an escape route to effect business decisions under the protection of ETO exceptions and those reasons may disingenuously be termed as ETO reasons. This is because the terms economic, technical or organisational reasons have no statutory definitions of what they are or what they may entail within the ARD or TUPE Regulations.

However, the Department for Business, Enterprise and Regulatory Reforms (BERR) (former Department for Trade and Industry (DTI)) and now the Department for Business, Innovation and Skills issued a guidance note on 28 June 2006[48] explaining what the terms economic, technical and organisational reasons may entail. However, the guidance did not give a definition of the terms but it gave an explanation of what the terms may involve, leaving the uncertainty unsolved. The guidance indicated that an economic reason may relate to the running or operations of the business. The guidance further provided that the term technical or organisational might include reasons relating to the nature of equipment or production process that the transferee operates.[49]

To this effect, the courts and tribunals through a case by case basis have interpreted and applied the ETO reasons variedly, basing their decisions on the facts existing in the case before them. However, the courts' and tribunals' varied approaches have also not provided a binding legal precedent to date from which guidance may be drawn.[50] This has created more tensions between the policies underlying employment protection and the policies underlying the rescue of insolvent but viable businesses during relevant transfers.

Moreover, the effect of regulation 7(2) on the employee is that, if dismissed either before or after the transfer in question, the employee has to show that the dismissal suffered was because of the relevant transfer. The burden in this instance falls onto the employee. As for employers, they may be able to justify why such a dismissal took place, whether it was for economic, technical or organisational reasons and whether any changes in the work force took place.

In *Ibex Trading v Walton & other*,[51] The EAT upheld an employer's (administrators') decision to dismiss 40 employees out of the 90 employed prior to

47 Amie J. Ahanchian, "Reducing the Impact of the European Union's Invisible Hand on the Economy by Limiting the Application of the Transfer of Undertakings Provisions" (2002) 2 *J. Int. Comp. L.* 29, 49.

48 Available at < www.berr.gov.uk/files/file20761.pdf> (accessed 5 June 2019).

49 Ibid., pgs. 14, 15.

50 For example, in *Whitehouse v Blatchford and Sons Ltd* [1999] IRLR 492, the EAT was of the view that an economic reason must be connected with the conduct or running of the business and not a dismissal made merely to achieve better returns for the undertaking being transferred. However, in *Wheeler v Patel* [1987] IRLR 211, the EAT had earlier held that the term economic must be interpreted as having the same contextual meaning as technical or organisational running or conduct of the business.

51 *Ibex Trading v Walton & Other* [1994] ICR 907, EAT.

the relevant transfer. The EAT was of the view that because there had been no transfer in contemplation at the time of the dismissal, the dismissals were not connected with the transfer and therefore not unfair. The EAT further acknowledged that the business needed to be made attractive to prospective buyers as it was uneconomic.[52]

ITC Limited that employed the claimants entered into administration in August 1991. The appointed administrators decided to downsize on the number of employees. The administrators also made some changes to the salaries of the non-transferring employees as a measure of reducing the company's debts with a view to selling the business as a going concern. Forty of the ninety employees were dismissed prior to selling the business in February 1992. A claim for unfair dismissal was brought against the transferee but the dismissals were held to be for an economic reason entailing changes in the workforce and therefore not automatically unfair.

It may be argued that this judgement may indicate that judges may interpret ETO reasons differently depending on the facts surrounding the employer's reasons for the decisions made under the ETO principle. In this instance, the decision was more on the side of business rescue than employee protection.

Similarly in *Enterprise Managed Services Ltd v Dance and Others*,[53] Enterprise Managed Services Ltd (EMS) which had contracts for building and maintenance services with the Ministry of Defence inherited ex-employees of Williams Ltd following a TUPE transfer. After the transfer, EMS consulted with the transferred employees to change their terms and conditions to bring them in line with those of its existing employees. EMS failed to reach an agreement with the transferred employees. The transferred employees rejected the changes and brought a claim for unfair dismissals. The EAT overturned the ET's decision which had stated that the dismissals were effected so as to harmonise the terms and conditions of the transferee employees with those of the existing employees so as to increase efficiency and productivity.

The EAT held that:

> ...[s]ince it is open to an employer to effect productivity changes in accordance with the ordinary law, this does not become unlawful when there has been a relevant transfer if the reason is connected to that drive for productivity changes.[54]

This is another judgement that gives employers a greater level of flexibility to exercise their business decisions. From the facts of this case, it seemed clear that the employer's intention was to harmonise the terms of the transferred employees with those of the existing employees which may be contrary to the procedural and substantive provisions of regulation 4(4). Although it has been acknowledged

52 Ibid., para. 14.
53 *Enterprise Managed Services Ltd v Dance and Others* [UKEAT/0200/11].
54 Ibid., para. 20.

that employers who inherit employees following TUPE transfers often find it difficult to manage them on different terms and conditions from their existing employees as it would be administratively challenging,[55] this judgement further highlights the courts' and tribunals' 'due-regard' to the employers' ETO reasons for making variations or dismissals during relevant transfers.

Liability for Pre–transfer and post-transfer dismissals: who assumes liability?

By virtue of regulation 7(1) of TUPE 2006, liabilities for unfair dismissals prior to a relevant transfer that are automatically unfair are inherited by the transferee courtesy of the automatic transfer provision in regulation 4(1) and (2). The automatic transfer of liabilities to the transferee is however, rebutted where the dismissals were for an ETO reason entailing changes in the workforce courtesy of regulation 7(2). In this instance, liabilities for pre-transfer unfair dismissals remain with the transferor.

In *Spaceright Europe Ltd v Baillavoine and Another*,[56] the chief executive officer Mr. Baillavoine was dismissed on the same day that the company (Ultralon Holdings Ltd) that employed him went into administration. A month following his dismissal, Ultralon was sold to Spaceright Europe Ltd as a going concern. Mr. Baillavoine brought a claim for unfair dismissal on the ground that his dismissal was necessitated by the transfer. Therefore, it was automatically unfair.

The ET and the EAT both held that Mr. Baillavoine's dismissal was connected with the business sale which made it automatically unfair. However, the decision of the EAT was appealed to the CA. The CA further upheld the ET and EAT's ruling that Mr. Baillavoine was unfairly dismissed by the transferor so as to make the business more attractive to the buyer, as the buyer would be at liberty to appoint a CEO of its choice following the relevant transfer.

Although regulation 7(1) (b) (the requirement for the dismissal to be connected with the transfer) has now been repealed by TUPE 2014, *Spaceright* is good authority and a warning to business owners that employee dismissals prior to a relevant transfer to make the business more attractive to potential buyers would be deemed an unfair practice and contrary to the spirit and intentions of the ARD and TUPE. The dismissals would also fall into the current provision of regulation 7(1) in TUPE 2014 that such a dismissal would be because of the transfer.

However, earlier in *Thompson v SCS Consulting Ltd*,[57] the EAT had held that Mr. Thompson who had been dismissed 11 hours before a relevant transfer took place was dismissed for an ETO reason entailing changes in the workforce. Therefore, the dismissal was not automatically unfair. The EAT was of

55 On this particular point, see the comments of Underhill L J. in *Hazel & Another v Manchester College* [2014] IRLR 392 (CA).

56 *Spaceright Europe Ltd v Baillavoine and another* [2011] EWCA Civ. 1565.

57 *Thompson v SCS Consulting Ltd* [2001] IRLR 801, EAT, (*Thompson*).

the opinion that the dismissal of Mr. Thompson was part of the need by the employer to reduce the size of the workforce as the business was overstaffed, inefficient and insolvent. Therefore, despite the fact that the dismissal was so close to the relevant transfer, it was held not to be a case of a dismissal to secure the sale of the insolvent undertaking. In this case, liability for the dismissal remained with the transferor.

However, on analysing both cases above, it may be submitted that both varying decisions illustrate that the interpretation and application of regulation 7 to relevant transfer cases is a still a major challenge to courts and tribunals. For example, in *Thompson*, it may be argued that the dismissal of Mr. Thompson would, on the normal principles of regulation 7(1), be unfair because of its closeness to the relevant transfer. Mr. Thompson was immediately employed until he was dismissed on the same day the transferor went into administration. Moreover, the fact that the dismissal was for the need to downsize on the workforce would be contrary to the jurisprudence of regulation 7(1), yet the dismissal was held to be for an ETO reason. However, in *Spaceright*, the dismissal was held to be automatically unfair mainly because of its 'connection with the transfer'.

From this perspective, it may be concluded that this area of TUPE is still proving a challenge both in application and interpretation to employers, employees and the courts and tribunals. Although the courts and tribunals ought to balance the interests of employees and employers in interpreting and applying ETO exceptions, the lack of a statutory definition or binding precedent in this area of TUPE is not helping to balance the tension between employment protection and the rescue of insolvent but viable business in the UK. This is an area of TUPE that Dworkin's interpretative approach to law would help to balance as discussed in the next chapter.

Regulation 7 under TUPE 2014 changes

Prior to the changes to the TUPE 2006 brought by The Collective Redundancies and Transfer of Undertakings (Protection of Employment)(Amendment) Regulations 2014,[58] it was a requirement of regulation 7 (1) (a) and (b) that a dismissal would be automatically unfair where the reason for the dismissal is the transfer, or a reason 'connected with the transfer', that is not an ETO reason entailing changes in workforce.[59] However, TUPE 2014 amended regulation 7(1) (b) so that it is no longer sufficient for the dismissal to be 'connected with' the transfer in establishing if the dismissal was automatically unfair or not. In effect, regulation 7(1)(b) has now been repealed by TUPE 2014.

On the backdrop of the changes to regulation 7(1), employees were already subject to a 'qualifying test' in terms of qualification period required to claim unfair dismissal from their employers in case of a relevant transfer. Employees

58 Hereafter cited as TUPE 2014.
59 TUPE 2006, regulation 7(1) (a) and (b).

are required to satisfy a two-year qualifying period, before a claim for unfair dismissal pursuant to regulation 7(1) may be made. This may be seen as being unfair to employees, especially those that may not have completed a two-year period of employment with their employer during which a TUPE relevant transfer takes place.[60]

Their employment relationship that is being terminated may be an employee's only source of livelihood. If that employment is unfairly terminated and employees are not awarded any compensatory damages because they have not been in that employment continuously for two years, this may leave them in an unfavourable position. This would be in contrast to their colleagues that are able to satisfy the two-year qualification period, and therefore, awarded some form of compensation for the loss of their jobs.

In addition, continuity of employment (for the purposes of regulation 7(1)) may be affected where there are breaks in employment which may affect the mutuality of obligation between the employee and the employer.[61] Similarly, under ERA 1996, s.94, an employee has a right not to be unfairly dismissed by the employer but there is a qualification requirement under s.108 for an employee to have been employed for two years prior to the dismissal before that employee may be qualified to initiate such a claim against the employer.

Therefore, per Briggs LJ,[62] there is a need to contain regulation 7 within its parameters, if both policies underlying employee protection during relevant transfers and those of boosting corporate rescue as intended by both the ARD and TUPE are to be pursued simultaneously. Regulation 7(2) ought to be approached as a balancing provision between the interests of employees and employers but its application to relevant transfers has so far failed to achieve the balance needed. Case law from the courts and tribunals on the interpretation and application of regulation 7(2) has highlighted a significant number of inconsistent judgements, which has not been helpful in balancing both policy objectives.

Protection from contractual terms and conditions variation

During relevant transfers, employees are protected from having their terms and conditions of employment varied by the transferor or transferee where the reason

60 However, in *Milligan & Another v Securicor Cleaning Ltd* [1995] IRLR 288, EAT, the EAT allowed unfair dismissal claims of some employees that had not completed the two years qualifying period with their employer to stand relying on the second part of Art. 4.1 of the 1977 Directive. The EAT however, was very specific that any such exception would have to be specifically identified by the Court.

61 *Carmichael & Another v National Power Plc.*, [1999] ICR 1226 (HL). However, continuity is preserved where gaps between employments are related to the machinery of the transfer. See, *Macer v Abafast Ltd* [1990] IRLR 477 (HL).

62 Per Briggs LJ, '...[t]he tie-breaker which must be applied to resolve the potential conflict between the Insolvency Code and the TUPE regime for the protection of employees in the UK, is at least, regulation 7 of the 2006 Regulations. It was designed to implement in the UK, the spirit and intendment of Art. 4.1 of the Directive...' Briggs LJ in *Crystal Palace*, para. 24.

for the variation is the transfer.[63] This pillar of employee protection was affirmed by the ECJ in the case of *Foreningen AF Arbedjsldere I Denmark v Daddy's Dance Hall*[64] which serves as the founding authority in relation to prohibiting employee contractual terms and conditions variation by employers before and after a relevant transfer.

The ECJ held in this case that an employment relationship may be altered with regard to the transferee to the same extent as it could have been for the transferor, provided the reason for the amendment is not the transfer itself.[65] The provision in regulation 4(4) is to ensure that employees enjoy the same terms and conditions of employment post-transfer as they did pre-transfer.

Regulation 4(4) provides that:

> Subject to regulation 9, in respect of a contract of employment that is, or will be transferred by paragraph (1), any purported variation of the contract shall be void if the sole or principal reason for the variation is the transfer.

However, despite the protection from variation to employee contracts pre-and post-relevant transfer, there is no statutory timescale within regulation 4(4) upon which an employer may or may not vary employment terms and conditions. The wording in regulation 4(4) places a prohibition on variations post transfer but do not give a specific timeframe within which such a prohibition on variation applies. This has meant that the scope of application of this provision has been decided by the courts and tribunals on a case by case basis.

However, these judgements highlight the lack of a single binding approach to be adopted by courts and tribunals in dealing contractual variations during relevant transfers. This further highlights the challenges that courts and tribunals face in interpreting and applying ETO reasons to facts before the courts and tribunals as the employer often has a wider scope within which to devise an ETO reason to justify the need for the variation or harmonisation of contractual terms and conditions. This has not helped ultimately to balance both the policy objectives of employment protection on the one hand and the policy objectives of corporate rescue on the other.[66]

For example, in *London Metropolitan University v Sackur & Others*,[67] the transferee University, London Metropolitan University (LMU) had been formed following a merger of two universities. After the merger, LMU proposed to harmonise the terms and conditions of employment contracts and started negotiations with employees. The negotiations broke down and LMU imposed new

63 TUPE 2006, regulation 4(4).

64 [1988] IRLR 315 ECJ. (*Daddy's Dance Hall*).

65 Ibid., para. 33.

66 J. McMullen, "TUPE: Ringing the (Wrong) Changes – The Collective Redundancies and Transfer of Undertakings (Protection of Employment) (Amendment) Regulations 2014" (2014) 43 Ind. L. J. 149.

67 *London Metropolitan University v Sackur & Others* [UKEAT/0286/06]. (Hereafter *London Met*).

terms and conditions. A claim for an unfair dismissal resulting from unlawful contractual variations was initiated against the transferee two years after the transfer. The ET found for the dismissed employees, holding that the dismissals were borne out of a variation (harmonisation) of contract terms following the transfer. At the EAT, the transferee's ETO defence was rejected as the harmonisation attempt did not entail changes in the work force.

However, in *Ralton v Havering College of Further and Higher Education*,[68] the EAT held that additional factors, such as economic, technical or organisational reasons may influence the employer to make business decisions, such as pay structural changes and may rely on these reasons as a ground to vary contract terms and conditions.

In this case, three college lecturers were employed on terms effected by a collective bargaining agreement between the local authorities and their recognised trade unions. Some of the employees were on fixed term contracts and upon expiry of those contracts, they were offered new contracts but on new terms in accordance with the College's terms and conditions. Some accepted the terms and promotion while others rejected them. An action was later brought against the employer for unfair contractual variations following a relevant transfer.

The main focus of the EAT in this case was to establish whether the changes to the terms of employment were as a result of the transfer which would render the variations invalid. The EAT held that as a requirement of the ARD on the automatic transfer of the employment relations, the lecturers would transfer on their existing terms and conditions. However, the college had the flexibility to offer new terms and conditions on promotions or renewals of fixed term contracts because some additional factors in the education sector, such as the demand for courses, need for promotions, et cetera would influence business decision.

From these two judgements, it may be submitted that despite the need to protect employees from unfair variations to their contract terms following a relevant transfer, the need to protect businesses to enable them to make changes so that they may operate successfully has not been overlooked by the Judges.[69] Very often, an employer's attempts to harmonise terms and conditions of employment involve changes to employees' term and conditions of employment.[70] When affected employees reject these harmonised terms and conditions, claims for unfair dismissal or constructive dismissal precipitated by the changes to their employment terms and condition may be initiated by the employees. However,

68 *Ralton v Havering College of Further and Higher Education* [2001] IRLR 743, EAT. (Hereafter *Ralton*).

69 For example, see cases such as; *Thompson v SCS Consulting Ltd* [2001] IRLR 801, EAT; *Spacerright Europe Ltd v Baillavoine and another* [2011] EWCA Civ. 1565; *Hazel v Manchester College* [2014] EWCA Civ. 72; *Crystal Palace F.C and Another v Kavanagh and Another* [2014] IRLR 139, (CA).

70 *Enterprise Managed Services Ltd v Dance and Others* [UKEAT/0200/11]; *Smith & Ors v Trustees of Brooklands College* [2011] UKEAT 0128/0509]; *Hazel v Manchester College* [2014] EWCA Civ. 72.

TUPE Regulations offer employers a broader scope within which to justify the reasons for the variation or harmonisation of contract terms and conditions via the ETO exception route.[71]

In *London Met*, although the claimants based their claim on unfair dismissal by the employer, their unfair dismissal claim was occasioned by the variation to their contractual terms and conditions through harmonisation. In *Ralton*, the claim was based on unfair variation to contract terms and conditions. However, despite both cases being initiated on different grounds, they both highlight the technicalities and challenges presented by TUPE Regulations, especially, on the interpretation and application of the ETO exceptions to contractual variations during relevant transfers.

The relevance of certain provisions, such as regulation 7(2) that provides employers with a degree of flexibility to justify their reasons for the need to vary contract terms and conditions for either economic, technical or organisational needs of their businesses has meant that business owners are not over burdened by TUPE Regulations from operating successfully.[72]

In addition to the lack of a specified timeframe upon which contractual variations may be justified, TUPE Regulations allow some other variations to contractual terms and conditions to be agreed under what is termed as 'permissible variations' under regulation 4(5) of TUPE 2006 as discussed below.

Permissible variation under regulation 4

Regulation 4(4) may not prevent an employer from varying employment contract terms and conditions where there are economic, technical or organisational reasons entailing changes in the workforce as reasons for the variations provided the variations are agreed between the employer and the employee.[73]

Regulation 4(5) of TUPE 2006 provides that:

> Paragraph (4) shall not prevent an employer and his employee whose contract of employment is, or will be transferred by Paragraph (1) from agreeing a variation of that contract if the sole or principal reason for the variation is:
>
> a a reason connected with the transfer that is an economic, technical or organisational reason entailing changes in the workforce
>
> b a reason unconnected with the transfer.

From the substantive reading of this provision, it may be construed that this provision aims at affording a certain degree of flexibility to employers to be able to negotiate with employees to agree to certain contractual variations through

71 Prassl, 'Freedom of Contract" (n 5).

72 S. Hardy and Richard W. Painter, "The New Acquired Rights Directive and its Implications for European Employees Relations in the Twenty-first Century" (1996) 6(4) *MaastJECL* 336, 378.

73 TUPE 2006, regulation 4(5).

peaceful measures. This would be a form of encouraging entrepreneurial relations between the employer and the employees which would be a welcome provision given the tension that exists between employment protection policy objectives and corporate rescue policy objectives during relevant transfers.[74]

However, note ought to be taken of the possibility that employers may use this flexibility afforded via regulation 4(5) for strategic purposes to vary contract terms and conditions. Employers often have stronger bargaining powers than employees, especially, during industrial negotiations between employers and employees.[75] Moreover, most cases involving negotiations between employers and employees during relevant transfer variations to contract terms and conditions have been in favour of employers.[76]

In addition, regulation 4(5) (b) of TUPE 2006 has now been amended by TUPE 2014. The new Regulation 4(5) of TUPE 2014 provides that:

> (5) Paragraph (4) does not prevent a variation of the contract of employment if—
>
> a the sole or principal reason for the variation is an economic, technical, or organisational reason entailing changes in the workforce, provided that the employer and employee agree that variation; or
>
> b the terms of that contract permit the employer to make such a variation.

Therefore, the new regulation 4(5)(b) of TUPE 2014 now affords an employer power to vary an employee's contract where the terms of the contract permit the employer to do so, which has further given an employer an edge over an employee during negotiations for variations of contract terms and conditions during relevant transfer.

Permissible variation during 'relevant insolvency proceedings'

In addition to agreed permissible variations to contracts terms above, other variations to contract terms and conditions are permissible during relevant transfers where the objective is to safeguard jobs and continuity of employment under regulation 9.[77] However, the variation should only be carried out if it would safeguard 'employment opportunities' by ensuring the survival and continuation of the business where the transferor is subject to 'relevant insolvency proceedings' as defined under regulation 8(6) of TUPE 2006.

74 F. Baumann, "On Unobserved Worker Heterogeneity and Employment Protection" (2010) 29 (2) *Eur. J. L. Econ.* 155, 175.

75 J. Armour and S. Deakin, "The Rover Case (2): Bargaining in the Shadow of TUPE" (2000) 29 *Ind. L. J.* 395, 402.

76 See cases such as *Nationwide Building Society v Benn & Others* [UKEAT/0273/09/JOJ]; *Ralton v Havering College of Further and Higher Education* [2001] IRLR 743 EAT; *Hazel and Another v Manchester College* [2014] IRLR 392, CA.

77 TUPE 2006, regulation 9(1).

Relevant insolvency proceedings are the types of insolvency proceedings that have been instituted not with a view to the liquidation of the business assets of the company and which are under the supervision of an insolvency practitioner under regulation 8(6) of TUPE 2006.[78]

Relevant insolvency proceedings are defined under regulation 8(6) as:

> …insolvency proceedings that have been opened in relation to the transferor, not with the view to the liquidation of the business assets and which are under the supervision of an insolvency practitioner.

In light of the substantive and procedural provisions of regulation 8(6), corporate rescue processes, such as administration may be termed as 'relevant insolvency proceedings' as these rescue processes are instituted with the aim of saving the company as a going concern and not the liquidation of the assets of the company,[79] even if this is not often the outcome in practice. Therefore, TUPE provisions, such as the automatic transfer of the employment relationships under regulation 4 and the protection from unfair dismissals because of a relevant transfer under regulation 7(1) apply to these relevant insolvency proceedings.

In this context, any variations to employees' terms and conditions by the employer are deemed invalid. The variations would only be valid if there is an agreement between the appropriately recognised representatives of the employees or specially elected employee representatives with their recognised trade unions. The agreement must be recorded in writing, signed copies and guidance given to the affected employees.[80]

Variation to contract terms and conditions post TUPE 2014 changes

The amendments to the TUPE 2006 in 2014 have changed the way through which protection to employees from having their contractual terms and conditions varied by their employers before and after a relevant transfer is currently approached by employers, courts and tribunals.[81] As a recap, regulation 4(4) of TUPE 2006 provided that any purported variation to an employee's contract would be void where; (a) the sole or principal reason was the transfer itself or (b) a reason connected with the transfer that was not an ETO reason entailing changes in the workforce.

78 TUPE 2006, regulation 8(6).

79 For example, see, IA 1986, Sch. B1, para.3(1) that sets out the hierarchical objectives of administration proceedings, the first being the rescue of the company as a going concern. See also, *Oakland v Wellswood* [2009] EWCA Civ. 1094; *OTG v Barke & Ors* [2011] IRLR 272; *Key2 Law (Surrey)LLP v De' Antiquis* [2011] EWVA Civ. 1564.

80 TUPE 2006, regulation 9(5)(a) – (b).

81 J. McMullen, "TUPE, Variation of Employment Terms and the ETO Reason" (2014) 43(3) *Ind. L. J.* 364.

However, by virtue of the TUPE 2014 amendments, regulation 4(4)(b) (the requirement for the variation to be connected with the transfer) to render it void has been repealed. Therefore, regulation 4(4) of TUPE 2014 provides that;

> Subject to regulation 9, any purported variation of contract of employment that is, or will be, transferred by para (1), is void where the sole or principal reason for the variation is the transfer.

Therefore, with effect from 31 January 2014, a variation to an employment contract is only void where the sole or principal reason for the variation is the transfer. A variation by the employer, is no longer void where it is for a reason connected with the transfer that is not an ETO reason entailing changes in the workforce as was the case under TUPE 2006 regulation 4 (4)(b).

In light of this change to regulation 4(4), it may be analysed that this change narrows the scope of application of regulation 4(4) to relevant transfers as compared with the scope originally under the TUPE 2006 Regulations. This is because, reasons, such as changes to the working patterns, working hours or conditions of employment that may be 'connected with' the contract of employment that is subject to a relevant transfer that would be argued to be 'connected with' the transfer by employees are no longer relevant to render such variations invalid.

As a result, this has arguably, presented employers with a broader scope within which they can devise circumstances under which variations to employment contracts may be justified than was the case prior to the 2014 amendments. For example, a loss of a tendering proposal, reduction in projected profits or changes in market trends may arguably, be used by an employer to justify contractual variations despite the fact that such changes would have exhibited a degree of 'connection with' the transfer which would have rendered such variations void.[82]

In *Hazel v Manchester College*,[83] Manchester College tendered for contracts to provide offender learning in prisons thereby acquiring 1,500 employees via a TUPE transfer. This was in addition to almost 2,000 other employees already working in the offender learning and 3,000 employees in other departments in the College. Following the transfer, the College sought to restructure employees' contracts on grounds of public funding cuts, especially in the offender learning service and other hidden costs. The other ground was that employees in the offender learning service were on different terms and conditions to the rest of employees in other departments which was administratively challenging and risked equal pay claims from other employees.

There were proposals by the College for staff to sign new contract terms and conditions. Employees that would reject the new proposed variations would be

82 For example, see, *London Metropolitan University v Sackur* [UKEAT/26/06]; *Abellio London Ltd (formerly Travel London Ltd) v Musse & others* [2012] IRLR 360; *Meter-U Ltd v Ackroyd* [2012] IRLR 367.

83 *Hazel v Manchester College* [2014] EWCA Civ. 72; [2014] IRLR 392 CA.

dismissed and offered re-engagement on new terms and conditions. The claimants objected to the changes. They were dismissed and brought a claim against the College.

The EAT's[84] earlier ruling that the dismissals (orchestrated by the proposed contractual variations) were automatically unfair was upheld by the CA.[85] The CA followed the formulation in *Berriman v Delabole Slate*[86] and held that the phrase ETO entailing changes in the workforce was part of the ETO reason.[87] Therefore, the dismissals followed by re-engagement of another would not constitute a change in the workforce.

However, earlier in *Smith v Trustees of Brooklands College*,[88] the EAT had held that a decision by the employer to vary contract terms and conditions following a relevant transfer to rectify a pay anomaly was not invalid and therefore, did not contravene the provisions of regulation 4(4). Four teaching assistants from Spelthorne College had transferred to Brooklands College via a TUPE Transfer. At Spelthorne College, they worked part time hours but were paid a full-time salary and also enjoyed the same benefits as full time staff. Brooklands proposed variations to salary terms and conditions so as to align them with the sector at large. The variations were to the material detriment of the transferred teaching assistants. They brought an action for unlawful variations to their salary terms and conditions. They also argued that 'but for' the transfer these variations would not have happened.

The EAT held that the contractual variations could have been done at any time irrespective of the TUPE transfer. It was an attempt to rectify a pay anomaly. It was the genuine belief by the decision maker (the employer) that the four teaching assistants had been mistakenly paid at a different rate which was out of step with the rest of the employees in the same sector.

HHJ McMullen held obiter that, the 'but/for' test, in other words, '...the contention by the claimants that 'but for the transfer, their pay structure would not have been varied...'" by their employer' was not the correct test to apply in such a case. Rather, 'what was in the mind of the employer'.[89] If the 'but for' test was to be applied, it would imply that 'but for the transfer', the four teaching assistants' pay would not have been reduced by the employer. HHJ McMullen further opined that the question would be; what was the reason that caused the employer to reduce the pay?

The decision in *Brooklands* may be seen as a policy decision by the EAT to let employers take business decisions that would benefit their businesses' restructuring and continuity prospects without fear of burdensome transfer liabilities.

84 *Hazel & Another v The Manchester College* [UKEAT/0642/11/RN] EAT, para. 59.
85 *Hazel v Manchester College* [2014] IRLR 392, CA, (Underhill LJ). Para. 6.
86 *Berriman v Delabole Slate* [1985] ICR 546. CA. 'A change in the terms and conditions of employees who are continuing in employment cannot be a change in the workforce. A change in the workforce means a change in the number or composition of the workforce'.
87 *Hazel v Manchester College* [2014] EWCA Civ. 72; [2014] IRLR 392 CA, para. 15.
88 *Smith v Trustees of Brooklands College* [EAT/0128/11].
89 Ibid., (HHJ McMullen), para. 28.

The judgement further highlights the different approaches through which the courts and tribunals interpret and apply employers' ETO reasons for effecting contractual variations pre and post relevant transfers, which has attracted some varied commentaries.[90]

However, despite the inconsistencies in the judgements above, it may be submitted that the changes brought by the TUPE 2014 to regulation 4, especially, on the requirement for an ETO reason to entail 'changes in the workforce' has somewhat narrowed the scope of protection for employees on the one hand, and widened the scope for employers on the other.

The effect of this change in the scope of employment protection is that, the narrower the scope of employment protection provisions, the less the potential liabilities on the employer (transferor) and prospective buyer of the business (transferee). Although this would be good for corporate rescue as insolvent but viable business may be more attractive to potential buyers due to fewer potential liabilities, however, narrowing the scope of protection to employee would arguably, create further imbalances between employment protection and corporate rescue.

In addition to changes brought about by the TUPE 2014, TUPE 2014 Regulations have incorporated a new regulation 4(5A) which provides that 'changes in the workforce' now include changes to the place where employees are employed or carry out their work. More still, agreed variations to workplace changes between the employer and employee following a relevant transfer would no longer be void.[91]

Regulation 4(5A) states that:

> (5A) In paragraph (5), the expression "changes in the workforce" includes a change to the place where employees are employed by the employer to carry on the business of the employer or to carry out work of a particular kind for the employer (and the reference to such a place has the same meaning as in Section 139 of the 1996 Act.

Although this may be seen as a move by the TUPE Regulation to consolidate a form of industrial democracy by encouraging employers and employees to negotiate and agree to certain contractual variations, such as to workplace concerns following relevant transfers, however, TUPE 2014 may have inadvertently widened the 'pool' of factors that may entail changes in the workforce that may weaken the protection to employees from contractual variations before and after relevant transfers that the ARD originally intended.[92]

90 See for example, J. Armour and S. Deakin, "Insolvency and Employment Protection: The Mixed Effects of the Acquired Rights Direct" (2003) 22 *Int. Rev. Law. Econ.* 443, 463; J. McMullen, "Restructuring and TUPE" (2012) 41(3) *Ind. L. J.* 358–362.

91 TUPE 2014, regulation 4 (5A).

92 Professor Albert Dicey's observations on law's unintended outcomes may be a guiding principle here. Professor Dicey observes that, '[t]he beneficial effect of state intervention, especially in

Contractual variations are also permissible where the terms of the contract allow the employer to make such variations pursuant to regulation 4(5)(b). However, it is worth noting that permissible variations as prescribed in regulation 4(5) require the ETO reasons for the variation to entail changes in the workforce, otherwise, a mere variation to the contractual terms and conditions, such as changes to employees' title,[93] without changes in the actual number of employees or changes in the activities would be void.[94]

As a consequence, genuine cases of dismissals or redundancies resulting from changes to workplace locations are no longer automatically unfair and employees may not be able to initiate claims against their employers in this regard as was the case under TUPE 2006. Moreover, it is a concern that where an employer fails to agree voluntary variations to work place changes with employees, the employer may arguably, be able to devise an ETO reason to justify the need for changes to employees' workplace locations due to the widened scope of regulation 4(5) (a) and such variations may not be held to be 'connected with' the transfer as this requirement is no longer applicable.

In addition, the widened scope of regulation 4(5A) may persuade employers to insert variation clauses, such as to workplace locations into employment contracts and may use such variation clauses to justify contractual variations before or after relevant transfers.[95] Moreover, new regulation 4(5A) may be construed as being in contrast with regulation 4(9) of TUPE 2006 which states that '… [w]here a relevant transfer involves or would involve a substantial change in working conditions to the employee's material detriment,… that employee may treat the contract of employment as having been terminated …and the employee shall be treated …as having been dismissed by the employer'.[96]

By analysing regulation 4(9) of TUPE 2006 above, one may infer that where an employer executes a contractual variation such as a variation to an employee's workplace location to that employee's material detriment, that employee would be at liberty to initiate a claim against that employer for constructive dismissal where the sole or principal reason for the variation is the transfer per

---

the form of legislation are indirect, immediate, and so to speak, visible, whilst its evil effects are gradual, indirect and lie out of sight…' see, Albert V. Dicey, "Law and Public Opinion in England in the 19th Century", in Richard Vande Wetering (ed.) *Lectures on the Relations between Law and Public Opinion in England during the 19th Century*, (Indianapolis, New Liberty Fund Book, 2008) 257–258.

93 For example, see *Green v Elan Care Ltd* [UKEAT/0018/01] where the court held that a change (demotion) in title from a senior manager to a senior carer did not entail changes in the workforce.

94 *Hazel v Manchester College* [2014] EWCA Civ. 72; [2014] IRLR 392 CA, Per Underhill LJ, para. 15.

95 See for example, *Bateman v Asda Stores Ltd* [UKEAT/0221/09] where the staff handbook contained a clause that the company (Asda) 'reserved the right to review, revise, amend or replace the contents of the employees' handbook from time to time reflecting the changing need of the business'. Asda used this clause to impose a pay structure on its employees without further consent from them.

96 See, TUPE 2006, regulation 4(9).

TUPE 2006.[97] However, this protective provision of TUPE 2006 is substantively weakened by regulation 4(5A).[98]

The term 'changes in the workforce' as stated under regulation 4(5A) TUPE 2014 now includes a 'change to the place where employees are employed by the employer to carry on the business of the employer or to carry out work of a particular kind for the employer'. Therefore, a change to a work location by an employer whether it is to the employees' material detriment or not may not provide sufficient grounds for an employer to treat that employment contract as terminated and claim constructive dismissal as it was under regulation 4(9) of TUPE 2006.

Contractual variations on collective bargaining incorporated terms and conditions

Employee contracts of employment whose terms and conditions have been incorporated from collective bargaining agreements may be varied by the employer following a period of one-year post-relevant transfer by virtue of regulation 4(5B) of the TUPE 2014 Regulations. This provision allows for contractual variations to terms and condition even where the reason for the variation is the transfer itself[99] provided that the relevant time period has elapsed.

However, the variation is subject to a condition that the rights and obligations in the employees' contracts should not be less favourable to the employees than would be following the variations if considered altogether. Nevertheless, this provision may be seen as being in contrast with the provisions of regulation 4(4) on the protection from non-CBA contractual variations before and after the transfer. This is because, regulation 4(4) does not contain provisions on prescribed timeframes within which an employer may vary contractual terms and conditions following a relevant transfer. Employees enjoy the protection in regulation 4(4) indefinitely unless the variations are for ETO reasons entailing changes in the workforce.[100]

From the provisions of regulation 4(5B), it is a concern that employees' contractual terms and conditions derived from CBAs may be vulnerable to variations by their employer. Where this is this case, it would be a form of creating a 'two-tier' level of protection categories; employees on general non-CBA incorporated terms contracts and those on CBA incorporated terms contracts. In view of this prospect, employees on CBA incorporated terms contracts would be on lesser protection than their counterparts which may weaken the notions underlying the policies for collective bargaining and trade union movement in the UK as a form of industrial democracy.

97 See cases such as *Tapere v South London and Maudsley NHS Trust* [2009] IRLR 972; *Abellio London Ltd (formerly Travel London Ltd) v Musse & others* [2012] IRLR 360; *RR Donnelley Global Document Solutionss Group Ltd v (1) Besagni and (2) NSL Ltd* [UKEAT/0397/13].

98 Charles Wynn-Evans, "Transfers of Undertakings – Principles and Pragmatism in the CJEU" (2014) 130 *Ind. L. J.* 202.

99 TUPE 2014, regulation 4(5B).

100 McMullen (n 66) 147.

Conclusion

By analysing the TUPE Regulations during relevant transfers in the UK, it may be concluded that TUPE Regulations were brought into force to serve a dual purpose. The first purpose is to safeguard the rights of employees during relevant transfers. The second purpose is to regulate the facilitation of relevant transfers. TUPE Regulations may achieve this by mitigating the effect that relevant transfers may present to the interests of employers and the interests of employees during relevant transfers. However, these two purposes of TUPE Regulations are in conflict with each other, if both purposes are pursued simultaneously.[101]

TUPE provisions, such as regulations 4(1) and 4(2) on the automatic transfer of employment relationships, rights and liabilities, regulation 4(4) on the prohibition on employers unfairly varying contractual terms and conditions and regulation 7(1) on employee protection from unfair dismissals because of relevant transfer are typical employee protection provisions.

On the other hand, regulations such as regulation 4(5) on agreed permissible variation, regulation 9(1) on permissible variation where the transferor is the subject of insolvency proceedings and regulation 7(2) on ETO exceptions to unfair dismissals in regulation 7(1) may be viewed as provisions that are aimed at empowering employers. These regulations may support employers to make business decisions that may enhance corporate rescue prospects of insolvent but viable business without being over-burdened by specific employee protection provisions of TUPE Regulations.[102] However, very often, employer decisions, especially, the decisions made under regulation 7(2) – ETO exceptions, may threaten employment protection provisions in regulations 4(1), 4(4) and regulation 7(1).[103]

Therefore, it may be concluded that pursuing these dual purposes of TUPE simultaneously creates a tension between the policy objectives of employment protection and the policy objectives of encouraging and promoting the rescue of insolvent but viable businesses that the ARD and TUPE Regulations may have sought to achieve. It should be noted that very often, an employer's attempt to rescue an insolvent but viable business by selling it as a going concern may involve the need to reduce labour costs as labour is one of the biggest costs of production or service provision.[104]

The employer may also consider making some changes to employees' terms and conditions of employment as a form of restructuring the operational structures of the business to enhance the chances of successfully selling the insolvent but viable business as a going concern. However, the employer may be constricted by

101 Samuel E. Etukakpan, "Business Rescue and Continuity of Employment: Analysing Policies through Lens of Theories" (2011) 32(4) *Company Lawyer* 99, 113.

102 S. Hardy and Richard W. Painter, "The New Acquired Rights Directive and its Implications for European Employees Relations in the Twenty-first Century" (1996) 6(4) *MaastJECL* 336, 378.

103 M. Sergeant, "Business Transfers and Corporate Insolvencies – The Effects of TUPE" (1998) 14(1) *I. L. P.* 8.

104 Lester C. Thurow, *The Future of Capitalism* (New York, W. Morrow & Co, 1996); J. E Stiglitz, "Employment, Social Justice and Societal Well-being" (2002) 141 *Int'l Labour Rev.* 9–29.

the fear of potential liabilities that may arise out of breaching the procedural and substantive provisions of the TUPE Regulations, such as regulations 4 and 7(1) which are aimed at employee protection during relevant transfers.

Moreover, the restrictions on the employer in regulations 4 and 7 may be compounded by the automatic and mandatory inheritance of several known and unknown liabilities on the transferee under regulation 4(2). The sum of all these concerns may mean that prospective buyers of insolvent but viable businesses may be less incentivised to acquire such businesses. Where this is the case, TUPE Regulations that seek to safeguard the rights of employees during relevant transfers may arguably, be counterproductive.

Therefore, there is a need to balance employment protection and business rescue during TUPE transfers to avoid a tension between employment protection and business rescue. However, as case law discussed in this chapter has demonstrated, the judicial judgements in this area have been quite inconsistent. Therefore, an interpretative approach would arguably, remedy these inconsistencies to achieve the balance needed between employment protection and corporate rescue during relevant transfers. This is the central argument in the next chapter, which applies Dworkin's interpretative approach to the judicial interpretation of TUPE Regulations during relevant transfers.

Bibliography

Books

Brewster, C, and Teague, P, *European Social Policy and its Impact on the UK* (London, Institute of Personnel Management, 1989).

Thurow, LC, *The Future of Capitalism* (New York, W. Morrow & Co, 1996).

Book chapters

Dicey, VA, "Law and Public Opinion in England in the 19th Century", in Richard Vande Wetering (ed.) *Lectures on the Relations between Law and Public Opinion in England during the 19th Century*, (Indianapolis, New Liberty Fund Book, 2008).

Legislation

United Kingdom

Limitation Act 1980, c.58.

The Collective Redundancies and the Transfer of Undertakings (Protection of Employment) (Amendment) Regulations 2014 (SI 2014/16).

Transfer of Undertakings (Protection of Employment) Regulations 1981 (SI 1981/1794).

Transfer of Undertakings (Protection of Employment) Regulations 2006 (SI 2006/246).

European Union

Directive 77/187/EC of 14 February 1977 on the approximation of the laws of the Member States relating to the safeguarding of employees' rights in the event of transfers of undertakings, businesses or parts of businesses [1977 OJ L 61/26].

Directive 98/50/EC of 29 June 1998 1977 amending Directive 77/187/EC on the approximation of the laws of the Member States relating to the safeguarding of employees' rights in the event of transfers of undertakings, businesses or parts of businesses [1998 OJ L 201].
Directive 2001/23/EC of 12 March 2001 on the approximation of the laws of the Member States relating to the safeguarding of employees' rights in the event of transfers of undertakings, businesses or parts of undertakings or businesses [2001, OJ L 82/16].

Cases

United Kingdom

Abellio London Ltd (formerly Travel London Ltd) v Musse & others [2012] IRLR 360.
Addison v Community Integrated Care [UKEAT/250779/11].
Bateman v Asda Stores Ltd [UKEAT/0221/09].
Bernadone v Pall Mall Services Group Ltd [2001] ICR 197.
Berriman v Delabole Slate [1985] ICR 546. CA.
Bolwell v Redcliffe Homes Ltd [1999] IRLR 485.
Carmichael & Another v National Power Plc., [1999] ICR 1226.
Celtec Ltd v Astley [2005] IRLR 647.
Crystal Palace F.C and Another v Kavanagh and Another [2014] IRLR 139, (CA).
Enterprise Managed Services Ltd v Dance and Others [UKEAT/0200/11].
Green v Elan Care Ltd [UKEAT/0018/01].
Hazel and Another v Manchester College [2014] IRLR 392, CA.
Hazel v Manchester College [2014] EWCA Civ. 72.
Ibex Trading v Walton & Other [1994] ICR 907.
Jackson v Computershare Investor Services Plc [2007] EWCA Civ. 1065.
Jefferies v Powerhouse Retail Ltd [UKEAT 1328].
Key2 Law (Surrey)LLP v De' Antiquis [2011] EWVA Civ. 1564.
London Metropolitan University v Sackur & Others [UKEAT/0286/06].
Macer v Abafast Ltd [1990] IRLR 477.
Martin v Lancashire County Council [2001] ICR 197.
Martin & Others v South Bank University [2004] ICR 1234, ECJ.
Meade & Baxendale v British Fuels Ltd [1998] ICR 387.
Meter-U Ltd v Ackroyd [2012] IRLR 367.
Milligan & Another v Securicor Cleaning Ltd [1995] IRLR 288.
Nationwide Building Society v Benn & Others [UKEAT/0273/09/JOJ].
Nokes v Doncaster Amalgamated Collieries Ltd [1940] AC 1014.
Oakland v Wellswood [2009] EWCA Civ. 1094.
OTG v Barke & Ors [2011] IRLR 272.
Ralton v Havering College of Further and Higher Education [2001] IRLR 743 EAT.
RR Donnelley Global Document Solutionss Group Ltd v (1) Besagni and (2) NSL Ltd [UKEAT/0397/13].
Smith v Trustees of Brooklands College [EAT/0128/11].
Spaceright Europe Ltd v Baillavoine and another [2011] EWCA Civ. 1565.
Stirling District Council v Allan [1995] ICR 1082.
Tapere v South London and Maudsley NHS Trust [2009] IRLR 972.
Thompson v SCS Consulting Ltd [2001] IRLR 801.
Wheeler v Patel [1987] IRLR 211.
Whent v T. Cartledge Ltd [1997] IRLR 153.
Whitehouse v Blatchford and Sons Ltd [1999] IRLR 492.

European Union

C-135/83 *Abels v Bedrijfsvereniging voor de Metallindustrie en de Electrotechnische Industrie* [1985] ECR 469.

C-186/83 *Arie Botzen and others v Rotterdamsche Droogdok Maatschappij BV* [1985] ECR 519.

C-324/86 *Foreningen AF Arbedjsldere I Denmark v Daddy's Dance Hall* [1988] IRLR 315 ECJ.

C-362/89 *D'Urso v Ercole Marelli Ellectromeccanica Generale SPA* [1991] ECR 1-4105.

Case C-499/04 *Alermo – Herron and Others v Parkwood Leisure Ltd* [2006] ECR 1-2397.

Journal articles

Ahanchian, A, "Reducing the Impact of the European Union's Invisible Hand on the Economy by Limiting the Application of the Transfer of Undertakings Provisions" (2002) 2 J. Int. Comp. L. 29, 49.

Armour, J, and Deakin, S, "The Rover Case (2): Bargaining in the Shadow of TUPE" (2000) 29 Ind. L. J. 395, 402.

Armour, J, and Deakin, S, "Insolvency and Employment Protection: The Mixed Effects of the Acquired Rights Direct" (2003) 22 Int. Rev. Law. Econ. 443, 463.

Baumann, F, "On Unobserved Worker Heterogeneity and Employment Protection" (2010) 29(2) Eur. J. L. Econ. 155, 175.

Etukakpan, SE, "Business Rescue and Continuity of Employment: Analysing Policies through Lens of Theories" (2011) 32(4) Company Lawyer 99, 113.

Frisby, S, "TUPE or not TUPE? Employee Protection, Corporate Rescue and 'One Unholy Mess'" (2000) CFIL 260.

Hardy, S, and Painter, R, "The New Acquired Rights Directive and its Implications for European Employees Relations in the Twenty-first Century" (1996) 6(4) MaastJECL 336, 378.

McMullen, J, "Atypical Transfers, Atypical Workers and Atypical Employment Structures – A Case for Greater Transparency in Employment Issues" (1996) 25(4) Ind. L. J. 286, 307.

McMullen, J, "An analysis of Transfer of Undertakings (Protection of Employment) Regulations 2006" [2006] Ind. L. J. 113.

McMullen, J, "Restructuring and TUPE" (2012) 41(3) Ind. L. J. 358–362.

McMullen, J, "TUPE: Ringing the (Wrong) Changes – The Collective Redundancies and Transfer of Undertakings (Protection of Employment) (Amendment) Regulations 2014" (2014) 43 Ind. L. J. 149.

McMullen, J, "TUPE, Variation of Employment Terms and the ETO Reason" (2014) 43(3) Ind. L. J. 364.

Prassl, J, "Freedom of Contract as a General Principle of EU Law? Transfers of Undertakings and the Protection of Employer Rights in EU Labour Law: Case C-426/11 *Alermo-Herron and Others v Parkwood Leisure Ltd*" (2013) 42 Ind. L. J. 434.

Sergeant, M, "Business Transfers and Corporate Insolvencies – The Effects of TUPE" (1998) 14(1) I. L. P. 8.

Stiglitz, JE, "Employment, Social Justice and Societal Well-being" (2002) 141 Int'l Labour Rev. 9–29.

7 Balancing corporate rescue and employment protection in the UK – applying Dworkin

Introduction

Although TUPE Regulations have been credited for enhancing employees' rights during relevant transfers in the UK,[1] TUPE Regulations have also been criticised for failing to facilitate a balanced form of entrepreneurial freedom between employers and protection or security of employees during relevant transfers.[2] The application of the TUPE Regulations to relevant transfers has been problematic and challenging to employers, courts and tribunals. This may be caused by the divergent policy objectives that UK insolvency law and employment law aim to achieve during relevant transfers.

The requirement for the UK courts and tribunals to follow the guidance and judicial precedents of the Court of Justice of the European Union (CJEU)[3] has also exacerbated the tension between the need to safeguard the rights of employees and the need to encourage and support the rescue of insolvent but viable businesses during relevant transfers in the UK. By virtue of the European Communities Act (ECA) 1972, s.3 (1), the UK, like other Members States of the EU is bound by the decisions of the CJEU on all matters of EU law. Consequently, UK courts and tribunals are required to interpret EU law and corresponding national legislation, such as TUPE Regulation in a manner that aligns UK law to the intentions of the ARD. This is the purposive interpretative approach.

According to Professor Ronald Dworkin in his Interpretative Theory of Law,[4] law as practice and law as legal theory are best understood as a process of

1 J. McMullen, "An Analysis of the Transfer of Undertakings (Protection of Employment) Regulations 2006" (2006) 35 *Ind. L. J.* 113; A. Garde, "Recent Developments in the Law of Transfers of Undertakings" (2002) 39 *Common Mkt L. Rev.* 523; V. Finch, "Corporate Rescue: A Game of Three Halves" (2012) 32(2) *Legal Stud.* 302–324.

2 S. Hardy and N. Adnett, "Entrepreneurial Freedom versus Employee Rights: The Acquired Rights Directive and the EU Social Policy Post-Amsterdam' (1999) 9 *J. Eur. Soc. Policy* 30; J. McMullen, "TUPE: Ringing the (Wrong) Changes – The Collective Redundancies and Transfer of Undertakings (Protection of Employment) (Amendment) Regulations 2014" (2014) 43 *Ind. L. J.* 149.

3 The Court of Justice of the European Union (hereafter CJEU) is the collective term for the European Union's judicial arm. The CJEU is made up of three courts: the European Court of Justice (ECJ), Court of First Instance (CFI) and the Civil Service Tribunal (CST).

4 R. Dworkin, *Law's Empire* (Cambridge, MA, HUP, 1986).

interpretation.[5] Dworkin posits that by applying the ideals of constructiveness and integrity in interpretation, a judge may be able to interpret the law based on legal principles that may fit perfectly into the legal context before the court to achieve a right answer to the legal question. This is as opposed to interpreting the law based on rules which may be static in application and may not fit perfectly into the legal scenario at hand[6] and the requirement for a purposive interpretation.

It is therefore the contention that by following Dworkin's interpretative approach, UK judges may be able to interpret TUPE Regulations in a manner that may remedy the tension between corporate rescue policy objectives and employment protection policy objectives during relevant transfers and remedy the interpretative inconsistencies that have failed to address this tension.

The interpretative challenges faced by UK courts and tribunals

Because TUPE Regulations owe their origin to the ARD, UK courts and tribunals are required to follow or seek guidance from the CJEU on all matters of EU law, including the ARD and TUPE Regulations.[7] The decisions of the CJEU bind all UK courts and tribunals including the UK Supreme Court.[8] The effect of this obligation on the UK is that courts and tribunals are required to interpret EU law in a manner that recognises the judicial precedents of the CJEU.

However, the CJEU's approach to interpreting the ARD and TUPE Regulations is the purposive approach.[9] The purposive approach is one rule of statutory interpretation that is grounded in the English Legal System, more commonly known as the 'mischief rule'. The mischief rule is the oldest rule of statutory interpretation in the UK which was established in *Heydon's Case*.[10] The rule is adopted by judges during statutory interpretation where there are ambiguities in the law or statutes. The aim is to establish the intentions of the legislature in passing the law to remedy the mischief or defect in the statute.[11]

The purposive approach as adopted by the CJEU involves the need to interpret TUPE Regulations in a manner that aligns TUPE Regulations to the purposes that the ARD sought to achieve. This is to safeguard the rights of employees during relevant transfers. In effect, the purposive approach to interpreting

5 R. Dworkin, "Pragmatism, Right Answers and True Benality" in M. Brint and W. Weaver (eds.) *Pragmatism in Law and Society*, (Boulder, CO, Westview Press, 1991) 365.

6 R. Dworkin, *Law's Empire* (Cambridge, MA, HUP, 1986) 255.

7 By virtue of the European Communities Act (ECA) 1972, s.3 (1), the UK at the time of writing this book like other Members States of the EU is bound by the decisions of the CJEU on all matters of EU law.

8 For example, see the reasoning by Lord Denning in *Bulmer v Bollinger* [1974] EWCA Civ. 14.

9 P. Wallington and R. Lee, "Transfers of Undertakings: EEC Law and Judicial Creativity" [1989] J. Bus. L. 513, 518.

10 [1584] *EWHC Exch. J.* 36.

11 See cases such as *Corkery v Carpenter* [1951] 1 KB 102; *Smith v Hughes* [1960] 1 WLR 380 and *Elliot v Grey* [1960] 1 QB 367.

TUPE Regulations involves giving TUPE Regulations a broader scope of interpretation where needed to 'carve out' the intended outcome that the ARD sought to address.[12] The requirement on the UK to adopt a purposive approach to interpreting EU law was emphasised by the House of Lords (HL) in *Litster v Forth Dry Dock and Engineering Company Ltd.*[13]

In *Litster*, the HL observed that it was incumbent on Member States' courts and tribunals to interpret TUPE Regulations in a manner that conforms to the spirit of the ARD. Lord Templeman observed that:

> ...[t]he courts of the United Kingdom are under a duty to follow the practice of the ECJ by giving a purposive construction of Directives and Regulations issued with the purpose of complying with the Directives.[14]

From this observation from Lord Templeman, it may be construed that UK courts and tribunals have a duty to take all appropriate measures to ensure the fulfilment of the obligation to interpret the ARD and TUPE Regulations in a purposive manner. This duty is binding on all authorities which would include the courts and tribunals of the UK.

In *Litster*, 12 employees that were employed by Forth Dry Dock Company were all dismissed by the receiver an hour before the company was sold to Forth Estuary Company. As a result of the dismissal, there would be no employees to transfer to the transferee and no liabilities would be inherited by the transferee as the dismissed employees would not be deemed to have been 'immediately employed' before the transfer took place. The dismissed employees brought an action for unfair dismissals on the ground that they were employed 'immediately before the transfer' which the company was strongly arguing against.

The HL were tasked to interpret the provision and jurisprudence of the term 'immediately before the transfer' under regulation 5(3) of TUPE 1981. Their lordships held that the automatic transfer under regulation 5(1) of TUPE 1981 (now regulation 4(1) TUPE 2006) not only applied to employees that were immediately employed before a transfer, but it also applied to employees that were able to show that they would have been so employed had they not been unfairly dismissed for a reason connected with a transfer under regulation 5(3) of TUPE 1981, (now regulation 4(3) of TUPE 2006). Therefore, the HL held that the reason for the dismissals was the transfer of Forth Dry Dock to Forth Estuary Company.[15]

It may be noted that the HL in this case had to give regulation 5(3) of TUPE 1981 a purposive interpretation which did not only align it within the

12 S. Hardy and Richard W. Painter, "The New Acquired Rights Directive and its Implications for European Employees Relations in the Twenty-first Century" (1996) 6(4) *MaastJECL* 336, 378.

13 *Litster v Forth Dry Dock and Engineering Company Ltd* [1989] 1 All ER 113; [1989] IRLR 161. (*Litster*).

14 *Litster*, para. 5.

15 *Litster*, para. 24.

spirit and intendment of Article 4 of Directive 77/187/EC,[16] but also aligned it within the jurisprudence of the ECJ's reasoning in the case of *P. Bork International A/S v Foreningen af Arbejdslederen i Danmark*.[17] Therefore, by following the decision in *Litster*, UK courts and tribunals, while addressing matters relating to relevant transfers, ought to adopt a purposive interpretation of TUPE Regulations to ensure that their decisions do not conflict with the intended purposes of the ARD, which is mainly to protect the interests of employees during relevant transfers.[18]

However, it may be submitted that sometimes, UK courts' and tribunals' adoption of the purposive approach in interpreting TUPE provisions during relevant transfers has been faced with both procedural and interpretative challenges. This is, especially, where the ARD does not provide prescriptive guidance on how certain provisions within it ought to be transposed into national laws of Member States. Other interpretative challenges have been witnessed where the CJEU has not provided binding precedents to Member States where certain aspects of the ARD are the subject of interpretation, rather, leaving Member States to find proper ways of solving such interpretative challenges.[19]

For example, when the CJEU was approached by the German Federal Labour Court to give a ruling on the effect of objection to the contract of employment where an employee had exercised a right to object to the transfer in *Katsikas v Konstantinidis*,[20] (discussed below), the CJEU left this matter to national courts of Member States to decide. In *Katsikas* the ECJ gave an opinion that the legal effect of an employee's objection to the automatic transfer and the fate of that employee's contract of employment was a matter for each Member State to determine.

In this case, Katsikas worked as a cook in a Greek restaurant in Germany which was sold to Mitossis. Katsikas refused to work for the new owner Mitossis. This resulted in Katsikas being dismissed by the transferor (Konstantinidis). Katsikas initiated a claim for accrued unpaid wages and compensation arising from his dismissal. The transferor (Konstantinidis) argued that he was no longer Katsikas' employer. This was a consolidated action that involved other cases relating to employees' objections to transfer to new buyers (transferees).[21]

16 Article 4.1 of Directive 77/187/EC provided that 'The transfer of an undertaking, business or part of a business shall not in itself constitute grounds for dismissal by the transferor or the transferee. This provision shall not stand in the way of dismissals that may take place for economic, technical or organisational reasons entailing changes in the workforce'.

17 *P. Bork International A/S v Foreningen af Arbejdslederen i Danmark* [1989] IRLR 41 (Hereafter *P. Bork*). See particularly, para. 20 of the judgment.

18 This point was emphasised by judges in *Litster*, para. 5.

19 S. Laulom, *The European Court of Justice in the Dialogue on Transfers of Undertakings: A Fallible Interlocutor in Labour in the Courts, National Judges and the ECJ*, (edited by S. Sciarra) (Oxford, Hart Publishing, 2001).

20 *Katsikas v Konstantinidis* [1993] IRLR 179. (*Katsikas*).

21 *Grigorios Katsikas v Angelos Konstantinidis* (C-132/91); *Uwe Skreb v PCO Stauereibetrieb Paetz & Co. Nfl. GmbH* (C-138/91) and *Günter Schroll v PCO Stauereibetrieb Paetz & Co. Nachfolger GmbH* (C-138/91), [1992] ECR I-6577, [1992] EUECJ C-132/91.

The claimants were relying on Article 613a of the German Civil Code which provided that

> where a part of an undertaking is transferred by a legal transaction to another owner, the objection of a person employed in that part of the undertaking prevents the transfer to the transferee of his employment and the employment relationship continues following the objection.

These concerns were referred by the German Federal Labour Court to the ECJ for a ruling on whether an employee may validly object to a transfer and whether that employee's employment relationship continues following that objection.

The ECJ held that it was not the ARD's purpose to ensure that continuity of the employment relationship between employees and transferors where employees did not wish to remain in the transferee's employment. However, despite the ECJ's ruling that an employee can legally object to a transfer to a transferee, the ECJ did not commit itself on ruling on the effect of objection on the employee's contract of employment with the transferor. This aspect was left to Member State's courts and tribunals to deliberate in accordance to their respective national laws.[22]

A similar situation arose in the UK on the right to object to a transfer and the effect such a rejection may have on the objecting employee's contract of employment. However, the UK court faced interpretative challenges as the provision in TUPE Regulations 2006 that dealt with an employee's right to object to a transfer was not elaborative on the effect of the objection on the employee's contract of employment. This was in the case of *New ISG Ltd v Vernon and Others.*[23]

The purposive interpretative challenge

Judicial interpretation of regulation 4(7) the right for employees to object to a transfer

Following the ECJ's failure in *Katsikas* to provide a binding ruling in relation to the treatment of an employee's contract of employment where the employee has objected to a transfer, a UK court was tested on the same issue in the case of *New ISG Ltd v Vernon and others.*[24] Under TUPE Regulations 2006, an employee is afforded a right to object to a transfer, where such an employee does not wish to continue to work for the transferee following a relevant transfer. This right is embedded in regulation 4(7) of TUPE 2006.

22 Laulom, (n 19) 173.
23 *New ISG Ltd v Vernon and Others* [2008] IRLR 115.
24 Ibid.

Regulation 4(7) provides that:

> Paragraphs (1)[25] and (2)[26] of Regulation 4 shall not operate to transfer the contract of employment and rights, powers, duties and liabilities under or in connection with it of an employee who informs the transferor or transferee that he objects to becoming employed by the transferee.

It follows therefore, from regulation 4(7) that an employee who wishes not to be involved in the automatic transfer of his employment to the new buyer (transferee) has a right to object to such a transfer. This is, especially, where the employee expects that by rejecting an automatic transfer of his employment to the transferee there may be a chance of being retained by the transferor where the transferor's business is not wholly transferred to the transferee. However, the effect of an employee's right to object to a transfer is a matter that is not adequately guided by either the CJEU or the TUPE Regulations in the UK.[27]

In *New ISG Ltd v Vernon and Others*,[28] the UK High Court was tasked to give a ruling on whether an employee can legally object to a transfer after a relevant transfer has been completed. In this case, the transferor (New Infrastructure Services Group Ltd) had gone into administration and the administrators sold part of the business to New ISG Ltd. The employees (those affected by the transfer) were not informed of the identity of the transferee until after the transfer was completed. However, this was contrary to the legal principle that decision making should be made upon the basis of informed consent or dissent. The employees were also not informed of their right to object to the transfer to the new buyer if they so wished. After the transfer was completed, affected employees were informed by the administrator that they had been transferred to UK Rail Services Ltd (UK Rail), a parent company to New ISG Ltd.[29]

UK Rail was a known company to some of the affected employees and the company was not well thought of by these employees. Some of the employees had indicated prior to the transfer that they would not work for UK Rail if it were to acquire their employer's business. Therefore, following the transfer, all of the affected employees resigned from their jobs with immediate effect and took employment with ESS Recruitment Ltd which was a known competitor to UK Rail. Moreover, these employees had prior to joining ESS Recruitment solicited some of New ISG Ltd's clients, an action that was prohibited by the post-termination restrictions / covenants in their employment contracts prior to the transfer.[30]

25 Paragraph 1 of regulation 4 automatically transfers the employment relationship to the transferee. The 'relevant transfer shall not operate to terminate' an employment.
26 Paragraph 2 of regulation 4 automatically transfers the transferor's rights, duties, and liabilities in relation to the employee to the transferor.
27 J. McMullen, "The Right to Object to Transfer of Employment under TUPE" (2008) 37(2) *Ind. L. J.* 167, 177.
28 *New ISG Ltd v Vernon and Others* [2008] IRLR 115. (*New ISG Ltd*).
29 Ibid., para. 22.
30 Ibid., para. 24.

New ISG argued that the resigned employees were bound by the post-termination restrictions / covenants as they had validly transferred to New ISG via a relevant transfer as they had not objected to the transfer. However, the employees argued that because they were not informed of the identity of the transferee until after the transfer, they were not in a position to exercise the right to object. The employees asked the court to 'purposively' interpret their right to object to the transfer under regulation 4(7). They argued that this would allow them to be treated as having objected to the transfer after it had been completed on the ground that the identity of the transferee was not disclosed to them until after the transfer had been completed.[31]

The High Court held that in circumstances such as these, (where the identity of the transferee was not disclosed), employees had validly objected to the transfer even though their objection had been made after the transfer had been completed. Therefore, their contracts of employment had not transferred to New ISG Ltd. Consequently, New ISG Ltd could not enforce post-termination restrictions / covenants on the employees.[32]

However, this ruling may serve as an indication that the purposive interpretation of TUPE Regulations may be vulnerable to abuse or manipulation by both employers and employees seeking the protection of the ARD. In this case, it may be noted that employees benefited from the purposive interpretation of regulation 4(7) by the High Court to release themselves from the post-termination restrictions / covenants in their employment contracts which would otherwise be binding on them.[33]

The impact of the court's decision on regulation 4(7)

In the UK, the treatment of an employee's employment contract in a case where the employee has objected to a transfer is governed by regulation 4(8) TUPE 2006. Regulation 4(8) provides that;

> Subject to paragraphs (9)[34] and (11),[35] where an employee so objects, the relevant transfer shall operate so as to terminate his contract of employment with the transferor but he shall not be treated for any purpose as having been dismissed by the transferor.

31 Ibid., paras. 22, 23.

32 *New ISG Ltd v Vernon and Others* [2008] IRLR 115, para. 87.

33 See also, *Credit Suisse First Boston (Europe) Ltd v Padiachy* [1998] IRLR 504; *Credit Suisse First Boston (Europe) Ltd v Lister* [1998] IRLR 700 where employees successfully argued that the new restrictive covenants agreed with their employer following a relevant transfer involved changes to their material detriment and were therefore invalid. The employees were paid to agree to these new changes. Nonetheless, they were invalid as they were to their material detriment.

34 Paragraph 9 of regulation 4 affords an employee a right to treat an employment contract as terminated where the transfer involves a substantial change in the employee's contract of employment to his material detriment.

35 Paragraph 11 of regulation 4 gives an employee power to terminate an employment contract without notice of acceptance to an employer's repudiatory breach of an employment contract.

From the procedural and substantive provision of regulation 4(8) above, it may be inferred that the ARD and TUPE Regulations sought to afford employees that are the subject of a relevant transfer some freedom to choose whether or not to work for the transferee following a relevant transfer. However, the effect of regulation 4(8) may imply that the contract of employment for the objecting employee is treated as being terminated by reason of rejection, neither by the transferor nor the transferee.[36]

Both regulations 4(7) and 4(8) are silent as to the manner or form that an employee's objection should take. Although the provision of regulation 4(7) states that an employee may inform the transferor or transferee of his objection, the format or timeframe within which an objection may be made is not elaborated. Questions remain unanswered as to whether an objection made by mere expression of unhappiness with the transfer,[37] an employee's activities of trying to secure alternative employment or attempts by an employee to negotiate a redundancy package[38] may all pass for forms of objection by an employee.

With these questions unanswered by regulations 4(7) and 4(8), it may be difficult for the employee to establish with certainty, the exact circumstances under which he may choose to exercise the right to object to a transfer. Moreover, if the protection afforded an employee under regulation 4(7) is compared to the protection afforded to the same employee via regulation 4(9),[39] the protection under regulation 4(9) may outweigh the protection under regulation 4(7). This is because the employee exercising a right under regulation 4(9) to resign because of a substantial change to his working conditions that is to his material detriment may have a claim for constructive dismissal from the transferor unlike an employee that exercises a right to object to a transfer under regulation 4(7).

At the same time, an employee exercising his right to treat his contract of employment as terminated without notice by his employer because of his employer's repudiatory breach of contract under regulation 4(11) has better protection than an objecting employee under regulation 4(7). Under regulation 4(11), an employee who treats his contract of employment as being terminated by reason of a repudiatory breach by his employer is not prevented from initiating a claim for constructive dismissal against his employer.[40]

Prior to *New ISG Ltd*, the EAT had held in *Secretary of State for Trade & Industry v Cook*[41] that an employer could not prevent an automatic transfer of employees' contracts by simply refusing to inform employees of the identity of the buyer (transferee). This is the same view that the House of Lords had reached

36 McMullen, (n 27).

37 For example, see, *Ladies Health and Fitness Clubs v Eastmond* [UKEAT94/03] (Unreported).

38 See, *Hay v George Hansen* [1996] IRLR 427.

39 See cases, such as *Nationwide Building Society v Benn & Others* [UKEAT/0273/09/JOJ]; *Tapere v South London and Maudsley NHS Trust* [2009] IRLR 972.

40 *Tapere v South London and Maudsley NHS Trust* [2009] IRLR 972.

41 *Secretary of State for Trade & Industry v Cook* [1997] IRLR 150.

in *North Wales Training & Enterprise Council Ltd v Astley and Others*[42] while applying the guidance from the ECJ in *Celtec v Astley*.[43]

The guidance from the ECJ in *Celtec* was that employees are automatically transferred from the transferor to the transferee regardless of what had been agreed between the parties to the transfer process and regardless of whether employees understood what was happening. The ruling in *Celtec* may also be said to be in conflict with the ruling in *New ISG Ltd* and it is contrary to the principle that decision making should be based on informed consent or dissent. Where employees are not given sufficient information to make informed decisions, it would be unfair to employees as it would impact on their ability to make informed decisions on whether or not to object to the transfer.

The ARD affords Member States power to introduce laws, regulations or administrative provisions that are more favourable to employees during relevant transfers.[44] However, in view of the challenges presented by regulations 4(7) and 4(8), these regulations may not be categorised as being favourable to employees during relevant transfers. The lack of clarity within regulations 4(7) and 4(8) remains a cause for concern.[45] It is an indication that an interpretative solution such as a change in the approach to interpreting TUPE Regulations is needed such that a form of a binding threshold or precedent is formulated to guide judicial interpretation of TUPE regulations. UK judges ought to balance the interest of employees and employers during relevant transfers, without moving away from purposive interpretation of TUPE Regulations.

Judicial interpretation of regulation 7 (2) – the ETO exceptions

The term 'economic, technical and organisational reasons' arises from regulation 7(2) of TUPE Regulations 2006. These terms or provisions may be used by employers as exceptions to the application of regulation 7(1) and regulation 4(4) of TUPE Regulations 2006 during relevant transfers to justify employee dismissals or variations to contract terms and conditions during relevant transfers.

Because of the requirement for UK courts and tribunals to interpret matters of EU law, especially, TUPE Regulations in a purposive manner to give effect to the intentions of the ARD, UK courts and tribunals have presided over a large number of cases in relation to ETO provisions. However, these cases have produced inconsistent judgements. The big number of cases and inconsistencies may

42 *North Wales Training & Enterprise Council Ltd v Astley and Others* [2006] UKHL 29 (HL).

43 *Celtec v Astley* [2005] IRLR 647 (*Celtec*).

44 See, Directive 2001/23/EC, Article 8 which states that; 'This Directive shall not affect the right of Member States to apply or introduce laws, regulations, or administrative provisions which are more favourable to employees'.

45 Paul Davies, "Opting Out of Transfers" (1996) 25 *Ind. L. J.* 247.

arguably, be attributed to the technical and procedural challenges within TUPE Regulations which may be traced back to the original ARD that the TUPE Regulations transposed into UK legislation.[46]

In the UK, the first point of interpretative challenge to note in relation to regulation 7(2) is the absence of a statutory definition of the terms economic, technical or organisational reasons within TUPE Regulations. The Department for Business, Enterprise and Regulatory Reform (BERR) now the Department for Business Innovation and Skills (BIS) offered a guidance report that tends to explain what these terms may entail.[47] However, the guidance does not give a definition of these terms. Rather, it gives an explanation of what the terms may involve, leaving the uncertainty unsolved.[48]

This has meant that UK courts and tribunals have interpreted and applied ETO reasons during relevant transfers on a case by case basis which has led to inconsistent judgements. Moreover, it is a substantive and procedural requirement that for the ETO exceptions under regulation 7(2) to be fully invoked, the ETO exceptions must entail changes in the workforce of the employer.[49]

Entailing changes in the workforce

'Entailing changes in the workforce' is part of the procedural and substantive requirements of regulation 7(2) that must be satisfied by the employer if the ETO defence is to be effective. The employer's reasons for dismissing employees or changing employees' contract terms and conditions would be void where no changes were entailed in the employer's workforce. In essence, 'entailing changes to the workforce' is the effect of the economic, technical or organisational reasons adopted by the employer.

However, the term 'entailing changes in the workforce' neither has a statutory definition under the TUPE Regulations nor in the ARD. Like the terms, economic, technical and organisational reasons, the courts and tribunals have through their adjudication tried to interpret what the term might mean or may

46 For example, see a report by the UK Department of Employment summarising a report by Prof. Dr. Rolf Birk, "Contracting Out in the Context of the Provisions of Community Law and National Laws relating to the Transfer of Undertakings" House of Commons Deposited Papers, Ref. HINF 94/1363.

47 This guidance is available at www.berr.gov.uk/files/file20761.pdf, (accessed 23 May 2019).

48 For example, the guidance indicated that an economic reason may relate to the running or operations of the business. The guidance further provides that a term technical or organisational might include reasons relating to the nature of equipment or production process that the transferee operates.

49 "...[f]or an ETO reason to be available, there must be an intention to change the workforce and to continue to conduct the business, as distinct from the purpose of selling it. It is not available in the case of dismissing an employee to enable the administrators make the business of the company a more attractive proposition to the prospective of a going concern" Per Mummery LJ in *Spaceright*, para. 47

involve.[50] For example, in *Berriman v Delabole Slate*,[51] the Court of Appeal (CA) observed that a change in the workforce was part of the ETO reason that must be satisfied if the ETO exception is to be invoked. The employer's plan must be to achieve changes in the workforce and must be an objective of the plan not a consequence. The CA emphasised that the term required changes in the numbers of employees in employment or to their functions. Mere changes in the identity of employees may not constitute changes to the workforce as long as the overall numbers and functions of the employees remain the same.[52]

In *Green v Elan Care*,[53] The claimant's role was changed from a senior manager's role to a senior carer following a relevant transfer involving the care home that employed her. This was following the transferee's restructure of the care home's senior management team. The claimant objected to the new role as it meant a demotion to her title. She initiated an unfair dismissal claim against her employer. The EAT held that the dismissal was for an organisational reason that entailed changes in the employer's workforce due to the management structural changes.

However, despite this ruling by the EAT to this effect, there had been no changes in the overall workforce in terms of numbers or a reduction in or addition to the workforce. The EAT rejected the claimant's contention that there had been no changes in the workforce. The EAT concluded that:

> ... [w]hile a minor change in the functions of one employee or a small number of employees in a large workforce might not be sufficient, considering the workforce as a whole, to amount to a change in the workforce, in our judgment where the steps taken by the employer involves a real change in the functions in a substantial or key area of the work force, it is open to a tribunal to find that changes in the workforce are entailed.[54]

Similarly in *Nationwide Building Society v Benn & Others*,[55] the EAT rejected a claim for unfair dismissals from employees who had resigned from their jobs following variations to their employment terms and bonus entitlements being downgraded. This was following a relevant transfer that took employees of Portman Building Society (PBS) to Nationwide Building Society (NBS). The employees claimed that variations to their employment terms and downgrading of their bonus entitlements did not entail changes (particularly numbers)

50 See cases such as *Berriman v Delabole Slate* [1985] IRLR 305; *Wheeler v Patel* [1987] IRLR 211; [1985] ICR 546*Whitehouse v Blatchford and Sons Ltd* [1999] IRLR 492; *Spaceright Europe Ltd v Baillavoine and Another* [2011] EWCA Civ. 1565.

51 *Berriman v Delabole Slate* [1985] IRLR 305; [1985] ICR 546.

52 See also, the EAT reasoning in *Crawford v Swinton Insurance Brokers Ltd* [1990] IRLR 42, EAT.

53 UKEAT/18/01/0403 (*Elan Care*).

54 Ibid., para. 25.

55 *Nationwide Building Society v Benn & Others* [UKEAT/0273/09/JOJ]. (*Nationwide*).

in the workforce. The EAT, rejecting the employees' claims for unfair dismissal observed that:

> ...[t]he term 'entailing changes in the workforce' did not imply that the dismissals must entail changes in the entirety of the workforce. Therefore, the dismissals were for an organisational reason.[56]

From the observation in both cases above, it may be submitted that the EAT's rulings in both *Elan Care* and *Nationwide* are exemplary of the UK courts' and tribunals' willingness to purposively interpret ETO terms during relevant transfers in order to keep their interpretation of TUPE Regulations within the spirit and intentions of the ARD. The judgements are a further indication that although the ARD and TUPE Regulations seek to protect employees' rights during relevant transfers, TUPE Regulations should however, not be seen as a 'weapon' used by employees to restrict employers from effecting economic, technical or organisational structural changes to their businesses that may enhance their going concern prospects which in turn may lead to employment security and continuity.[57]

Therefore, regulation 7(2) should be used as a balancing provision between the interest of employees and the interest of employers during relevant transfers. However, it may be submitted that judicial approaches to interpreting and applying regulation 7(2) to solving employers' and employees' concerns during relevant transfers have so far failed to reach the balance needed. The varying judicial approaches to interpreting and applying regulation 7(2) were recently tested in the Court of Appeal case of *Crystal Palace F.C Limited and Another v Kavanagh and Others.*[58]

This case is the subject of detailed analysis below. In particular, the case will be analysed in light of Dworkin's interpretative approach. This is to examine whether, Dworkin's approach to interpretation if adopted by the ET, EAT and CA, would have led to a better and balanced outcome for both employees and employers in all of the three hearings.

Crystal palace F.C limited and another v Kavanagh and others – the background

Crystal Palace F.C went into administration and the appointed administrator who dismissed the claimant employees on the grounds that the football club had run out of money to pay for employee wages. At the time of the dismissals, the football club was facing serious prospects of becoming liquidated as it had

56 Ibid., para. 7.

57 J. McMullen, "Atypical Transfers, Atypical Workers and Atypical Employment Structures – A Case for Greater Transparency in Employment Issues" (1996) 25 (4) *Ind. L. J.* 286, 307.

58 *Crystal Palace F.C and Another v Kavanagh and Another* [2014] IRLR 139, CA. (*Crystal Palace*).

become insolvent. The administrator claimed that he dismissed the claimant employees in a bid to cut the wage bill to continue running the football club on skeleton staff in the hope that a buyer would be found. The dismissed employees brought a claim against the football club on the ground that their dismissals were connected with the transfer and were for the purposes of selling the football club.

The employment tribunal (ET) held that although the dismissals were connected with the transfer, they were however, for an economic reason that entailed changes in the workforce. Therefore, the dismissals were not automatically unfair by reason of regulation 7(1). The ET drew a distinction between the administrator's 'reason for the dismissal' which was to 'reduce the wage bill' in order to continue running the football club, and the administrator's 'ultimate objective' which was the sale of the football club.[59] The ET therefore, concluded that the administrator did not dismiss the employees to make the sale of the football club more attractive. The football club had genuinely run out of money to pay for staff wages and salaries. The intention was to run the football club on a 'skeleton staff' in the hope of selling the football club in the future.[60]

The ET decision was appealed to the EAT. However, the EAT did not agree with the ET's conclusions above. The EAT was of the view that the ET's finding that the administrator's reason for the dismissal was to continue running the football club was untenable and ambiguous.[61] The EAT's conclusion was that the dismissal of the employees by the administrator was for purposes of selling the football club although at the time there was no serious buyer in contemplation.[62] The EAT observed that dismissing a proportion of employees to reduce the wage bill in the hope that a buyer would be found, who in fact bought the football club a week later, may closely be linked to the administrator's ultimate objective which was the selling of the football club, rather than the desire to continue running the football club as a going concern.

The EAT drew a distinction between a dismissal necessitated by the desire to entail changes in the workforce, which would pass for an ETO exception and a dismissal as 'part and parcel of a process' for the purposes of selling the business which may not be covered by an ETO exception.[63] The EAT drew on Mummery LJ's formulation in *Spaceright* in their distinction that for an ETO reason to be available to an employer, the employer must have had the intention to make changes in the workforce and to continue operating the business as opposed to making the business attractive for sale.[64]

However, the EAT observed that a dismissal by the employer as 'part and parcel of a process' to sell the business should not be covered by an ETO exception.

59 *Crystal Palace*, EAT, para.8.
60 Ibid., para. 8.
61 Ibid., para. 30.
62 Ibid., para. 31.
63 Ibid., para. 26.
64 Ibid., para. 47.

In the EAT's observations, the administrator's reasons for the dismissal could only point to one conclusion. This was the ultimate objective of selling the football club. Therefore, the dismissals would not pass for an ETO reason so they would be automatically unfair.[65]

The EAT judgement was also appealed to the CA. The CA was not in agreement with the EAT's observations above as it restored the ET's original ruling that the dismissals were for an ETO reason that entailed changes in the workforce.[66] According to the CA, the dismissals were necessitated by the desire by the administrator to cut the wage bill to continue running the business.

However, Briggs LJ observed that this case (*Crystal Palace*) had raised some fundamental issues about the interaction between two statutory regimes of TUPE and insolvency. The TUPE regime that protects employees on transfer of an undertaking and the insolvency regime (administration in this case) that aims to rescue an insolvent but viable business that would save jobs where the business is sold as a going concern.[67] Interesting to note, his Lordship observed that:

> ...[i]n the context of insolvency, dismissal of employees is a principal method by which administrators can achieve the economies necessary to "maximise" the period before a lack of resources compels closure and to make the business more attractive to buyers.[68]

From the observation from Briggs LJ above, it may be construed that judges are aware of the potential conflict that arises between the two protective regimes of TUPE and Insolvency law during relevant transfers. Each protective regime seeks to protect its principal objective. TUPE Regulations protecting employees while insolvency law seeking to protect business rescue and continuity. The observation above is also a further indication that the courts and tribunals are aware that sometimes business owners may try to dress up a dismissal under the guise of ETO exceptions.[69] Therefore, a balance, through Dworkin's interpretative approach to law may be the solution.

The interpretative theory of law – Ronald Dworkin

Dworkin writes about an interpretative approach to law as the best approach to interpreting the laws of a legal system.[70] Dworkin observes that both law as practice and legal theory are best understood as processes of constructive interpretation. This is the form of interpretation that makes the law the best it can

65 *Crystal Palace*, EAT, para. 31.
66 Ibid., para. 8.
67 Ibid., at para. 18.
68 Ibid., para. 22.
69 For example, see, *Dynamex Friction Ltd and Another v Amicus and another* [2008] EWCA Civ. 381.
70 R. Dworkin, *Law's Empire* (Cambridge, MA, HUP, 1986) 44–48.

be, which makes it the best example of the form and genre to which it is taken to belong.[71]

Dworkin argues that constructive interpretation is the proper approach to artistic and literary interpretation of laws. According to Dworkin, constructive interpretation is based upon the ability of a judge to assign a distinctive value or purpose to the object of interpretation. It is the value or purpose that serves as the criterion for determining whether one interpretation of an object is better or worse than the alternative. The purpose of the law is to justify the exercise of government powers.[72] For example, the governmental power to enact legislation such as TUPE Regulations 2006 to transpose the ARD that serves to protect the rights of employees during relevant transfers.

Dworkin writes that along with legal rules, legal systems also contain legal principles.[73] Legal principles are moral propositions that are stated in, or implied by past official acts such as statutes, judicial decisions or constitutional provisions. Therefore, principles are part of a legal system that judges ought to consider where appropriate in balancing the interests of competing stakeholders. This is especially where the outcome of the case before the court appears to be contrary to relevant precedents (if any) or departs from the 'real meaning' or 'true spirit' of the law.[74]

Dworkin states that by using legal principles, a judge may be able to test a variety of theories regarding what the law requires in that particular field of law to reach a fair and balanced judgement. The judge may be able to disregard legal principles that do not adequately fit past official judgements, precedents or actions and consider legal principles that fit the moral vision that the law seeks to achieve. This would make that law the best it can be in that particular area.

Dworkin also writes about the concept of 'integrity' in interpretation in *Law's Empire*.[75] Dworkin argues that judges should decide cases in a manner that makes the law more coherent, more like a product of a single moral vision. Dworkin opines that 'judges who accept the interpretative ideal of integrity decide hard cases by trying to find, in some coherent set of principles about peoples' rights and duties, the best constructive interpretation of the political and legal doctrine of their community.'[76]

Therefore, by following the concept of law as integrity, propositions of law such as the need to balance employment protection and corporate rescue during relevant transfers would be approached by a judge in a manner that conforms to the principles of fairness, equality and justice. These principles are part of the procedural due process that provide the best constructive interpretation

71 Ibid., 52.

72 Ibid., 93, 109, 127.

73 R. Dworkin, "Pragmatism, Right Answers and True Benality" in M. Brint and W. Weaver (eds.) *Pragmatism in Law and Society*, (Boulder, CO, Westview Press, 1991) 365.

74 Brian Bix, "On the Dividing Line between Natural Law Theory and Legal Positivism" (2000) 75 *Notre Dame L. Rev.* 1613.

75 R. Dworkin, *Law's Empire* (Cambridge, MA, HUP, 1986) 255.

76 Ibid., 46–48.

of the law. Law as integrity would provide an approach to judges to decide cases or approach legal questions before the courts in a methodological and novel manner that is structured on coherent principles because according to Dworkin, law must speak with one voice. This model of constructive interpretation of the law would therefore, express a coherent conception of justice and integrity.[77]

Dworkin's interpretative ideals of constructive and integrity as a remedy

Dworkin writes about constructiveness[78] and integrity[79] as two factors in judicial interpretation that would aid a judge to reach a right answer[80] to the legal question before the court. Constructive interpretation would involve analysing past government actions, judicial judgements with the *ratio decidendi*, and legislative statutes to draw up a theory of what the law is or ought to be in answering the legal question before the court.[81]

Dworkin observes that in making the law or an area of the law the best it can be, the judge must consider the criteria of 'fit and 'moral value' in assessing whether the legal principles before him can lead to the right answer to the question before the court.[82] This is, especially, where the law is unsettled or inconsistent with the answer to the legal question before the court. This is because some legal principles would fare better on the 'fit' criterion while others would do better on the 'moral value' criterion. The 'fit' criterion may involve legal principles that fit into the purposes underlying the passing of the law and would inform a decision that is parallel to the law. The 'moral value' category may involve principles that would aim to ensure moral fairness or equity in the law that is subject to application to specific areas or legal questions.[83]

Legal principles that hold moral value of the law not only fit into the law at hand, but also carry with them the ideals of fairness and reasonableness to the demands of competing stakeholders. For example, legal principles on the 'moral value' of law would inform a judge's analysis of the law in establishing that law's moral vision for the legal question before the court. For instance, should the availability of an economic reason to justify an employee's dismissal be invoked at the slightest opportunity by an employer even where there are other viable options to address a company's financial difficulties? Would it not be fair and reasonable to exhaust other options where possible before effecting a dismissal because the laws states so?

77 Ibid., 225.
78 R. Dworkin, *Law's Empire* (Cambridge, MA, HUP, 1986) 44–48.
79 Ibid., 255.
80 Dworkin claims that all or almost all legal questions have a unique right answer, even the hardest of cases. See, R. Dworkin, *Taking Rights Seriously* (London, G. Duckworth, 1977) 85.
81 R. Dworkin, *Law's Empire* (Cambridge, MA, HUP, 1986) 52.
82 Ibid., 228–258.
83 Ibid., 46–48.

Therefore, by devising a theory that compares these legal principles (on both the 'fit' and the 'moral value' criteria), a judge may be able to choose the legal principles that have better weight to fit both into the 'fit and moral value' criteria. This model of constructive interpretation of the law would express a coherent conception of justice and integrity.[84] This may be seen as a form of a decision-making process that is consistent with the spirit and intentions of the policies underlying the principles of fairness and justice.

It should be noted that in reaching the decisions in *Crystal Palace*, both the EAT and CA, in addition to interpreting the provisions of regulation 7(1) and 7(2) of TUPE 2006 purposively, they also applied the formulation of Mummery LJ in *Spaceright* that

> [f]or an ETO to be available, there must be an intention to change the workforce and to continue conducting the business as opposed to the purpose of selling it. It is not available in the case of dismissing an employee to enable the administrators make the business of the company, a more attractive proposition to prospective transferees of a going concern.[85]

By following this formulation and applying it to the facts before it, the EAT in *Crystal Palace* concluded that the administrator's decision to dismiss a proportion of the workforce and mothball the football club in the hope that a buyer would be found could only point to one conclusion. This was to sell the football club as the ultimate objective which could not have been for an ETO reason entailing changes in the workforce.[86]

However, the CA concluded that Mummery LJ's observations were made in a fact-intensive case of *Spaceright*. The CA therefore distinguished the facts in *Crystal Palace* from the facts in *Spaceright*. The distinction was that in *Spaceright*, the dismissals were made to attract the buyer as the buyer would be able to appoint a new chief executive of its choice. However, the dismissals in *Crystal Palace* were not to attract the sale of the football club but were necessitated by need to avoid liquidation.[87] Therefore, the CA observed that the EAT had given more weight to the concept of 'mothballing' the club in reaching its conclusion that the dismissals were for the sale of the football club.[88]

Judicial balancing of policy objectives – in light of Dworkin

According to Dworkin, 'judges who accept the interpretative ideal of integrity decide hard cases by trying to find, in some coherent set of principles about peoples' rights and duties, the best constructive interpretation of the political and

84 Ibid., 225.
85 *Spaceright*, para. 47.
86 *Crystal Palace*, EAT, para. 12.
87 *Crystal Palace*, CA, para. 28.
88 *Crystal Palace*, CA, Per Maurice Kay, LJ, para. 14.

legal doctrine of their community.'[89] Constructiveness and integrity in interpretation would present judges and policy makers with the advantage to reflect on whether the law is serving the purposes for which it was intended to serve. If inconsistent with the current desired demands of fairness, equality and justice to the interests of stakeholders, that law may be subjected to change or reform. The weaknesses in that particular law would have been exposed through constructiveness and integrity in interpretation.

The decision of the ET, as supported and reinstated by the CA, and that of the EAT, highlight the interpretative challenges and technicalities involved in applying TUPE Regulations to relevant transfers. The decisions further highlight how the purposive approach to interpreting TUPE Regulations by UK courts and tribunals may lead to different judgements which have not helped to address the tension between corporate rescue and employment protection policy objectives during TUPE transfers in the UK.[90]

It may be submitted that the decision of the EAT above would be more protective of employees than the decisions of ET and CA respectively. It is the concern that the ET's decision and that of the CA were based on the distinction between the administrator's 'reason for the dismissal' and the administrator's 'ultimate objective'. Although the factors leading to the activities that necessitated the dismissals were interpreted purposively, the distinction formulated by the ET and followed by the CA may not have given the necessary weight to the need to safeguard the rights of employees during relevant transfers as required by the ARD.[91]

It is the argument that if indeed, the administrator's reason for the dismissals was to continue running the football club as a going concern, it is questionable why the administrator did not consider other cost cutting mechanisms as opposed to dismissing the employees in question. Why did the administrator not consider selling some of the playing staff (footballers) as a cost reduction strategy? On occasion, UK courts and tribunals have tended not to interfere in the business decisions made by an employer, especially in non-TUPE business sales and transfers where the business decisions are for 'sound business reasons'.[92] However, whether the administrator's decisions for the dismissal would pass for a 'sound business reason' remains a moot point.[93]

The sale price of a professional footballer may arguably, be of greater return (in terms of generating income) than the income obtained from dismissing

89 R. Dworkin, *Law's Empire* (Cambridge, MA, HUP, 1986) 255.

90 Hamiisi J. Nsubuga, "Corporate Insolvency and Employment Protection: A Theoretical Perspective" (2016) 4(1) *NIBLeJ* 4.

91 *Crystal Palace*, CA, paras. 13–14, 28.

92 For example, in *Catamaran Cruisers v Williams and others* [1994] IRLR 384, the ET held that an employer's decision to dismiss claimant employees was for 'sound business reasons' and therefore fair. See paragraph [9] of the judgment. The employer company was in a serious financial state that required drastic measures to avoid receivership or liquidation.

93 Charles A. Wynn-Evans, "TUPE and Mothballs – *Crystal Palace FC Ltd and Another v Kavanagh and Others*" (2014) 43(2) *Ind. L. J.* 185.

administrative members of staff. The income obtainable from the sale of a professional footballer may arguably, sustain a football club for some considerable period as a going concern as opposed to dismissing non-playing staff whose annual salaries may constitute a fraction of the costs of maintaining a professional footballer.

There may be sense in the argument that continued operation of a football club would mainly depend on winning football matches and retaining good footballers. This may safeguard the football club against other losses of revenue, such as from fans who may stop attending football matches. However, the fact that the administrator may not have considered the possibility of selling some of the footballers as a cost saving measure may cast further doubt into the administrator's reasons for the dismissal. This may echo the argument that on corporate insolvency, employers find employee dismissals as a soft target for costs reduction. With the availability of statutory protection, such as in regulation 7 (2) in the form of a shield to potential unfair dismissal claims, employment protection may be compromised.[94]

Therefore, the possibility that the administrator in *Crystal Palace* did not consider other cost cutting mechanisms than employment termination would raise questions as to whether the administrator used regulation 7(2) disingeniously. Legal principles such as fairness and reasonableness may have been overlooked by the administrator. Questions of whether invoking TUPE provisions for own protection would be fair, reasonable and would conform to the 'moral value' that commercial morality would demand may have been overlooked by the administrator. This is why Dworkin's ideals of weighing up legal principles that would conform to the 'fit and moral value' would help to balance the potential unfairness in the use of TUPE Regulations for own protections by both the employers and employees.[95]

Therefore, in light of this perspective, the EAT's observations that the administrator's reasons for the dismissals were for the sale of the football club, ought to be given some weight. This may be supported by the fact that the football club was sold a week later following the dismissals of the employees. With the ET and CA departing from the observations of the EAT, it casts doubt as to whether the ET's and CA's purposive interpretation of the administrator's 'reasons for the dismissal' and the administrator's 'ultimate objective' took the intentions of the ARD into consideration.[96]

Prior to the CA's decision in *Crystal Palace*, the CA had in *Dynamex Friction Ltd and Another* v *Amicus and Another*[97] held that in determining the reasons for the dismissal, what counts most is the 'thought process of the decision maker'. In this case, the CA was tasked to give a ruling on whether a dismissal

94 F. Toube and G. Todd, "The Proper Treatment of Employees' Claims in Administration" (2005) 18 *Insolvency Intel.* 109.

95 R. Dworkin, *Taking Rights Seriously* (London, G. Duckworth, 1977) 85.

96 Wynn-Evans, (n 93).

97 *Dynamex Friction Ltd and Another v Amicus and another* [2008] EWCA Civ. 381. (*Dynamex*).

prior to a relevant transfer was for economic reasons or simply carried out to facilitate a business sale to escape potential liabilities. After realising that the company had a potential approximate liability of around three million pounds from potential unfair dismissal claims, Mr. Smith (the sole director of Dynamex Friction Ltd) instructed an administrator to file for administration, arguably to escape potential liabilities.

Upon appointment, the administrator dismissed all of the employees that had taken part in a strike action on the basis that there was no money to pay for their wages. The transferor's business was sold to an ex-employee who formed a new company assisted by Mr. Smith who later took control of the company. The dismissed employees brought claims for unfair dismissals.

The ET initially held that the dismissals were for an economic reason. However, the EAT disagreed and the case was appealed to the CA. The CA held that the dismissals were not for a reason connected with the transfer. The dismissals were for an economic reason.[98] The CA further held that in determining the reasons for the dismissal, what counts most is the 'thought process of the decision maker'. However, despite the ruling by the CA, it remained a point of contention that the employer (Mr. Smith) had contemplated a sale of the business through an administrator to escape potential unfair dismissal liabilities.[99]

By giving regard to the 'thought process of the decision maker' (the administrator), the CA was of the view that the decision maker (the administrator) dismissed the employees for lack of money to pay wages. Therefore, for the CA, the reason for the dismissal was not the impending or prospective transfer but the reason was purely economic, necessitated mainly by the poor cashflow state of the company at the time.[100]

The decision of the CA was a majority decision, with Lawrence Collins LJ dissenting. His Lordship gave a statement which if followed, may support the argument that by using the purposive approach to interpreting TUPE Regulations especially the ETO exceptions under regulation 7(2), judges give too much attention to activities that fall within the ETO exceptions rather than balancing the reasons for the dismissals.[101]

Collins LJ observed that if TUPE stood alone, he would agree that it was appropriate to focus on the thought process of the person who made the decision to dismiss. However, taking into account a purposive construction in light of the ARD, rather than looking only at the motives of the person who effected the dismissals, it would be relevant if the tribunals were to find that Mr. Smith stage-managed the administration and used the administrator as his unwitting tool to regain the business without having to pay liabilities for unfair dismissal claims.[102]

98 Ibid., para. 62.
99 Per the submission of Lawrence – Collins LJ, in *Dynamex*, paras. 63–68.
100 *Dynamex*, para. 59.
101 Ibid., para. 63.
102 Ibid., para. 64.

Although a majority of the judges were not persuaded by this approach, it may be seen as a school of thought that if adopted, would balance the policy objectives of corporate rescue while also offering the social employment protection to employees during relevant transfers that the ARD sought to achieve. Collins LJ's observations above would echo Dworkin's ideals of constructiveness and integrity in interpretation as two fundamental factors that may aid a judge to reach a right answer to the question before the court.[103]

The point of concern is that judges in *Crystal Palace* and *Dynamex Friction* above relied too much on the employers' reasons for the dismissals. It is the contention that by the judges in *Crystal Palace* relying on the distinction between the administrator's 'reasons for the dismissal' and the administrator's 'ultimate objective' they may have been constructive but may not have taken the ideal of integrity into consideration. Integrity would ensure that fairness and reasonableness into the administrator's reasons to dismiss employees is given consideration alongside a constructive analysis of the facts surrounding the activities that led to the dismissals. This would be the interpretative approach that Dworkin posits that would express a coherent conception of justice and integrity.

Would Dworkin's approach fit into the UK legal structure?

It may be argued that in the UK, particularly, in the field of insolvency law, there have not been specific hard cases that are analogous to Dworkin's hard case thesis that would arguably, warrant the application of Dworkin's hard case thesis as a remedy. This is because in the UK, in contrast to the US, bankruptcy judges are more involved in a greater range of decisions whereas judges in the UK insolvency proceedings, do not typically have to ask themselves, whether, a company faced with financial difficulties, can or should be rescued.

Judges in the UK do not rule on administration proposals as US bankruptcy courts do with Chapter 11 reorganisation plans. The UK judges do not consider economic and business decisions as part of their role in adjudication. They are willing to leave these matters to experts in these particular fields, such as insolvency practitioners and business experts.[104] However, UK judges may be called upon to interpret contentious issues during insolvency proceedings, such as interpreting economic, technical and organisational reasons (ETO reasons) or the meaning of the term 'wages or salary' during insolvency proceedings which may arguably, be analogous to Dworkin's hard case thesis.[105]

In addition, Dworkin's hard case theory is more judge-focused and UK insolvency law is more insolvency practitioner-focused and therefore, there is a high level of contrast which means that interpretative issues would not arise in the

103 R. Dworkin, *Law's Empire* (Cambridge, MA, HUP, 1986) 46–48.

104 See Hansard, HL Deb, vol. 638, col.768 (29 July 2002).

105 *Re Huddersfield Fine Worsteds Ltd and Re Ferrotech Ltd & Granville Technology Ltd* [2005] EWCA Civ. 1072.

same ways. However, what could be drawn from Dworkin's hard case thesis is the ability to analyse the administrator's role and capacity to discharge his duties in a manner that is analogous to that of a judge. This notion is premised on the fact that the IA 1986, Sch. B1 that deals with the administration procedure, is about how the administrator 'thinks'.[106] The administrator therefore has the same level of expectation, especially, in deciding which rescue objective would serve the interests of creditors as a whole during insolvency proceedings that is analogous to that of judge presiding over a case in a court of law.[107]

A hard case analogy – *Re Huddersfield Fine Worsteds Ltd and Re Ferrotech Ltd & Granville Technology Ltd*

The Court of Appeal (CA) decision in *Re Huddersfield Fine Worsteds Ltd and Re Ferrotech Ltd & Granville Technology Ltd* [108] may serve as a good example where Dworkin's hard case thesis may be drawn. This case presented interpretative challenges to the courts that would be analogous to a hard case. Although the case may not be categorised as a hard case per se, the level of challenges encountered in interpreting the legal and policy provisions around paragraph 99 of Schedule B1 of the IA 1986, draws it closer to what Dworkin would term as a hard case upon which an administrator's and a judge's ability to adopt a novel interpretative approach to finding a fair and balanced answer may be drawn.

In this case, the CA was tasked to determine whether liabilities for protective awards and payments in lieu of notice to employees of a company in administration, whose contracts of employment had been adopted by the administrator would be interpreted within the scope of 'wages or salary' pursuant to paragraph 99(4) – (6) of Schedule B1 to the Insolvency Act 1986. Another practical importance of this case was that the CA had to hear this case at a short notice. The administrators of the company were due to decide whether or not to adopt the contracts of employment of over 150 employees, as the 14-day period for doing so was due to expire and their decision would depend on the outcome of the case.

A protective award arises under s.189 of the Trade Union and Labour Relations (Consolidation) Act 1992 (the 1992 Act), where an employer has failed on the obligation to hold consultations with employees where more than 19 employees are to be dismissed by reason of redundancy under s.188 of this Act.[109] A payment in lieu of notice arises where, either, with express or implied agreement, an employer gives proper notice of termination of employment to the employee, or the employer summarily dismisses the employee and tenders

106 IA 1986 Sch.B1, para 3(3) (a). This provision gives the administrator power to exercise discretion in deciding which rescue objective would best serve the interests of creditors as a whole.

107 Hamiisi J. Nsubuga, "Corporate Insolvency and Employment Protection: A Theoretical Perspective" (2016) 4(1) *NIBLeJ* 4.

108 [2005] EWCA Civ. 1072.

109 See the reasoning in *Re Hartlebury Printers Ltd* [1993] BCLC 902.

a payment in lieu of proper notice as such action would amount to a breach of contract of employment.[110]

In *Re Huddersfield Fine Worsteds Ltd*[111], Peter Smith J had given judgement on 27 July 2005 that protective awards and payments in lieu of notice were paid in priority to administration expenses. However, on 09 August 2005, Etherton J, gave a judgement that both protective awards and payments in lieu of notice were not payable in priority to administration expenses in respect of two different companies in the *Re Ferrotech Ltd and Granville Technology case*[112] that led to two conflicting first instance decisions and led to this appeal.

By virtue of paragraph 99(5), sub paragraph 99(4) applies priority status to liabilities arising under a contract of employment which was adopted by the former administrator or predecessor. However, paragraph 99(5) (C) states that no action is taken of a liability to make a payment other than for wages and salaries. Interestingly, under paragraph 99(6), wages and salaries include among other things, holiday pay and sick pay. However, the challenge in interpretation mainly centred on the interpretation of paragraph 99(6) (d) and paragraph 99(5) (c).

Paragraph 99 (6) (d) states:

> in respect of a period, a sum which would be treated as earnings for that period for the purposes of an enactment about social security.

The CA had to consider four versions of interpreting this sub paragraph, which all gave different meanings which had been put forward by the legal teams and the Attorney General during this case. However, more interesting, is the fact that the CA was not prepared to accept the submission of the Attorney General that the problem of interpretation before the court was as a result of a drafting error. Therefore, it may be argued that this is the sort of a hard case that Dworkin would help to guide the judge to choose the best approach to interpreting the subsection that was the subject of interpretation.

Second, the test to ascertain whether protective awards or payments in lieu of notice are payable in priority to administration expenses centred on two conditions being satisfied in paragraph 99(5):

- That the liability arises out of a contract of employment.
- That the liability falls within the category of 'wages and salaries.

In their judgement (delivered by Neuberger J), the judges allowed the appeal of the administrators against the decision of Peter Smith J in *Re Huddersfield* holding that protective awards and payments in lieu of notice were not payable in priority to administration expenses. Interestingly, they upheld the decision of

110 The four principle categories of payments in lieu of notice as set out by Lord Browne – Wilkinson in *Delaney v Staples* [1992] 1 AC 687, at 692D – H.

111 [2005] EWCA Civ. 1682 (Ch).

112 [2005] EWCA Civ. 1072.

Etherton J in the *Re Ferrotech Ltd and Granville Technology* which was in conflict with Peter Smith J's decision.

The judges opined that analysing both issues involved a gateway, that is, a consideration of two issues in paragraph 99(5) that gave rise to difficulties on any view and if the gateway was correct, protective awards would not enjoy super priority because they cannot be described as liabilities arising under a contract of employment, but liabilities that no doubt, arise because of the existence of a contract of employment.[113]

Notably, the judges opined that:

> [t]he argument involved giving the words 'arising under' in paragraph 99(5), their ordinary and natural meaning, the notion that such expression should not be given an artificially wide meaning...[114]

There is sense in the argument that allowing protective awards and payments in lieu of notice to be paid in priority over administration expenses would make adoption of employment contracts by administrators substantially costly and burdensome to rescue attempts. However, Peter Smith's judgement would be favourable to employees.

Therefore, this case highlighted the extent to which the courts may be prepared to analyse what the legislature intended in passing this legislation. This is the interpretative approach that carries with it, the integrity and constructiveness in exploring extant legal rules and principles to derive at a unique answer or approach that would balance both employees' and employers' interest during corporate insolvency. Therefore, Dworkin's interpretative approach would fit the UK legislative structure if adopted by courts and tribunals.

Conclusion

The tension between corporate rescue and employment protection policy objectives during relevant transfers has been a major challenge to the UK Courts and tribunals since TUPE Regulations were enacted into UK law, giving effect to the ARD. This tension has to a larger extent been created by the purposive interpretation of TUPE Regulations and the provisions of the ARD adopted by UK Courts and tribunals. This tension can however, be remedied through an interpretative solution to achieve the balance needed to pursue the policy objectives of corporate rescue and employment protection simultaneously.

Competing policy objectives of rescuing insolvent but viable businesses and those of protecting, and promoting employment within the ARD and TUPE Regulations are not totally incompatible.[115] Where business rescue is pursued successfully, it saves jobs and promotes continuity of employment. However, the

113 [2005] EWCA Civ. 1072, para. 17.
114 Ibid., para. 17.
115 P. Walton, "Pre-packin' in the UK" (2009) 18 *Int. Insolv. Rev.* 85, 104.

problem arises where these policy objectives conflict with each other during relevant transfers. This is because both policy objectives are difficult to achieve simultaneously, rather, a compromise ought to be made.

However, as discussed in this chapter, the requirement for UK Courts and tribunals to interpret TUPE Regulations purposively, as a form of aligning TUPE Regulations to the intentions of the ARD, has created further problems and challenges. In a bid to interpret TUPE Regulations purposively by the UK Courts and tribunals, inconsistent judgements have been witnessed which have not been helpful in trying to balance employment protection and corporate rescue objectives through interpretation. On other occasions, the CJEU, has not provided binding judgements to Member States on how to approach certain provisions relating to EU law, especially, the ARD.

Therefore, Dworkin's interpretative approach, if adopted by UK judges in interpreting and applying TUPE Regulations to relevant transfers, may provide an approach that would achieve the balance needed. Dworkin's ideals of constructiveness and integrity in interpretation should be adopted and used as the criteria for devising a theory or threshold upon which factual arguments before the court are analysed and applied to relevant laws and policies applicable in that particular area of law.

Bibliography

Books

Dworkin, R, *Taking Rights Seriously* (London, G. Duckworth, 1977).

Dworkin, R, *Law's Empire* (Cambridge, MA, HUP, 1986).

Laulom, S, *The European Court of Justice in the Dialogue on Transfers of Undertakings: A Fallible Interlocutor in Labour in the Courts, National Judges and the ECJ*, (edited by S. Sciarra) (Oxford, Hart Publishing, 2001).

Book chapters

Dworkin, R, "Pragmatism, Right Answers and True Benality" in M. Brint and W. Weaver (eds.) *Pragmatism in Law and Society*, (Boulder, CO, Westview Press, 1991).

Cases

United Kingdom

Berriman v Delabole Slate [1985] IRLR 305.

Bulmer v Bollinger [1974] EWCA Civ. 14.

Catamaran Cruisers v Williams and others [1994] IRLR 384.

Celtec v Astley [2005] IRLR 647.

Corkery v Carpenter [1951] 1 KB 102.

Crawford v Swinton Insurance Brokers Ltd [1990] IRLR 42.

Credit Suisse First Boston (Europe) Ltd v Lister [1998] IRLR 700.

Credit Suisse First Boston (Europe) Ltd v Padiachy [1998] IRLR 504.

Delaney v Staples [1992] 1 AC 687.

Dynamex Friction Ltd and Another v Amicus and another [2008] EWCA Civ. 381.
Elliot v Grey [1960] 1 QB 367.
European Union.
Hay v George Hansen [1996] IRLR 427.
Katsikas v Konstantinidis [1993] IRLR 179.
Ladies Health and Fitness Clubs v Eastmond [UKEAT94/03] (Unreported).
Litster v Forth Dry Dock and Engineering Company Ltd [1989] 1 All ER 113.
Nationwide Building Society v Benn & Others [UKEAT/0273/09/JOJ].
New ISG Ltd v Vernon and Others [2008] IRLR 115.
North Wales Training & Enterprise Council Ltd v Astley and Others [2006] UKHL 29 (HL).
Re Hartlebury Printers Ltd [1993] BCLC 902.
Re Huddersfield Fine Worsteds Ltd and Re Ferrotech Ltd & Granville Technology Ltd [2005] EWCA Civ. 1072.
Secretary of State for Trade & Industry v Cook [1997] IRLR 150.
Smith v Hughes [1960] 1 WLR 380.
Spaceright Europe Ltd v Baillavoine and Another [2011] EWCA Civ. 1565.
Tapere v South London and Maudsley NHS Trust [2009] IRLR 972.
Wheeler v Patel [1987] IRLR 211.
Whitehouse v Blatchford and Sons Ltd [1999] IRLR 492.

European Union

C-101/87 P. Bork International A/S v Foreningen af Arbejdslederen i Danmark [1989] IRLR 41.
C-132/91 Grigorios Katsikas v Angelos Konstantinidis (1991).
C-138/91 Uwe Skreb v PCO Stauereibetrieb Paetz & Co. Nfl. GmbH (C-138/91) and *Günter Schroll v PCO Stauereibetrieb Paetz & Co. Nachfolger GmbH* (C-138/91), [1992] ECR I-6577, [1992] EUECJ C-132/91.

Journal articles

Bix, Brian, "On the Dividing Line between Natural Law Theory and Legal Positivism" (2000) 75 Notre Dame L. Rev. 1613.
Davies, Paul, "Opting Out of Transfers" (1996) 25 Ind. L. J. 247.
Finch, V, "Corporate Rescue: A Game of Three Halves" (2012) 32(2) Legal Stud. 302–324.
Garde, A, "Recent Developments in the Law of Transfers of Undertakings" (2002) 39 Common Mkt L. Rev. 523.
Hardy, S, and Adnett, N, "Entrepreneurial Freedom Versus Employee Rights: The Acquired Rights Directive and the EU Social Policy Post-Amsterdam' (1999) 9 J. Eur. Soc. Policy 30.
Hardy, S, and Painter, R, "The New Acquired Rights Directive and its Implications for European Employees Relations in the Twenty-first Century" (1996) 6(4) MaastJECL 336, 378.
McMullen, J, "Atypical Transfers, Atypical Workers and Atypical Employment Structures – A Case for Greater Transparency in Employment Issues" (1996) 25(4) Ind. L. J. 286, 307.
McMullen, J, "An Analysis of the Transfer of Undertakings (Protection of Employment) Regulations 2006" (2006) 35 Ind. L. J. 113.

McMullen, J, "The Right to Object to Transfer of Employment under TUPE" (2008) 37(2) Ind. L. J. 167, 177.

McMullen, J, "TUPE: Ringing the (Wrong) Changes – The Collective Redundancies and Transfer of Undertakings (Protection of Employment) (Amendment) Regulations 2014" (2014) 43 Ind. L. J. 149.

Nsubuga, HJ, "Corporate Insolvency and Employment Protection: A Theoretical Perspective" (2016) 4(1) NIBLeJ 4.

Toube, F, and Todd, G, "The Proper Treatment of Employees' Claims in Administration" (2005) 18 Insolvency Intel. 109.

Wallington, P, and Lee, R, "Transfers of Undertakings: EEC Law and Judicial Creativity" [1989] J. Bus. L. 513, 518.

Walton, P, "Pre-packin' in the UK" (2009) 18 Int. Insolv. Rev. 85, 104.

Wynn-Evans, CA, "TUPE and Mothballs – *Crystal Palace FC Ltd and Another v Kavanagh and Others*" (2014) 43(2) Ind. L. J. 185.

8 Conclusion – latest legislative developments and substantive matters

Introduction

Some jurisdictional observations

The US and the UK both are common law jurisdictions and they both share a form of similar objectives when dealing with debtor-creditor relationships during corporate insolvency.

Both countries' corporate insolvency laws, policies and processes set out to achieve the same goal: to offer companies in financial difficulties a chance to either reorganise their business affairs to enable them to continue operating as going concerns, or support them through a liquidation process in an orderly and controlled manner where corporate rescue is not achievable.[1]

However, there are some fundamental differences between the UK and the US corporate insolvency laws and employment laws that govern the employer-employee relationships during corporate insolvency proceedings. These differences are born out of the differences in the business, political and social cultures inherent in both jurisdictions that are attuned to the contention that 'while US law is pro-debtor law, UK law is pro-creditor law'[2] which has attracted various debates on both sides of the Atlantic.[3]

Although both jurisdictions have provisions in their insolvency laws that seek to balance the debtor-creditor (employer-employee) concerns during corporate insolvency, a majority of the provisions in these insolvency laws more protective of corporate rescue than employment protection. Moreover, corporate rescue laws and processes inherent in both jurisdictions highlight a level of disparity between corporate rescue and employment protection objectives during corporate rescue.

1 See, for example, IA 1986, Sch. B1, para. 3(1) (C); Bryant P. Lee, "Chapter 18? Imagining Future Uses of 11 U.S.C 363 to Accomplish Chapter 7 Liquidation Goals in Chapter 11 Reorganizations" [2009] 2019 (2) *Columb. Bus. L. Rev.* 520, 524.

2 G. McCormack, "Control and Corporate Rescue – An Anglo- American Evaluation" (2007) 56(3) *Int. Comp. L. Quart.* 515, 551.

3 E. Warren and J. L. Westbrook, "Financial Characteristics of Businesses in Bankruptcy" (1999) 73 *Am. Bankr. L. J.* 499, 553; C. E. Vance and P. Barr, "The Facts and Fictions of Bankruptcy Reform" (2003) 1 *De Paul Bus. & Com. L. J.* 361, 410.

For example, in the US Bankruptcy Code, provisions such as s.362, s.365 and s.1113 offer more protection to business reorganisation /rescue imperatives than employment protection. In the UK, corporate rescue processes such as administration considered the rescue of the company as a going concern as the main objective.[4] Although successful rescue of the company as a going concern may save jobs, employment protection is not a specific objective of administration.[5] However, certain employee claims such as claims for unpaid wages, accrued holiday pay, maternity and paternity benefits are treated as preferential debts on their employer's insolvency.[6]

Employee participation in the bankruptcy and insolvency proceedings processes

There is a certain degree of disparity in terms of control and participation between extant stakeholders during corporate insolvency proceedings in the UK and the US. For example, in the US, there exist strong consensus within the bankruptcy and business communities that the DIP is best positioned to manage and execute rescue operations successfully post-petition. However, this is in contrast to the practice in the UK, where outside professionals, such as administrators in the form of a practitioner-in-possession model are preferred to oversee the business rescue operations of the debtor company on corporate insolvency, especially, under the administration process.

In the US, the DIP is equipped with powers to exercise discretion on how best to implement the reorganisation plan successfully. In the classic Chapter 11 model, the DIP would run the business in an ordinary sense and where needed, may acquire post-petition finance debts[7] where doing so would boost the reorganisation prospects of the debtor's business. The DIP may execute these duties with less interference from the bankruptcy courts, except where, a cause arising out of incompetence, dishonesty or fraud arose.[8]

In addition, corporate failure in the US is primarily viewed as a result of external factors, not management failings that put the company business in financial difficulties which is not the practice in the UK. There is a social cohesion that is borne with a commitment to an entrepreneurship ethic of giving the current management of the company a chance to steer the company back to solvency.[9] There is belief that the DIP model is cost effective, the DIP is well appraised of the business activities of the debtor company's business from past dealings, and time saving in implementing reorganisation plans.[10]

4 IA 1986, Sch. B1, para. 3(1)(a).
5 IA 1986, Sch. B1, para. 3(1).
6 IA 1986, Sch. 6.
7 11 U.S.C. s.341.
8 11 U.S.C. s.1104; see also the decision in *In Re Cybergenics Corp.*, 330, F. 3d 548.
9 B. A. Henoch, "Post-Petition Financing: Is there Life After Debt?" (1991) 8 *Bank. Dev. J.* 575, 577.
10 Bethany C. Suhreptz, "Key Employee Retention Plans, Executive Compensation, and BAPCA: No Rest for Congress, No More for Execs" (2009) 35 *Wm. Mitchell L. Rev.* 1194, 1199.

However, in the UK, the attitude towards corporate failure is predicated on the assumption that the current management of the company had failed in their obligations. The general consensus within the UK is that the company becomes insolvent because of management failures. Therefore, the failed management are replaced with an external professional, such as an insolvency practitioner to oversee the rescue operations of the company business.[11]

In addition, the lending market culture in the UK is strongly premised on the notion that the price for failure is replacement.[12] The lending market is comfortable in replacing management failures with professional outsiders, such as insolvency practitioners, rather than assuming more risks with the failed management. In fact, leaving the failed management in control of the rescue operations was likened to leaving an alcoholic in charge of a pub.[13]

Nonetheless, in terms of employee participation and control in rescue proceedings, both jurisdictions do not afford employees equal participation and control rights equivalent to those of the DIP (in the US) or administrators (in the UK). However, the UK system, especially, the administration procedure provides an otherwise inclusive model of protection to employees during corporate insolvency in comparison to that available to US employees in Chapter 11 reorganisations. This is because the administration procedure requires the administrator to pursue rescue operations in the interest of creditors as a whole,[14] including employees, without cherry-picking whether, or not, some employees are members of labour unions or parties to collective bargaining agreements, like it is the position in the US.

Latest legal development: Brexit and European Union (Withdrawal) Act 2018

A substantive part of the literature used in this book in relation to the UK employment protection law covered the ARD, TUPE Regulations and CJEU case law.[15] TUPE is UK law that was enacted as a form of transposing the Acquired Rights Directives into the UK law. However, the latest political changes in the UK at the time of writing this book may affect the future impact of TUPE Regulations in the UK.

On 23 June 2016, citizens of the UK voted in favour of leaving the EU via a referendum.[16] The vote in favour of leaving the EU by the UK has since become

11 See, R. Goode, *Principles of Corporate Insolvency Law* (4th edn, London, Sweet & Maxwell, 2011) 39.

12 McCormack, (n 2) 515.

13 G. Moss, "Chapter 11: An English Lawyer's Critique" (1998) 11 *Insol. Intel.* 17, 18–19.

14 IA 1986, Sch. B1, Para. 3(2).

15 By virtue of the European Communities Act (ECA) 1972, s.3 (1), the UK at the time of writing this book, like other Members States of the EU, is bound by the decisions of the CJEU on all matters of EU law.

16 Alex Hunt and Brian Wheeler, "Brexit: All You Need to Know About the UK Leaving the EU" *BBC News* (London, 28 August 2017) <www.bbc.co.uk/news/uk-politics-32810887> (accessed 12 May 2019).

known as 'Brexit'.[17] On 29 March 2017, the UK government started the formal process of the UK exiting the EU by triggering Article 50 of the Treaty of Lisbon which gives EU Member States a right to exit the EU.[18] This was followed by the UK government tabling the Great Repeal Bill highlighting the government's agenda for dealing with EU-derived legislation pre-and post-Brexit and other provisions to repeal the European Communities Act 1972 that took the UK into the EU. The EU Withdrawal Bill has now been adopted as the European Union (Withdrawal) Act 2018 (Withdrawal Act)[19] as of 26 June 2018.

One of the key provisions of the Withdrawal Act is the provision that the European Communities Act 1972 (ECA 1972) will be repealed on exit day.[20] In addition, case law of the CJEU existing at the time of the UK's exit from the EU will continue to have effect in the UK post-Brexit to ensure continuity and certainty in the interpretation of EU-derived legislation post-Brexit.[21] However, pre-Brexit CJEU decisions will have the status of UK Supreme Court judgements and therefore will continue to have effect unless the UK Supreme Court decides otherwise. The point of concern is that the UK courts and tribunals have been interpreting EU-derived legislation such as TUPE Regulations purposively to align TUPE Regulations to the ARD.[22] This has meant that the ARD's intention of safeguarding and protecting employees during relevant transfers is maintained. However, the repeal of the European Communities Act 1972 may affect the UK courts' and tribunals' interpretation of TUPE regulations post-Brexit.

Section 6 of the European Union (Withdrawal) Act provides that:

1 A court or tribunal—

  a is not bound by any principles laid down, or any decisions made, on or after exit day by the European Court, and
  b cannot refer any matter to the European Court on or after exit day.

This may impact the way courts and tribunals deal with technical and challenging interpretative approaches, especially the matters relating to TUPE Regulation as TUPE will continue to have effect under UK domestic legislation post-Brexit.

17 Brexit is the popular term for the withdrawal of the United Kingdom from the European Union. See also, Hunt and Wheeler, (n 27).

18 Laura Kuenssberg, "Brexit: Theresa May to Trigger Article 50 by End of March" *BBC News* (London, 2 October 2016) <www.bbc.co.uk/news/uk-politics-37532364> (accessed 20 June 2019).

19 European Union (Withdrawal) Act 2018, c.16.

20 European Union (Withdrawal) Act 2018, s.1. Currently, the UK is scheduled to exit the EU on 31 October 2019.

21 European Union (Withdrawal) Act 2018, ss.3 and 7.

22 The requirement on the UK to adopt a purposive approach to interpreting EU law was emphasised by the House of Lords in *Litster v Forth Dry Dock and Engineering Company Ltd* [1989] 1 All ER 113; [1989] IRLR 161.

Moreover, the Withdrawal Act gives flexibility to the UK Parliament to repeal, amend or otherwise change any law existing by virtue of the EU after the exit day. This is because no UK court or tribunal will be bound by any retained case law it would otherwise not be bound by.[23] It is therefore the concern that TUPE Regulations may be subjected to either amendment or repeal post-Brexit and the purposive interpretation of TUPE Regulations may be disregarded by the UK courts and tribunals post-Brexit. This may affect TUPE's protection to employees during relevant business sales and transfers. Nonetheless, the UK is schedules to exit the EU on 31 October 2019 and any changes to EU derived / retained legislation have yet to be witnessed.

The EU preventive restructuring framework directive

The European Union Commission (EU Commission) published a proposal for a Directive on preventive restructuring framework, second chance and measures to increase the efficiency of restructuring, insolvency and discharge procedures and amending Directive 2012/30/EU on 22 November 2016.[24] The text to the proposed Directive was formally adopted by the EU Commission on 6 June 2019 and will be officially signed and entered into force on the 20th day, following its publication in the official journal of the EU. Member States of the EU will have two years to transpose it into corresponding domestic laws, with a potential extension of one year to Member States that encounter transposition challenges within the two-year period.

The Directive's key objective is to reduce the most significant barriers to the free flow of capital stemming from differences in Member States' restructuring and insolvency frameworks. The aim is for all Member States to have in their national insolvency and restructuring laws key principles on preventive restructuring and second chance frameworks, and measures to make all types of insolvency procedures more efficient by reducing their length and costs and improving their quality.[25]

However, prior to the proposal for this Directive, in 2014, the EU Commission had made a recommendation for a new approach to business failure and insolvency across EU Member States.[26] The 2014 Recommendations had

23 European Union (Withdrawal) Act 2018, s.6 (4) (c).

24 European Commission, *Proposal for a Directive on Preventive Restructuring Frameworks, Second Chance and Measures to increase the Efficiency of Restructuring, Insolvency and Discharge Procedures and amending Directive 2012/30/EU.* (Com (2016) 723/0359) final.

25 Maria-Thomas Epeoglou, "Comments on the Commission's Proposal for a Directive on Preventive Restructuring Frameworks and Second Chance for Entrepreneurs: The Third Step to the European Cross-border Insolvency Saga" (2017) 14 *Int. Corp. Rescue* 1.

26 European Commission, *Commission Recommendation of 12 March 2014 on a New Approach to Business Failure and Insolvency*, (2014/125/EU). See also, G. McCormack, A. Keay and S. Brown, *European Insolvency Law: Reform and Harmonisation* (Cheltenham, Edward Elgar, 2016) Ch.6 on the EU Commission recommendation for a new approach to business failure and insolvency.

provisions for Member States to adopt procedures such as the introduction of the debtor-in-possession (DIP) model like that of the US, out of court restructuring model, creditor cram-down mechanisms, use of moratoria and discharge period mechanisms.[27]

To achieve these recommendations, Member States had to review their domestic insolvency restructuring laws and processes, or introduce new ones where needed. However, the EU Commission's Evaluation Reports on the implementation of the 2014 Recommendations concluded that it had not been successful in achieving the intended outcomes.[28] This was mainly due to compliance issues across Member States and the divergence in relative national insolvency laws and restructuring frameworks within Member States.

It is therefore noteworthy, that the Directive on preventive restructuring frameworks may be seen as building on or carrying forward the 2014 Recommendations by requiring Member States to adopt the Directive and set up measures on preventive restructuring frameworks and second chance provisions in their national/domestic restructuring laws.[29]

The Preventive Directive also seeks to broaden the scope of harmonisation of cross-border insolvency restructuring frameworks across the EU. This is through the Directive's increased proposals for convergence of insolvency and restructuring frameworks across Member States that would create a degree of legal certainty on cross-border investment, and also, certainty on a timely framework for restructuring insolvent but viable businesses in financial difficulties.[30]

Potential impact of the preventive restructuring directive on the UK

The new Preventive Directive has provisions that if adopted by the UK and transposed into domestic insolvency and restructuring laws, certain substantive and procedural safeguards, especially on improved iteration for worker / employee protection and involvement during corporate insolvency and restructuring may be impacted.

Under Article 3(1), Member States are to ensure that debtors have access to one or more clear and transparent early warning tools, which can detect circumstances that could give rise to insolvency and can signal them to act without delay.[31] Moreover, Member States are to ensure that debtors and

27 G. McCormack, "Something Old, Something New: Recasting the European Insolvency Regulation" (2016) 79(1) *Mod. L. Rev.* 121–146.

28 European Commission, *Evaluation of the Implementation of the Commission Recommendations of 12 March 2014 on a new approach to business failure and insolvency*, <http://ec.europa.eu/justice/civil/files/evaluation_recommendation_final> (accessed 12 April 2019).

29 Maria-Thomas Epeoglou, "Comments on the Commission's Proposal for a Directive on Preventive Restructuring Frameworks and Second Chance for Entrepreneurs: The Third Step to the European Cross-border Insolvency Saga" (2017) 14 *Inter. Corp. Rescue* 1.

30 Preventive Directive, Art.1.

31 Ibid., Art. 3(1).

employee representatives have access to up-to-date information about the availability of early warning tools and as well as of the procedures and measures concerning resolution and discharge of debt.[32] In addition, Member States may provide support to employees' representatives for the assessment of the economic situation of the debtor.[33] All these provisions are geared towards improved worker involvement and protection if adopted and transposed into UK domestic law.

Another key provision of the Preventive Directive is article 13. This article offers addition protection to individual and collective workers' rights. Once transposed, the UK will have to ensure that its labour and restructuring laws have provisions that ensure workers' rights to bargain collectively through collective bargaining arrangements, and engaging in industrial actions are not affected by preventive restructuring frameworks.[34]

In addition, where an employer's proposed restructuring plan involves measure leading to changes in employees' work or contractual arrangements, and those arrangements are part of collectively agreed arrangements, any changes to those arrangements shall have to be approved by the workers and their representatives to the collective arrangement.[35] It should be noted that collective bargaining and trade unionism are key factors in industrial relations in the UK. Therefore, upholding these employee rights during corporate insolvency and restructuring is of fundamental importance. However, the full impact of the new Preventive Directive is subject to harmonisation and whether the UK leaves the EU on 31 October 2019 as currently scheduled.

Bibliography

Books

Goode, R, *Principles of Corporate Insolvency Law* (4th edn., London, Sweet & Maxwell, 2011).

McCormack, G, Keay, A, and Brown, S, *European Insolvency Law: Reform and Harmonisation* (Cheltenham, Edward Elgar, 2016).

Cases

United Kingdom

Litster v Forth Dry Dock and Engineering Company Ltd [1989] 1 All ER 113.

United States

In Re Cybergenics Corp., 330, F. 3d 548.

32 Ibid., Art. 3(3).
33 Ibid., Art. 3(5).
34 Ibid., Art. 13 (1) (a).
35 Ibid., Art. 13(13) (2).

Journal articles

Epeoglou, Maria-Thomais, "Comments on the Commission's Proposal for a Directive on Preventive Restructuring Frameworks and Second Chance for Entrepreneurs: The Third Step to the European Cross-border Insolvency Saga" (2017) 14 Int. Corp. Rescue 1.

Henoch, BA, "Post-Petition Financing: Is there Life After Debt?" (1991) 8 Bank. Dev. J. 575, 577.

Lee, P Bryant, "Chapter 18? Imagining Future Uses of 11 U.S.C 363 to Accomplish Chapter Liquidation Goals in Chapter 11 Reorganizations" [2009] 2019 (2) Columb. Bus. L. Rev. 520, 524.

McCormack, G, "Control and Corporate Rescue – An Anglo- American Evaluation" (2007) 56 (3) Int. Comp. L. Quart. 515, 551.

McCormack, G, "Something Old, Something New: Recasting the European Insolvency Regulation" (2016) 79(1) Mod. L. Rev. 121–146.

Moss, G, "Chapter 11: An English Lawyer's Critique" (1998) 11 Insol. Intel. 17, 18–19.

Suhreptz, C. Bethany, "Key Employee Retention Plans, Executive Compensation, and BAPCA: No Rest for Congress, No More for Execs" (2009) 35 Wm. Mitchell L. Rev. 1194, 1199.

Vance, C, and Barr, P, "The Facts and Fictions of Bankruptcy Reform" (2003) 1 De Paul Bus. & Com. L. J. 361, 410.

Warren, E, and Westbrook, JL, "Financial Characteristics of Businesses in Bankruptcy" (1999) 73 Am. Bankr. L. J. 499, 553.

Other – news articles

Hunt, Alex, and Wheeler, Brian, "Brexit: All You Need to Know About the UK Leaving the EU" *BBC News*, (London, 28 August 2017) <www.bbc.co.uk/news/uk-politics-32810887> (accessed 12 May 2019).

Kuenssberg, Laura, "Brexit: Theresa May to Trigger Article 50 by End of March" *BBC News*, (London, 2 October 2016) <www.bbc.co.uk/news/uk-politics-37532364> (accessed 20 June 2019).

Legislation

United Kingdom

European Union (Withdrawal) Act 2018, c.16.

European Union – other

European Commission, *Commission Recommendation of 12 March 2014 on a New Approach to Business Failure and Insolvency*, (2014/125/EU).

European Commission, *Proposal for a Directive on Preventive Restructuring Frameworks, Second Chance and Measures to increase the Efficiency of Restructuring, Insolvency and Discharge Procedures and amending Directive 2012/30/EU.* (Com (2016) 723/0359) final.

Index

Note: Page numbers followed by 'n' denote footnotes.

Acquired Rights Directives (ARD) 94, 95, 101, 118, 123, 126, 129, 133, 145, 151
administrative receivership 7, 14–16
Alermo-Herron and Others v Parkwood Leisure Ltd 94, 95
American Bankruptcy Institute Recommendations 54–5
automatic transfer: of liabilities on business rescue 99–100; provision under regulation 4 of 96–9

Bankruptcy Amendments and Federal Judgeship Act (1984) 52
Bankruptcy Code 33, 39, 46, 55–7, 58n90, 64, 69–73, 75, 86, 91; provisions 5; s. 365(a) of 49; s.1113 of 50; s.1114 of 60
bankruptcy laws 24, 27, 30, 35, 69, 70 74, 79
bankruptcy legal theory 24–6; interpretative theory of law 36–8; theoretical divide analysis 26–34; theoretical limitations analysis 34–6
bankruptcy policies 27
bankruptcy proceedings 92; formal participation in post-petition 64; in US 81, 82
bankruptcy process 25, 34
Bankruptcy Reform Act (1978) 36
bankruptcy reorganisation 5, 66, 70, 78, 91; corporate 58; policies 5; proceedings 82
bankruptcy reorganisation proceedings in US: American Bankruptcy Institute Recommendations 54–5; legislative response post-Bildisco 50–3; *NLRB v Bildisco & Bildisco* 49–50; post-petition employee claims 64–5; pre-petition and post-petition employee claims 56–64; role of labour union movement 47–8; US social policy 43–7
bankruptcy venue forum shopping: impediment to employee participation 75–7; *In re* WorldCom Inc. 77–8
Bankruptcy Venue Statute 75
benefit pension plan 58
Bernadone v Pall Mall Services Group Ltd 98
BERR *see* Department for Business, Enterprise and Regulatory Reform (BERR)
Berriman v Delabole Slate 114, 132
BIS *see* Business Innovation and Skills (BIS)
Brexit and European Union (Withdrawal) Act (2018) 151–3
Brotherhood of Railways, Airline and Steamship Clerks v REA Express, Inc. 90
Business Innovation and Skills (BIS) 131
business judgement rule 85, 86
business reorganisation policy objectives 83
Butner v United States 29

CA *see* Court of Appeal (CA)
capital 1; liquidity issues 63; mobility 48; *see also* human capital
CBA *see* collective bargaining agreement (CBA)
Celtec v Astley 130
"changes in the workforce" 115, 117
Chapter 11 of the US Bankruptcy Code 5, 43, 46, 54, 90
coherent bankruptcy law 24

collective administration process 35
collective bargaining 19, 44, 48, 51–3, 72–5, 155; contractual variations on 117; and labour unionism 45–7; paradigmatic shift in 49–50; rights on employees 5
collective bargaining agreement (CBA) 45, 50, 57, 79, 86, 88, 109, 117
collective debt collection regime 28
Collective Redundancies and Transfer of Undertakings Regulations 2014 (TUPE 2014) 7
Collective Redundancy Directive 3
Commerce Clause 69
common law 95; rule 45
company voluntary arrangement (CVA) 4, 12–14, 16
compatible legal precedents 84
compulsory liquidation 16
congressional policy 88
constructive interpretation 82, 136; of law 137, 138
contractual liabilities 98
contractual variations 116; on collective bargaining 117
Cork Committee Report 4, 13
Cork, Kenneth 13
corporate bankruptcy reorganisations 58
corporate investment decisions 46
corporate liquidations 27
corporate reorganisations 27–8
corporate rescue 17–19; laws 149; policy objectives 14; process 8, 15, 16, 150; and reorganisations 27–8; in UK 2–5; in US 5–7
corporate restructuring 2
Court of Appeal (CA) 132, 135
Court of Justice of the European Union (CJEU) 94, 122–3, 122n3, 125, 146
court's decision on regulation 4(7) 128–30
Creditors' Voluntary Liquidation (CVL) 16, 17
Crystal Palace F.C Limited and Another v Kavanagh and Others 101, 133–5, 138, 140, 142
CVL *see* Creditors' Voluntary Liquidation (CVL)

debtor-creditor relationship 27, 33, 38, 69
debtor-in-possession (DIP) 6, 7, 30, 51, 64, 79, 150, 151, 154
decision-making processes 46, 138
Delaware state law 71–5
Department for Business, Enterprise and Regulatory Reform (BERR) 103, 131
divergent policy objectives 122
Dworkin, Ronald 83, 84, 122; bankruptcy proceedings 81; interpretation approach 89–91, 133; interpretation as balancing tool 82–4; interpretative approach 92, 123; interpretative ideals of constructive and integrity 137–8; interpretative theory of law 36–9, 135–7; judicial balancing of policy objectives 138–42; judicial interpretation approaches to U.S.C. s.1113, 84–9; UK legal structure 142–5
Dynamex Friction Ltd and Another v Amicus and Another 140, 142

ECA *see* European Communities Act (ECA)
economic models 25
economic, technical and organisational (ETO) reasons 102–6
employee benefit plan 59
employee claims 77; in bankruptcy 65
employee contracts of employment 117
employee involvement, federal-state uniform model of 79
employee participation: in bankruptcy 150–1; impediment to 75–7
employee pension 57–9
employee post-petition claims 64
employee protection: under TUPE 96; from unfair dismissals under regulation 7, 100–2
Employers in Insolvency Directive, Council Directive 80/987/EEC 3
Employment Appeal Tribunal (EAT) 109, 114, 132–4, 139–41; in *Crystal Palace* 138; judgement 135
employment-at-will 43–5
employment laws 149
employment protection 17; concerns 26; and continuity 16; policies 5, 14, 83; provisions 115; provisions under Delaware state law 71–5; in UK 2–5, 7; in US 5–7
Employment Retirement Income Security Act (ERISA) 58–9
Employment Rights Act (ERA) 4, 7; s.94 107; s.98 (1) (b) 102
employment tribunal (ET) 134, 139, 140
English Legal System 123
'entailing changes in the workforce' 102, 105, 110, 115, 131–5

Enterprise Act 2002 (EA 2002) 8, 11, 35
entrepreneurial freedom 122
equity receiverships 35
ERA *see* Employment Rights Act (ERA)
ERISA *see* Employment Retirement Income Security Act (ERISA)
ET *see* employment tribunal (ET)
EU preventive restructuring framework directive 153–4
European Communities Act (ECA) 122, 152
European Union (EU) 94, 98; Council Directive 77/187/EC, Article 4 125; Council Directive 80/987/EEC 3; Council Directive 98/59/EC 3; Council Directive 2001/23/EC 2–3; preventive restructuring framework 153–154; social employment legislation 4, 17; social policy directives 2; Withdrawal Bill 152
"ex WorldCom5100," 78

'fair and equitable' standards 86–7
Fair Labour Standards Act (1994) 45
federal-state law division 70–1, 79
federal-state uniform model of employee involvement 79
'fit and moral value' 137, 138, 140
Foreningen AF Arbedjsldere I Denmark v Daddy's Dance Hall 108
formal administration process 11
formal corporate rescue processes in UK 7–8; administration 8–10; administrative receivership 14–16; company voluntary arrangements 12–14; liquidation 16–17; pre-pack administration 10–12
free market approach 34

General Motors (GM) 77
Genetic Information and Non-Discrimination Act (2008) 45
German Civil Code, Article 613a 126
global economic recession 2
Green v Elan Care 132, 133

Hazel v Manchester College 113
Heydon's Case 123
House of Congress and Senate conference committee 52
Howard Johnson Co. v Detroit Local Joint Executive Board 74
human capital 1; contributions 12; investment 12

individual debt collection regimes 33
In re WorldCom Inc. 77–8
Insolvency Act 1986 (IA 1986) 3–4, 8, 11, 13, 18, 39; Sch.B1, para 3(3) (a) 143n106; Sch.B1, para 99 143
insolvency law 24, 25, 27–9, 32, 35, 135, 142; contractarian approach to 30; policies 4; traditionalist perspectives on 36
insolvency regimes 26
insolvency setting: judges role in 32–4; legal system in 26–7
insolvent practitioner (liquidator) 17
'internal affairs' doctrine 71
interpretation: as balancing tool 82–4; constructive 82, 137–8; Dworkin's approach to 89–91, 133; ideal of integrity 38, 136–8, 142; inconsistencies 92; judicial 81, 84–9
interpretative theory of law 36–9, 82, 84, 122, 135–7

Jackson v Computershare Investor Services Plc. 97
John Wiley & Sons, Inc. v Livingston 73
judicial balancing of policy objectives 138–42
judicial interpretation 81; approaches to U.S.C. s.1113, 84–9; of regulation 4(7) 126–8, 130–1
'just cause' dismissal 45
'justice and convenience' of stakeholders 76

Katsikas v Konstantinidis 125
known (contractual) liabilities 100, 119

labour 1, 17, 48; costs, reduction in 2; organisation 54; transformational policies 86
labour law 91; policies 74; statutes 69
labour union(ism) 20, 44–7; movement 19, 47–9, 51, 53
law as integrity 136, 137
Law of Corporations 71
Law's Empire 136
legal precedents 38, 83, 84
legal rules 83, 84, 136
legal system 32; in insolvency setting 26–7
legal theory 82
liabilities: automatic transfer of rights and 97–9; on business rescue, automatic transfer of 99–100; contractual 98;

known 119; known contractual 100; non-contingent 18; non-contractual 98; for post-transfer dismissals 105–6; unknown 98, 100, 119
liquidation 16–17
Litster v Forth Dry Dock and Engineering Company Ltd. 124
'London Approach' 4, 4n27
London Metropolitan University v Sackur & Others 108, 110

market culture, in UK 151
market economy functions 29
Martin v Lancashire County Council 99
Members' Voluntary Liquidation (MVL) 16, 17
'mischief rule' 123
Mitchell, Stephen S. 54
'Mobility Clauses' 48n31
Model Employment Termination Act (META) 44
'moral value' category 137
MVL *see* Members' Voluntary Liquidation (MVL)

National Conference of Commissioners on Uniform State Laws (ULC) 44
National Insurance Fund 3, 17
National Labour Relations Act (NLRA) 5, 19, 44, 45, 47, 65, 69, 74, 75; s.8 (d) of 51; s.158 of 53; s.158 (a) of 48
National Labour Relations Board (NLRB) 49, 90
Nationwide Building Society v Benn & Others 132, 133
natural disasters 63
natural law theory 37
'necessary' standards 86–7
New ISG Ltd v Vernon and Others 126, 127
NLRA *see* National Labour Relations Act (NLRA)
NLRB v Bildisco & Bildisco 49–50, 84
Nokes v Doncaster Amalgamated Collieries 95
non-bankruptcy laws 59, 69–71
non-contingent liabilities 18
non-contractual liabilities 98
non-insolvency creditor 25
non-insolvency setting 30, 32
non-structural mandatory rules 31
non-unionised employees 20
Northern Pipeline Construction Co. v Marathon Pipe Line Corporation 52
North Wales Training & Enterprise Council Ltd v Astley and Others 130

Occupiers Liability Act (1957) 99
offender learning service 113
Omnibus Bankruptcy Bill 52
'open texture' 83

Parkwood, Robert William 52
P. Bork International A/S v Foreningen af Arbejdslederen i Danmark 125
Pension Benefit Guaranty Corporation (PBGC) 58, 59
permissible variation: to contract terms and conditions 112–17; under regulation 4, 110–11; 'relevant insolvency proceedings,' 111–12
post-Bildisco, legislative response 50–3
post-petition bankruptcy proceedings, formal participation in 64
post-petition employee claims 56–65
post-transfer dismissals, liability for 105–6
practitioner-in-possession model 150
pre-pack administration 10–12
pre-pack business sales 7
pre-petition bondholder claims 77
pre-petition employee claims 56–64
pre-transfer dismissals, liability for 105–6
Preventive Directive 154, 155
preventive restructuring directive on UK 154–5
private sector workforce 19, 44, 65
proceduralist bankruptcy scholars 25
proceduralist perspectives on issues 35

quasi-formal corporate rescue processes in UK 7–8; administration 8–10; administrative receivership 14–16; company voluntary arrangements 12–14; liquidation 16–17; pre-pack administration 10–12
quasi-legal rescue process 10

Ralton v Havering College of Further and Higher Education 109, 110
RBBPA *see* Retiree Benefits Bankruptcy Protection Act (RBBPA)
receiverships: administrative 7, 14–16; equity 35
re Delta Airlines Inc. 86

Re Huddersfield Fine Worsteds Ltd and Re Ferrotech Ltd & Granville Technology Ltd 143–5
'relevant insolvency proceedings' 111–12
Retiree Benefits Bankruptcy Protection Act (RBBPA) 60
retiree benefits protection 57–62
rights and liabilities, automatic transfer of 97–9

Schwartz, Alan 30, 31
Secretary of State for Trade & Industry v Cook 129
selfish debt collection regime 29
shareholders' investment 1, 12
SIP 16 *see* Statement of Insolvency Practice 16 (SIP 16)
Smith v Trustees of Brooklands College 114
social effects 1–2
social employment protection 5; policies 2
social policy 43
stakeholders: collection processes 33; non-insolvency 31
state labour laws 70, 71; objectives 74
Statement of Insolvency Practice 16 (SIP 16) 12
state non-bankruptcy laws 70
statutory dismissal requirements 45
statutory interpretation 84
statutory moratorium 8
Supremacy Clause 70, 74

temporary financial situation 29
theoretical divide analysis: corporate reorganisations and rescue 27–8; judges role in insolvency setting 32–4; legal system in insolvency setting 26–7; uniform application of law, inside and outside bankruptcy 29–32
theoretical limitations analysis 34–6
Thurmond, James Strom 52
Title 11 of the US Bankruptcy Code 65
Trade Union and Labour Relations Act (TULCRA) 3; s.188 of 10, 143
trade unionism 65, 155
traditional bankruptcy lawyers and scholars 24
Transfer of Undertakings (Protection of Employment) Regulations (TUPE) 3, 7, 11, 15, 17, 94, 95, 118, 119, 123, 129, 133, 135, 141, 145, 146, 152; automatic transfer of liabilities on business rescue 99–100; automatic transfer provision under regulation 4 of 96–9; contractual variations on collective bargaining 117; economic, technical and organisational reasons 102–6; employee protection from unfair dismissals under regulation 7, 100–2; obligation 9, 18; protection from contractual terms and conditions variation 107–17; Regulation 4(4) 113; Regulation 4(5) 110, 111; Regulation 4(5A) 115, 117; Regulation 4(5)(b) 111; Regulation 4(7) 126; Regulation 4(8) 128; Regulation 4(9) 116; Regulation 5(1) 124; Regulation 5(3) 124; Regulation 7 100–2, 106–7, 138; Regulation 8(6) 111, 112; scope of employee protection under 96
Treaty of Lisbon, Article 50 of 152
Truck Drivers Local 807 v Carey Transportation Inc. 87–91
TULCRA *see* Trade Union and Labour Relations Act (TULCRA)
'two-tier' level of protection categories 117

UK: corporate insolvency laws and employment laws 149; corporate rescue and employment protection in 2–5, 7; courts and tribunals, interpretative challenges faced by 123–6; formal corporate rescue processes (*see* formal corporate rescue processes in UK); general employment legislation 17; insolvency law 8, 17, 142; insolvency law's administration process 17; legal structure 142–5; preventive restructuring directive on 154–5; quasi-formal corporate rescue processes in (*see* quasi-formal corporate rescue processes in UK)
UK Insolvency Service 8
UK Rail 127
unfair employer prerogatives 7
uniform application of law, inside and outside bankruptcy 29–32
unknown liabilities 98, 100, 119
US: collective bargaining 45; constitution 69; corporate insolvency laws and employment laws 149; corporate rescue and employment protection in 5–7; labour law contractual relationships 44; legal system 81; legislation 20; market economy 48; private sector labour

market 45; private sector workforce 19, 44, 65; upstream labour market 44
US Bankruptcy Code 150; Chapter 11 of 5, 43, 46, 54, 90; s.1113 of 82, 84; s.1113(a) of 53; s.1114 of 60–2; 11 U.S.C. 362 and 11 U.S.C. 365 of 30
US social policy: collective bargaining and labour unionism 45–7; employment-at-will 43–5
US State of Delaware 44, 70–1
US v Whiting Pools Inc. 6

Wheeling-Pittsburgh Steel Corp. v United Steelworkers of America 87–91
winding-up process 16
Withdrawal Act 152–3
Worker Adjustment and Retraining Notification (WARN) Act (1988) 62–4
workforce: changes in 102, 105, 110, 115, 117, 131–5; private sector 19, 44, 65

'zero-hours' contracts 2